Fell's Collector's Guide to Valuable Antiques

Fell's
Collector's Guide
to
Valuable Antiques

by

HOWARD R. BLACK, Jr.

FREDERICK FELL, INC. • *Publishers* • NEW YORK

TABLE OF CONTENTS

Fell's Collector's Guide to Valuable Antiques

Chapter I

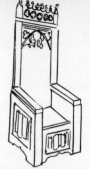

INTRODUCTION

Acquiring a collection of first-quality antiques presents little or no problem to a person who is handy with a checkbook. He can afford to hire appropriate experts, pay the highest market prices, and write off whatever mistakes he and his assistants may make. A book such as this is not intended for him.

There is another for whom this book is not intended. This is the person who hopes to go into any shop and buy a piece of merchandise for ten dollars and sell it the next day for a thousand. Rather than get something for nothing he is likely to get nothing for something.

As you look in shops, shows and museums and see many wonderful antiques, you will notice that they are held at wonderful values. If worth-while antiques must be inordinately expensive, you may begin to wonder, "Just what kind of antique can I afford to own?" If it is a tiara set with large diamonds, the chances are that you can't afford to own that kind of antique. However, if you wish to collect representative pieces of almost any other sort and are willing to learn about the various sorts before you leap at buying something, you can own genuine antiques of the type you want much more easily and cheaply than you think.

The advice I shall give in the pages that follow is intended to serve the person who wants to own antiques because he likes them. I hope to show you, as I have done in my lectures at City College, how to make your collection on even a slender budget. In order to make the best use of my suggestions, you will have to decide for yourself why you like antiques and why you want to own them.

Are you interested in them because they are attractive? Many handsome things are not antique, nor are antiques always beautiful. Perhaps your interest in antiques comes from the fact that they are in a sense frozen history and that they have the mysterious power of transporting you into the past when you see them. The romantic attitude toward the stage settings of historic events is certainly one of the strongest motives of collectors. Historically, it is the mark of "antiquarian" periods of art.

Before you can start to apply directions for getting genuine antiques at reasonable prices, there are a few things to remember about what you are trying to do. Certainly, one of the most important things you must learn is to find ways of distinguishing an antique from something that is not an antique. This distinguishing of the actuality from the appearance, the reality from the illusion, is generally called connoisseurship.

CONNOISSEURSHIP

The art of the connoisseur lies in making mountains out of molehills. The smaller the molehill and the larger the mountain into which it is made, the more accomplished is the connoisseur. We must, if we are to make any progress at this difficult art, train hand, eye, and ear to work together with the greatest sensitivity to the smallest differences in texture, in shape, and in color, as well as in expression and, above all, in style.

We can call to our aid the mechanics of science, history, or technology to help us confirm our observations. But we should always remember that reliance on the comparison microscope, ultraviolet photography, and X-ray machines, as well as dependence upon a check list of productions at a given time and place, historical trivia, or a particular artist's technique, can lead us woefully astray. Moreover, the calling in of the expert to solve his problems for him is not only an admission on the part of the connoisseur that he cannot do the job he set out to do, but also that his whole thesis is wrong; that the job to be done is impossible and that the differences he claims exist are but figments of his imagination.

The antique is embodied in its style. All other characteristics it has may be successfully imitated. Then what is the

task of the connoisseur? It is simply to supply an identity
to the object under examination, to give it a name, a country,
a place of manufacture, a maker, and a time. It is the
connoisseur's job to answer the questions, What? Where?
When? Whose? Why? and To what good? With these questions answered, the problem is solved.

This would be enough of a job if each unknown were a
straightforward case of identification, but such is not the case.
At least five or six different disguises are used to confuse
and confound the connoisseur. His first problem then is to
penetrate these disguises and find the reality beneath them.

THE MASQUERADERS

Many objects in antique shops are masquerading as antiques.
It is the province of connoisseurship to show them up for
what they are. There are five classes of things not antique
that are offered as such to the unwary. They are: the fake,
the reproduction, the secondhand piece, the overrestored
(or transformed) piece, and the glorified piece.

THE FAKE

Consider, first, the fake. By definition, it is made to
deceive and to defraud. The fake is made to look like something it is not. It is a carefully or not so carefully made
imitation of some object that is accepted as antique. In addition, various attempts have been made to give it the appearance
of having been around a long time. It is, to use a familiar
term, antiqued. How accomplished is this antiquing and how
successful it is in deceiving the public varies in inverse
proportion to that public's sophistication in such matters. The
fake in its emergence from the workshop, then, has two
aspects, the copy of a work of art and the imitation of a work
of nature. The new-made piece is the echo of the work of art;
its antiquing is the copy of nature and thus a work of art in
its own right.

A second inherent quality of any fake is that it does not come through the regular channels of trade but reaches the shops and ultimate consumer in devious ways. The output of fakes is controlled by the value of the antiques they copy and the ease with which they can be marketed. As the value of an antique rises, the likelihood of its fake being made tends to increase. This tendency is held in check by the cost of modern production. On the other hand, a high-priced fake would be the object of so much scrutiny that the chances of its getting by are extremely unlikely. Consequently, those antiques in which much faking is done range from the small, inexpensive, attractive articles to those of moderately high prices, where the difference between the cost of production and the selling price of the antique is large enough to make the project worth while.

This does not necessarily mean that any category of antique is exempt from the work of the faker. What may be too expensive to fake now may not have been so thirty years ago. On the other hand, things that were not worth faking a few years ago may be worth faking tomorrow. It is for this reason that all antiques should be suspect as fakes from the start; for the making of imitations is as old as time.

THE REPRODUCTION

Whereas the fake is a fly-by-night, a thief, a blackguard and an impostor, the reproduction is under no such stigma. Reproductions are frank copies of works of art or antiques, made as nearly like the originals as we care to make them. They differ from fake antiques in that no attempt is made to antique them, at least with no attempt to deceive. They are examples of contemporary taste in an age of eclecticism. They vary from adaptations of older styles, as in the so-called traditional furnishings available through any outlet for mass-produced items, to carefully made-to-order, detailed copies of pieces actually on exhibit in museums and galleries.

Reproductions are respectable. Many writers on antiques advise readers of limited means to add or use good reproductions

in their homes to complete the total effect when the comparable antique is of such quality or rarity as to be unobtainable. This advice has been followed very consistently in
various restorations of villages and towns here and there
about the country. Sometimes whole blocks of buildings have
been restored to something even transcending their original
glory. The reasons for this are varied. Some extreme
restorations may be necessary to furnish backgrounds for the
antiques displayed therein in much the same way that a
museum of natural history will carefully construct a habitat
group to give the viewer an idea of what a forest or desert
biome really looks like. Antiques do look better displayed
against backgrounds like those for which they were originally
made than against the bare-bones background of a plain gallery.

For all such uses, as for a stage setting in the theater,
there is ample justification for using reproductions. However,
the average collector is not planning to restore anything. For
this reason, my advice is to avoid reproductions, and if you
plan to make use of new-made pieces, be sure that they are
examples not of what we think the middle of the eighteenth
century was but of the best-designed and made pieces of
twentieth-century contemporary style. As antiquarians, we
should be against both the fake and the reproduction. Aut
totus aut nullus.

THE SECONDHAND PIECE

The next type of antique represents a group of items that
fashion laid aside only yesterday. It represents the taste of a
time that is too close to the present to be romantic. It is
most usually described as nineteenth-century (as many of
these things doubtless are) in the hopes that the buyer's
nineteenth century ends in 1830 instead of in 1899. The distance
from 1830 to 1899 is only sixty-nine years, less than a life-
time. What is contained within those sixty-nine years, however, is such a multitude of styles as the world has not seen
before nor since. I suppose in all fairness we ought to admit
that our century is no stranger to multitudes of styles.

Most secondhand pieces are of mediocre character, to say the least, but they are salable to the inexperienced under the portmanteau term Victorian. Some, but not all, Victorian things are eagerly sought after by collectors. Therefore, it is well to learn which Victorian things are now collectible or are likely to be collectible in the near future. As for the other Victorian secondhand hand-me-downs, take Mark Twain's advice: "When in doubt, leave it out."

THE OVERRESTORED PIECE

One group of antiques that stands midway between legitimate antiques and fakes consists of overrestored, overrepaired, and overrefinished items. It falls into two subgroups. The first we can call the transformed group. These are objects that, intended for one use, have been converted or transformed to another. They might be typified by the spinning wheel converted into a lamp, tops to double chests into chests of drawers or melodeons into desks. The point is that in these transformations some portion of the antique is antique all right, but it is either a fragment of an antique or the antique has been dismembered and rearranged into "something new and strange." It is the newness and the strangeness of the result that should admonish us at once to leave it where we found it, no matter whether it is called a Rhode Island lowboy or not.

THE GLORIFIED ANTIQUE

There are always some for whom the best is none too good. I mean the lily gilders. Wherever we have antique collectors, we have them. What do we mean by glorification as applied to an antique? Well, we mean doing something to it that cannot be undone, with the purpose of making it look more important. We might cite as typical examples the carving of a plain piece or the application of veneering, inlay, or marquetry to a plain piece. Paint the bisque figurine or the Rogers group Indian red or antique white; you have done nothing except injure it.

The glorified antique is a ruined antique and not all your
piety or wit will uncarve the legs or restore the vanished
marquetry.

****

Now that the problems facing the collector at each purchase
have been enumerated, the next thing to decide is whether
they can be solved or not. Is it possible to make eighteenth
century objects in the twentieth century or is the worker a
prisoner of time in this respect? I believe that he is. The
relation of the worker to his time is the only certain way we
have to distinguish the works of one time from those of another.
If we are familiar with a time, we can recognize its works,
and vice versa.

The first tool we have is an understanding of how it is
that we recognize anything. Although a work exists as a thing
in itself, we cannot perceive it as such. The essential nature
of the work remains a mystery, since in order to perceive it
at all, we must perceive it in terms of such symbols as we
have at hand. Most of these symbols are verbal descriptions
of what we are looking at, but they may be visual symbols as
well. The symbols are not attached to the work but are con-
cepts and relationships built up over a long period of time by
the viewer. Many are peculiarly his own; most are peculiar
to his time.

Hence, it is clear that the work is accomplished by the
worker to fulfill his purposes in terms of his own and his
time's symbols, and they will be peculiar to him and to his
time. Time goes on, symbols used in the perception of a
thing change, while the work remains unchanged. For each
separate time, the work evokes a new set of symbols.

How does this apply to separating the fake from the genuine?
Consider an example: A chair actually made in the eighteenth
century remains, however, we describe it, a chair made in
the eighteenth century. For us to recognize it as an eighteenth-
century chair, we must have a generalized description of such
a chair in our minds. We apply it to the chair and if the
chair fits the description, then we believe we have an antique
chair.

Now, in the case of an eighteenth-century chair made in the twentieth century, the faker will work from the symbols he has to the actuality. Regardless of what care he takes in framing his description of the eighteenth-century chair, more characteristics will escape him than he includes, and since he must wind up with a chair in the end, he supplies their lack from within himself. The new eighteenth-century chair now differs from the old chair because of these omissions and substitutions. This combination of old and new in the fake leads to anachronistic inconsistencies that the faker cannot see because for him they do not exist.

The student of the past or the connoisseur has a collection of symbols that differ from those of the faker because they are different people and because to them the antique has different meanings. The connoisseur will, if he examines the fake closely, notice the inconsistencies and thereby uncover the fraud.

We can say that our technique of separating the alleged from the genuine antique is based on the following principles:

The first is simply this: History does not repeat itself or, as Heraclitus phrased it, "You can't step into the same river twice." If a man working in 1960 can make something undistinguishable from another something made in 1660, a mockery is made of antique collecting and even of the study of history.

The second principle with which we will work is that there is an intimate connection between the worker and the work and that antiques are products of time, place, and personalities.

The third principle is that any antique, as it appears to us now, is a combination of what it was when new and the things that have happened to it as a result of the passage of time. Since the vicissitudes of time are the work of nature, any attempt to imitate them results in a work of art. A work of art has purpose and pattern; in nature, the purpose and pattern are not revealed.

Now, with these three principles in mind, we are in a position to study what an antique is and also what it is not. How old must it be to be numbered among the acceptable?

Chapter II

THE ANTIQUE

What is an antique? At first, we are likely to make the assumption that it is something old. In fact, <u>old</u> and <u>antique</u> are frequently put together, as in the phrase <u>old antiques</u>. Thus: "She is living down there in the country with that house full of those old antiques." Another word is so consistently associated with the word <u>antique</u> that it goes together with it as <u>heinous</u> does with <u>crime</u>. I mean the word <u>valuable</u>. Any antique is always assumed to be valuable even when it isn't worth thirty cents!

The antique, then, must be old, and it is valuable <u>because</u> of its age. Is this the whole story? Waterworn pebbles of Triassic sandstone are millions of years old, yet no one would consider these antiques.

Antiques are things made by men that are valuable because of their age. Does this exclude all things not antique and not exclude things generally accepted as antique? No, for we must remember that there are a great many products of human activity (usually called artifacts) that are not of the order of things we would call antiques.

Suppose we start out with a general definition of an antique that runs something like this: An antique is a man-made object of a kind no longer made that is valuable because of its age and its historic implications.

VALUES OF ANTIQUES

If it were not for the existence of pack rats, magpies and jackdaws, one might conclude that the instinct for collecting and hoarding the uneatable was a purely human one, and if it were not for the existence of bower birds and others of their ilk, one would feel the same way about the ostentatious display of acquisitions. The moment we begin to collect, we want to

display our collections and use them in a kind of rivalry with
our fellow collectors. This rivalry gets to be very intense;
all one has to do is attend an auction or two to see it. As
soon as we have rivalry, we have a general degree of ranking
of items as good and bad or acceptable and not so acceptable.

A great deal of the ranking in the early periods of collecting
was a hit-or-miss proposition, since there were not enough
facts on which to set up standards. This ranking came rather
from the buying and selling of antiques.

The first collectors bought from original owners on any
basis that would complete a deal. However, as more and more
persons decided to collect antiques seriously, it became
inevitable that some of them would go into antique collecting
for profit and become dealers. Now this group was primarily
interested in antiques as a source of profit. It is obvious that
the higher-priced item or the one from which the dealer
could expect to get the most profit looked to him like the best
antique. In seeking these, he was bound at least to come into
conflict with other dealers doing the same thing. When this
happened, his ideas that one kind of antique was better than
another were reinforced. These conflicts often took place
in public, as at auction sales, where dealers, collectors,
and other interested parties were assembled.

Thus, long before many studies of the subject were undertaken and long before information about relative rarity,
desirability, and antiquity was assembled, relative values
had already been set up in the market place. Nothing has
really superseded this ranking, although it differs at many
points from the rank due these things as antiques. In price
valuation, dealers in particular frequently speak of an antique
as "a five-hundred-dollar table" without any reference to
style, age, or antiquity. It is for this reason that market-
price values are so likely to be capricious and can so easily
be changed by the appearance of an article or book on one
kind of antique or another. It is also possible to manipulate
the market price of an item.

I do not believe that this is a good way of ranking antiques,
but it is certainly the one that will persist for a long time,
because any attempt to set up any other system will, if

successful, merely cause another market-price fluctuation
rather than cause price to cease being equated with rank or
value.

There is not necessarily a one-to-one relation between the
desirability of an antique and its price, for the fashion of the
moment, the latest craze, frequently overrides established
values. At a moment such as the present when elegance is
emphasized in all departments of modern life, it is not surprising that the antiques that look the most elegant are the
rank leaders. This means that currently antiques of the
eighteenth century are most sought after. For this reason,
simpler, less elegant pieces of the seventeenth century are
relatively more easily obtainable and at lower prices.

Also, it may happen for a variety of reasons, not the least
of which is the vast army of casual, uninformed buyers, that
two objects sell for about the same price, although no one at
all familiar with what an antique ought to be would rank one
as the equal of the other. For example, early eighteenth-
century pieces of simple style will bring little more than
similar items from the early nineteenth century. However,
with the exception of things temporarily out of fashion, the
market place rules supreme and the value of a piece is its
money value.

There are other things meant when the value of a piece is
discussed, and one of them most certainly is: "How does
this antique stand in relation to other antiques?" This particular meaning of value comes up all the time in many different ways. It may present itself to you in the question of
whether to spend the money you have available on a pair of
chairs when what you were looking for was a chest of drawers.
Rank of the market place kind is not going to resolve this
kind of value problem (since both have the same money value)
but ranking of another kind may.

There are a large number of experts and collectors who
would like to think of antiques possessing in the aggregate
something called quality. That one antique is made of gold or
silver instead of copper or pewter or that one antique is better
designed and executed than another is certainly true, but
whether these factors really affect its antiquity or not is

questionable. Is an antique made of silver or gold any more
antique than one made of wood?

Quality is a characteristic chosen by the authorities in
much the same way that a political party constructs a platform.
Today's group may very well esteem what yesterday's group
decried. For this reason, quality is somewhat illusory, like
the Emperor's new clothes. But it has a magical aspect; it
rubs off on those who possess things having it. Sleeping in the
house where Washington slept or owning a bed exactly like the
one that belonged to Charles Carroll of Carrollton by some
sympathetic magic lifts the sleeper or owner above the ranks
of ordinary men.

Is there, then, no way of ranking antiques? That is, once
an object has been accepted in the proper circles as an
antique, is it then representative of a special class like aleph-
null, where each member is equal to any of the others or to
all of them put together? I am inclined to believe that in
general this is indeed the case. Once a thing becomes sought
after as an antique, it is equal to any other antique in its
antiqueness.

However, here, are two methods of ranking, neither of
which is precisely like that of the market place. The first is
ranking according to rarity. How easily can you find its
match? Bearing in mind that all antiques are rare, we can
classify them according to relative rarity. The classification
would start with common, thence proceed to relatively common, not common, somewhat scarce, scarce, rare, very rare,
and end with unique. The next question is, To what degree is
a unique pressed-glass cup plate equal in rarity to a unique
signed Boule cabinet? The uniqueness of each is undeniable,
but the rarity and desirability of signed Boule pieces is of a
much higher order than of cup plates, so the cabinet is in-
comparably higher in rank than the piece of glass. Thus,
uniqueness must be located within the class. We can then
compare classes for rarity and desirability, and the unique
piece of the class that is rarest and most desirable is the
highest-ranking antique. Unfortunately, rarity is not necessarily constant. Once a duplicate of the cup plate is found, it
is no longer unique, and its rank suffers accordingly.

Here is a way to set up a value system of your own that
will be as permanent as you care to make it, based primarily
on the kind of antique you like best. First, the most important
antique is the one that best exemplifies its type, style, and the
age that produced it. It is this consideration that should out-
weigh all the others. Second, in general, the older the antique,
the better it is. Third, the signed piece is more desirable
than the unsigned. Fourth, condition is of great importance
in giving value to antiques; the better the condition, the
better the antique. Fifth, a pedigree or history of the piece
is of great help in establishing an antique's claim to importance.

Nevertheless, I still feel that each antique (with obvious
exceptions, such as two chairs of the same set) is so individual
that one can hardly be compared with another.

I think we are now ready to re-examine our definition of
an antique to see whether we want to add anything to it. I
think we shall. An antique is a man-made object of a kind
no longer made that is valuable because of its age and historical implications. To this end, it should be a clear expression
of a time, a place, and a maker; for it is this quality above
all others that makes the antique.

HOW OLD MUST THE ANTIQUE BE?

How old must the antique be? The first problem is, must
the antique be older than a fixed number of years, say one
hundred, before it becomes antique? The second is, must all
classes of antiques possess the same age qualifications?
Let's take these problems one at a time.

Assume that an antique is anything over one hundred years
old. This means that all kinds of things that were secondhand
merchandise yesterday will be antique tomorrow. This
process, which will elevate the nonantique to the antique, being
continuous, would add constantly to the supply faster than the
supply was used up. Nonantiques do become antiques finally,
but at a pace much slower than the passage of time. That is,
of the many nonantiques that are now almost, or even more

than, one hundred years old, some may soon become antiques, but most of them will not.

When the Tariff Act of 1930 allowed things that were made before 1830 to come in free of duty as antiques, it was clear that those sponsoring it had in mind the one-hundred-year limit but were also aware of the problem posed above, so that they set a date before which a thing must have been made in order to be considered antique. Now, even with this system there is some latitude in deciding whether a thing belongs to a date prior to 1830. Currently, the tendency is to decide that if a thing <u>could</u> have been made before 1830, it is sufficient for customs purposes. This means that if a style started before 1830, even though it continued after 1830, things in this style will be considered as <u>circa</u> (around) 1830 and thus admitted duty-free. We shall see that setting a fixed date before which things have to be made to be antique, called by our hard Latinists a <u>terminus ante quem</u> (<u>boundary before which</u>), is probably preferable to the one-hundred-year rule.

Consider the next problem: Must all antiques have the same qualifications or does one kind of antique become antique earlier than another? At the present time, there are enthusiasts for the collecting of antique automobiles. The automobile has not been around for a hundred years, yet nevertheless we do have antique automobiles. Are they really antique? I can imagine the collector of Sèvres porcelains or of Flight and Barr Worcester saying, "Perish the thought!" Yet his collectibles were considered antique three or four score years ago when they were no older than the early automobiles are now. Thus, the answer to the second question is Yes, some kinds of things do become antique earlier than others. Therefore, using fixed dates or the <u>terminus ante quem</u> system, we can give a series of these fixed dates, one for each kind of antique.

Here I would like to call your attention to this odd fact: Writing about antiques and antique collecting began about the turn of the century, and the books of various sorts that discussed antiques set forth the classes and set fixed dates then acceptable as upper limits for antiques. With few exceptions, both classes and time limits remain as then set. Still more curious is the fact that in sixty years there have been added to this list only three types of glass and minor items.

Following is a list of dates older than which a thing must be to be antique in its class. The reasons for these dates will be apparent when each class is taken up.

Furniture

Before 1830

Ceramics

European c. 1830
Chinese Export c. 1840
Staffordshire c. 1850
American ceramics c. 1890

Glass

Blown glass, ordinary sorts c. 1830
Blown glass bottles and flasks c. 1860
Pressed glass of early types c. 1827-1850
Pressed glass of early pattern types c. 1840-62
Pressed glass of later pattern types c. 1863-1900
End-of-day blown types c. 1890
Opaque white, blue, green, black c. 1870-90
Paperweights c. 1915
Cut glass (with reservations) c. 1915
Art glass c. 1840
Iridescent glass (Tiffany et al.) c. 1926

Silver

American c. 1815-1830
European c. 1800

Pewter

English c. 1750-1800
European 1750-90
Oriental 1750

<u>Pewter</u> (cont'd.)

American 1860
English Britannia 1790
American Britannia 1860

TOMORROW'S ANTIQUES

What are the things unwanted today that will be antique tomorrow? Collectors all know of someone who collected the unwanted and found out later that he was only the first of a new crop of collectors whose follies became wise buying. All of us would like thus cheaply to assemble an enviable collection. Is there a way to do it?

There are many things unwanted today that will be wanted tomorrow. There are also a lot of other things equally unwanted today that will still be unwanted tomorrow. How are we going to distinguish one from the other? The advice I am going to give here is of the most general sort. As you study the style periods of the remote past and the nearer past, you may encounter something not now antique that takes your fancy. See how it fits the description of the antique of today. If the two tally and you like the piece and it has the air of belonging closely to a time and a place, it will likely be antique tomorrow. Most of the antiques of tomorrow, however, will be not something that today's antiquarian forgot from a past that lies near at hand, but rather something that is being made today.

Chapter III

Style has many meanings for us. We can relate it to a formalized mode of execution, like the Doric or the Gothic style in architecture, or to a peculiar personal style, like the style of Praxiteles or of Scopas in sculpture. We can extend it to mean the style of a given time and place, the mode of expression used in, for instance, seventh-century Egypt or twentieth-century France.

All of us are familiar with the way in which fashions change. We expect a style to last longer than a fashion, but the principle is much the same. If we think of the fashions of only a few years back, they seem to belong to another world. If we go back a generation or so, we are astonished to see how different was the appearance of the actual from the remembered.

But as we move back along the sequence of fashions and styles, we notice a curious fact: as past styles recede into the distance, they reach a point at which they seem no longer silly, and from there on they earn more and more the respect and admiration of the viewer. Distance lends enchantment in time as well as in space. When a style or sequence of fashion is thus removed from us in time, we discover a pattern in it. We can assign a cause for it. We can understand it by what prepared the way for it.

Another characteristic of style is that it is in a constant state of change. What makes it change in this way rather than in another way is something yet to be discovered. No one can recognize the moment when the style is changing. He can only recognize that it has changed. Styles evolve; they do not originate. Each new style has much more of the previous style in it than it does of innovation.

The unconscious evolution of styles is characteristic of most of the past. There have been periods in the history of art when everyone was acutely aware of style and was seeking to lay the foundations for a new one by picking over the bones of the past. Such periods are known as periods of eclecticism. It is hard to think of an eclectic style in the same way as one thinks of other styles, because it seems to contain no limits and no unity. Anything goes. It "praises in enthusiastic tones every century but this and every country but . . . our own."

It is odd and almost magical in a way that styles have such a broad base among the people. For why should the populace have decided en masse in 1788 or 1789 that they were through with curving lines and preferred furniture without these embellishments? Old bandy legs were banished to the attic and the new furniture produced was all in the new style with legs as straight as pokers.

The changes that must take place simultaneously in seemingly unrelated fields in order to produce a style change are remarkable. Sometimes the development of a new material such as porcelain makes possible designs of a kind not used before. Sometimes the needs of a design evoke new methods of construction and new tools. Sometimes new social and political changes bring about needs that can only be filled with new designs. Mostly, however, all of these changes take place together. Style changes, then, involve not just an aspect of the life of a people; they are a record of the changes that, in the large, we call history.

Take the style popular in the reign of King Charles II of England as an example. What are some of the things we can discover from it? One of its characteristics was the popularity of exotic materials. From all over the world came products —cottons from India, leather from Spain, silks from Italy and France, ceramic wares from China. These tell us of an extensive trade abroad. The elaborate carvings and the use of Classic patterns tell us of trade with countries to the south. The forms of the design and the materials in which they were executed show us the paths by which the Classical styles were reaching England. Flemish and Portuguese scrolls in the designs and the presence of "S" curves of a type different from those of France show that the styles of that country were not being picked up on their way north. Why are influences from farther off having more effect on the styles than those so close to home?

At first blush, there seems to be no relationship between a chair of Charles II style and one of Louis XIV, yet they show the selfsame elements. The French work is more polished, more sculptured, and more modeled. The forms have been assimilated. For the English, the forms are still new, they have not been polished. At the same time, the chairs look and are more sturdily made than those of the rival across the Channel. They are carved in solid wood and the surface is not coated with gesso and gilt. This forthrightness may be the result of poorer tools, workmen skilled in other manners of carving, or poorer glues for gesso making and a damper climate—but only in part. British suspicion of frills and belief in maintaining sturdiness of both form and construction were also important.

A style is not alone the result of material conditions. Workmen may be capable, the society may be opulent, the knowledge of the design forms may exist, but the way in which material, wealth, skills, and knowledge are used to produce an art form depend on the emotional responses of the people to the totality of their experience and to the things that went before. In the long run, this totality is the style. For each kind of work demands the tools, materials, skills, knowledge, and will to do it. They must all develop together or it cannot be accomplished. Style is mankind in his everchanging aspects.

Now that we have considered what style means as it expresses humanity, let us turn our attention to what we mean by a style. The meanings are several because they have different applications. A style is a group of related forms, materials, and ways of working that are sufficiently self-consistent to form a class of things different from all other things.

This group of objects will also be held together by contemporaneity of a wide or narrow range. For example, the term Renaissance style would refer to anything made between the beginning and the end of the Renaissance. This is generally accepted to mean from the end of the thirteenth through the sixteenth centuries in the Western world. We can limit the range by saying the Italian Renaissance or High Italian Renaissance to specify the fourteenth or fifteenth century.

Although long, the styles of the Renaissance resemble each
other much more closely than they do any other styles. The
styles of the eighteenth century or of the third quarter of the
nineteenth century may show that same consistency within
the narrow limits that we find in larger ones.

Finally, we can refer to styles as characteristic of a place,
as, for example, French (without reference to time). Things
can be said to be urban or provincial in style. They can even
be assigned to a single city, as in comments like "This work
is Parisian in style" or "This is Philadelphia cabinetwork."
We ought to remember that a chair can be Parisian, French,
Renaissance, and sixteenth-century all at the same time.
Each of these terms is general and therefore each refers to
different qualities a piece may have. Thus, the characteristics
that make a thing French are not the same as those that make
it Renaissance.

We can narrow the number of qualifying terms further.
Styles can be attached to the names of reigning monarchs and
thus we have a style of Louis XIV or of Francis I. A style
can be associated also with a designer or a cabinetmaker,
as was the case with Sheraton and Chippendale.

This is a good time to emphasize the considerable difference in meaning between saying "This is a chest in the style
of Louis XIV" and "This is a chest in the style of Boule."
In the one case we are giving it a place in time, and in the
other we are giving it a creator. Here is also a good place
to point out the difference between saying a chair is in the
Chippendale style and a chair is in the style of Chippendale.
The first statement relates to a type of design that the chair
has and the second implies, although it does not so state,
that the chair came from the shop of Thomas Chippendale.

There is yet another way in which we must apply the term
style. This is to use a descriptive name, such as Neo-Classic
or Baroque. Here the terms Neo-Classic and Baroque are
shorthand descriptions that tell us that the style uses this
kind of ornamentation and those sets of designs that are
associated with Neo-Classic or Baroque.

Styles also apply to the way an element of design or construction is handled, such as "This is a Newport ball-and-claw
foot," or "This chair has Philadelphia-style corner blocks."

Style, then, may mean any or all of the following things:

1. The purely personal methods of an individual cabinetmaker ("This is in the style of Thomas Tuffts.").
2. A manner of working peculiar to a place or a group
   ("The style of the London silversmiths").
3. A manner determined by the kind of ornamentation
   used ("Early ceramic productions at Meissen are in
   the Rococo style.").
4. The manner of working peculiar to a country ("This
   elaborate use of ormolu mounts is characteristic
   of French style.").
5. The manner of designing and working characteristic
   of a given monarch's reign ("This is in the style of
   Louis XIV.").
6. The manner of working peculiar to a given time ("This
   use of seaweed marquetry is peculiar to the style
   of the seventeenth century.").
7. The way of designing and building used over a period
   in history of some length ("The application of the
   acanthus leaf to the finials of a chair is characteristic of the Renaissance style.").
8. The distinctive feature of a great division of time
   ("The use of the five orders is a characteristic of
   Classical architecture.").

These eight applications of the word style are the major
ones.

How can we learn about the styles of individual workmen
and place them in time? To try to learn in detail the work of
even a few individuals entails a great deal more time than
anyone has. Fortunately, the situation is not entirely hopeless,
although trying to be an expert in all fields at once is. The
differences in design, workmanship, and finish between two
eighteenth-century chests made by different cabinetmakers
are a great deal less than those that separate the eighteenth
from the seventeenth and nineteenth centuries. Thus, once
one has learned to distinguish eighteenth-century furniture
from seventeenth- and nineteenth-century styles, learning
the differences from one cabinetmaker to another is not too
difficult.

Learning to distinguish one style from another requires that you have a good guide, good illustrations, a good memory, a good museum nearby, and a good set of arches. For those of you who find getting to the museum impossible, the next best thing is to look at pictures. Even fairly small libraries have picture books. Certainly one way to become familiar with what you want to know is to take every opportunity to examine, handle, and study every authentic relic that you can; for looking, testing, examining, and thinking about the nature of your quarry is the way to track it down.

The connoisseur is one who takes advantage of small differences. These cannot be appreciated if we are not aware of large differences between one era and another. The most important aspect of our knowledge of style for help in recognizing the genuine antique is the ability to use style differences and similarities to put the thing in its proper place chronologically. Once this has been done successfully, the major job is finished, since this establishes its antiquity or lack of it. Style can, then, be used successfully to rank the antique, that is, to show the extent to which the piece is representative of a style. A high style piece is more representative of a style than a piece not so high in style.

Remember Buffon's "Le style est l'homme même" (Style is mankind itself). Style is most certainly the antique.

Chapter IV

THE STYLES OF THE LAST
THREE HUNDRED YEARS (1600-1900)

INTRODUCTION

Styles, as we have seen, vary considerably from time to time and from place to place. What I will do here is to point out similarities in the various styles of several countries and group together those things that seem to belong together. We can then note what the variations in form of a given style are as it travels from place to place and develops in time.

Of the two kinds of change, that due to the development in time seems to be the greater. It is for this reason that a style originating in Italy in the sixteenth century may not make its appearance in England, for example, until the middle of the seventeenth. The style will have changed somewhat in the process of passing from country to country. But during the same time, the style in Italy will have changed in quite a different way, so there may often be a closer correspondence in style between the work of two countries a hundred or so years apart in time than there is between the work within one country over the same length of time. For example, the English were creating an English Renaissance out of the Gothic tradition at the same time that the Italians were fairly well launched on the Baroque style.

Thus, style of a given kind varies in two ways simultaneously: horizontally, from country to country; and vertically, from time to time.

What I propose to do is to look first to similarities rather than differences and group together styles that share a common tendency, describe this tendency, and then proceed to the next later style until we have come to the end of the sequence. As we do this, you will notice that these styles come in gradually, develop slowly, overriding—that is, combining with —existing styles, changing them, assimilating them, and finally reaching the point at which no vestige of the earlier style remains. When the style reaches its fullest development, you can see the faint beginnings of a new style.

Many books on the subject, especially the ones of the early years of this century, treat styles in an anthropomorphic fashion, assigning them birth, youth, maturity, old age, and decay. Decay suggests deterioration from good to bad, but today we prefer to think of changes as changes, without trying to decide whether they are good or bad according to some arbitrarily selected standard. This is primarily because, at this moment, we cannot find any general agreement on a standard.

It is well to remember one self-evident truth, and that is, simply, that style does not appear in all objects that are intended for use by men. Styles do not exist or change very much when life is at the subsistence level. Consequently, a certain amount of security and opulence is necessary before there is much in the way of possessions except those absolutely necessary to continued existence. In the past, possessions of any important kind were the prerogative of the powerful and well-to-do. As we approach our own time, the number of things an average family can have increases considerably and comes nearer to what we today feel is necessary to comfort and convenience. With this fact in mind, we can now get down to the business of tracing the development of styles of the last three hundred years.

For many reasons, but especially because England in 1600 was in transition from the styles of the Middle Ages to those of the Renaissance, which were founded in the Classical style, we will start at the beginning of it all with the Classical style. We can distinguish two tendencies in Europe. One follows the other in time, and it is possible, although little proof exists for it, that the one is southern and Mediterranean in origin, the other northern—Scandinavian, Germanic. The one we call Classical, the other Gothic

****

Classical refers particularly and specifically to the art and culture of Greece and Rome. The most characteristic quality of Classical art is, first of all, simplicity. The designs are arranged in orderly fashion with due regard to proportion and symmetry. The same element may be repeated to give rhythm, or different elements may be put together to provide harmony and balance. Most of Classical art is designed to be taken in as a whole at a glance.

The very foundation of Classical architecture is the orders. These orders, together with some other design elements, constitute the legacy of Classical design. We shall find it worthwhile to recognize them, since the details of the orders and the orders themselves constantly recur as decorative motifs in later styles of the centuries following the Renaissance.

The orders are as follows: Doric, Ionic, Corinthian, Aeolic, Tuscan Doric, Composite (Figs. 1-6). The basis of each of

Fig. 1 – Doric order   Fig. 2 – Ionic order   Fig. 3 – Corinthian order

Fig. 4 – Aeolic ·
column capital

Fig. 5 – Tuscan Doric
order

Fig. 6 – Composite order

these orders is the column or <u>stylos</u>, whence the word <u>style</u>.

The Doric column has twenty flutes, meeting in sharp edges. The column shaft tapers toward the top with a slight swelling in the center. On top of the shaft sits the capital, with its bulging echinus supporting the square abacus.

The columns support the entablature, which consits of three parts—the architrave, frieze, and cornice. The architrave, ornamented with taenia, rests directly upon the column capitals and, at intervals below it, are regulae, with their dependent drops. The frieze consits of two elements. The first is a triglyph, a block with three grooves in it.

Between the triglyphs is a metope, which may or may not be carved. The cornice, which slopes slightly downward, is ornamented below with a series of blocks called mutules, each containing three rows of six drops. The face of the cornice consists of a flat band over which is a small bed molding, a flat fillet and, finally, a crowning molding of cyma recta. The Doric order was otherwise not ornamented except by color.

The next order is called Ionic. It differs from the Doric in being more ornamented. Its column stands on a base, which in turn stands on a plinth. The base is round and consists of a turned molding of convex-concave-convex profile. The column has twenty-four flutes separated by fillets. Although the capital may be ornamented with additionally elaborate carving, the distinguishing thing about this order is the presence of two spirals or volutes at each side. The side of the Ionic capital adjacent to the volutes is called the baluster side. The architrave of the Ionic order consists of three bands and a crowning series of moldings. The usual set is a bead-and-reel carved astragal, above which is a cyma molding carved with Lesbian leaf.

The Ionic order of antiquity sometimes omitted either the frieze or the dentils, which were a row of projecting blocks above the architrave. Later, both frieze and dentils occur. In this case, the dentils surmount the frieze and are occasionally separated from it by a base molding such as an ovolo carved with egg and dart.

The cornice may or may not spring from a base molding. The soffit or undersurface of the cornice is plain. The face consists of a flat band surmounted by bead and reel and by ovolo carved with egg and dart or a cyma carved with Lesbian leaf. The crown is a plain cyma molding.

The Corinthian order differs from the Ionic in being still more ornamented. The base and shaft of the Corinthian order resemble those of the Ionic. The capital is quite different. First, it has a bell shape. Around the bell shape are two ranges of acanthus leaves from which double tendrils rise and curl on the outside to support the corners of the abacus, and on the inside to support an acanthus flower or anthemion

ornament. The entablature of the Corinthian order is the same
as the Ionic, except that it has both frieze and dentils. In
later Roman work, the entablature is enriched still more by
having extra bed moldings and a course of modillions or
brackets added between the dentils and the cornice.

The Aeolic order resembles the Corinthian in most details.
The capital again is different. It consists of a double range
of flutes becoming leaflike as they turn over at the top.

The Tuscan Doric or simply the Tuscan order differs
from the Doric in having a base similar to that of the Ionic,
more than one triglyph between columns, and, frequently, no
fluting on the column shaft. In the entablature, the mutules
are replaced by dentils.

The Composite order is similar to the Corinthian, from
which it differs only in its capital. This capital resembles a
Corinthian capital in which the spirals supporting the projecting angles of the abacus have been replaced by the volutes
of the Ionic order.

The Tower of the Winds capital (Fig. 7) gets its name
from a building in the Roman Agora in Athens.
In this capital, there is one range of acanthus
leaves and, above it, one range of water
leaves.

Before we end the description of the Classical style, we should look at the moldings
and carved ornaments most often used. They
are as follows:

Fig. 7 – Tower
of Winds capital

The torus, a molding of semicircular profile, ornamented
with several patterns, of which the scale and the guilloche are
the most common (Fig. 8a).

The fillet, a flat band, unornamented (Fig. 8b).

The astragal, a small half-round molding. It is usually
carved with a bead and reel (Fig. 8c).

The ovolo, an egg-shaped molding frequently carved with
a pattern known as egg and dart (Fig. 8d).

The cyma molding, which is S-shaped in profile. When the
lower section is convex and the upper concave, the cyma is
called a cyma recta. When the lower section is concave and

Fig. 8a – Torus molding

Fig. 8b – Fillet

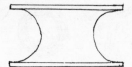

Fig. 8f – The Scotia

Fig. 8c – Bead and reel

Fig. 8d – Egg and dart

Fig. 8g – Cavetto with water leaf

Fig. 8e – Lesbian leaf

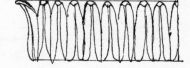

Fig. 9a – Anthemion

Fig. 9b – Maeander

Fig. 9c – Rinceau

Fig. 9d – Laurel wreath

Fig. 9e – Wave pattern

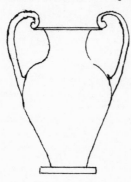

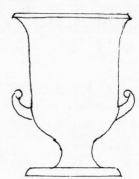

Amphora

Krater

Fig. 10 – Greek vases

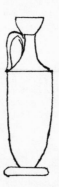

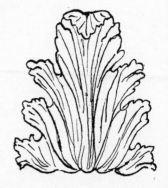

Hydria

Lekythos

Fig. 11 Acanthus

the upper convex, the molding is called a cyma reversa.
The usual carved ornament for the cyma recta or reversa is
the Lesbian leaf (Fig. 8e).

The cavetto, a particular kind of convex curve. A convex
curve is called a scotia (Fig. 8f); when one side only is convex,
dying away to a flat plane, the molding is called a cavetto. It is
occasionally ornamented with a water leaf (Fig. 8g).

The anthemion, a pattern alternating two forms of palmette
(palmette and honeysuckle and palmettes in bands) or a single
palmette (as in a finial). (Fig. 9a).

The fret or meander, sometimes called a Roman key,
of which there are many varieties (Fig. 9b).

The rinceau, which is a woven, continuous interlace of
acanthus leaves and branches, sometimes sprouting human
heads and mythical monsters (Fig. 9c).

The laurel wreath and ox skulls or bucrania (Fig. 9d).

The wave pattern (Fig. 9e).

I have also chosen to show some shapes of Greek vases as
they are frequently reflected in the shapes of various objects
at later dates (Fig. 10). The acanthus plant and leaf are also
frequently recurring ornaments (Fig. 11).

****

If Classical design was ordered and simple, intended to
be seen at a single glance, Gothic was not. Gothic art is
involved, intricate, and not regulated by symmetry or proportion. Variety, surprise, and magic were qualities emphasized by Gothic design.

Whereas simple construction is characteristic of Classical
architecture, the Gothic order consists of arches and vaults.
Arches, vaults, buttresses, piers, and colonettes achieved
the aim of Gothic art, which seemed to be to get as near to
heaven as the materials of earth would let it. Gothic architecture soars. The means of its soaring are, in part, its
structure, and so, we are told, Gothic art is an example of
form following function. This is pure nonsense. It is true,
however, that the creaking machinery that lifted the spires to
heaven and raised the tremendous naves 150 feet above the

pavement was always in evidence. In actuality, the forms of Gothic architecture have little to do with Gothic engineering, as witness the fact that the same dimensions or even greater ones were achieved at later dates when no vestige of Gothic forms was left.

You may wonder why there is this concentration on architecture when what we are concerned with is small objects— pieces of furniture, glassware, china, and such things in which there is nothing that could be called engineering. The reason for our quick glimpse at the nature and spirit of the Gothic style in architecture is that it represents a treasury of style forms that affect all the areas of Medieval or Gothic design. Gothic decoration on small objects is but an echo of the larger forms. Chairs and chests and seats are built like churches and ornamented in the same way. Gothic ornamentation consists of almost anything that human observation and fancy might dictate. It is complicated and involved and for this reason difficult to describe in general terms. Here, however, are some of the general features that are characteristic:

Sturdiness and largeness of scale with emphasis on structure.

Emphasis on vertical lines as opposed to Classic horizontality.

Network-like patterns of complicated form, generally called tracery (Fig. 12).

Pattern forms such as the pointed arch (Fig. 13), the trefoil (clover leaf) (Fig. 14), the quatrefoil (four-leaf clover) (Fig. 15)

Leaflike forms derived from the acanthus but much different in appearance from the Classic version (Fig. 16).

Ugly or fantastic human and animal forms not organically related to the designs, called grotesques, e.g., gargoyles (Fig. 17-18).

Columns of exceedingly varied forms, of polygonal cross section, molded, twisted, in pairs and groups (Fig. 17-18).

The crocket, a curl of leaves sprouting along the ribs or vaulting but mostly on exterior surfaces (Fig. 19 a, b).

Fig. 12 – Tracery

Fig. 13 – Pointed arch

Fig. 17 – Grotesque

Fig. 18 – Gothic columns

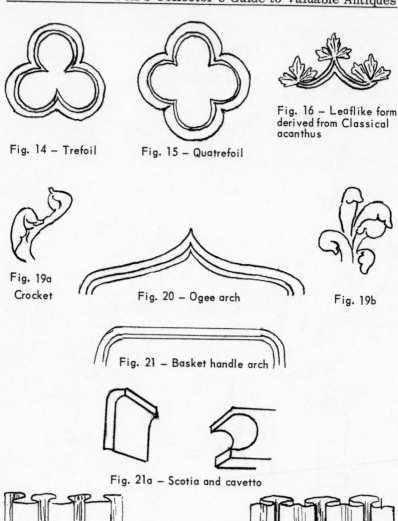

Fig. 14 — Trefoil

Fig. 15 — Quatrefoil

Fig. 16 — Leaflike form derived from Classical acanthus

Fig. 19a Crocket

Fig. 20 — Ogee arch

Fig. 19b

Fig. 21 — Basket handle arch

Fig. 21a — Scotia and cavetto

Fig. 22 — Linen fold

The ogee arch or the arch in form of a basket handle (Figs. 20, 21).

Moldings: These are varied but consist mostly of the fillet, the quarter-round, the half-round, the scotia and the cavetto (Fig. 21a). They seem to be used as fancy dictates and do not have the same relation to structure as do Classic moldings.

Gothic art was to be studied piecemeal, to be seen from a constantly changing point of view, and to be read like a book. During the great periods of Gothic art, the twelfth and thirteenth centuries, the greater part of the population was illiterate, and art took the place of books; hence the need for symbolism and the complicated iconography. Together with each saint went his special symbol, a wheel for St. Catherine, a lion for St. Mark. Symbolism and complexity are typical of Gothic ornament.

From these two styles, Classical and Gothic, was made the subsequent art of the Renaissance and modern times. The styles of the last three hundred years show the gradual progress of Classicism and the retreat of the Gothic. The causes of the Renaissance and the nature of this great cultural period are not going to be discussed here in detail, except for some dates.

One date for the beginning of the period is the collapse of Constantinople in 1453, some 147 years before we take up the study of styles. However, it is rather hard to accept a single cause as exciting so much change so suddenly. And, as a matter of fact, this is not the case. The Duomo in Florence was begun and almost finished before the fall of Constantinople. The constant exchanges of peoples and ideas between the East and the West during the periods of the Crusades had made the Classical heritage more accessible, and enriched the city-states of Italy at the expense of the East.

The Renaissance as it affects art seems to begin in Italy at the end of the thirteenth century and in England about the middle of the sixteenth century.

****

The Renaissance differs from both the Classical and Gothic periods in that it was a conscious effort on the part of the

Italians to regain for themselves and for Italy the form and appearance of past glories. They sought to restore the glory of Greece and the grandeur of Rome to the best of their abilities. The ground soil and conditions in which the new style grew was the style of the Gothic world, and the continued classicization of this Gothic world makes the story of the styles of Western Europe from this moment on.

We first see Classicism appear as a minor decorative feature in connection with other kinds of decoration. At the beginning, the nature of the form is imperfectly understood and the detail is added as an encrustation on an essentially Gothic structure. As time goes on, and more and more Classical details are added, there comes about a change of structure to accommodate more of the classicizing ornament. When this change is complete, Classicism has triumphed. The elements and forms used are all Classic-inspired but the way in which they are used and combined is not Classical. Finally, the forms and decoration correspond to a large degree with the Classical past, and the triumph of Classicism is now complete; so is the Renaissance, and we have passed from the Medieval to the Modern world.

Since there are several recognizable steps along the way, we can give these steps names. It is well to remember that the process was gradual and continual and that all chronological limits are arbitrary, but the following names can be given to the style periods of the last three hundred years:

Late Gothic, including Flamboyant and Perpendicular Gothic and its transitional phases to the commencement of the next type.

Renaissance or Classicizing, including Early and High Renaissance.

Baroque, including variations of this theme as long as it lasts.

Rococo, a style originating in France, and its extensions to other countries.

Neo-Classicism — first phase.
With this comes an end to the sequence of evolving styles.

Greek Classic Revival.

<u>Eclectic</u> styles or styles of the nineteenth century:

> Late Neo-Classicism (continuation of Greek Revival)
> Gothic Revival
> Italian Revival
> Rococo Revival
> Neo-Feudalism
> Antiquarianism
> Naturalism
> Art Nouveau

THE LATE GOTHIC STYLE

This style is the one popular at the end of the Medieval period. Here and subsequently, I shall describe style in terms of furniture, because this is where, next to architecutre, style is most easily seen.

The majority of Gothic pieces are plain, rectangular forms, fastened together with mortise and tenon joints, and pinned. Panel construction is used. The wood is usually oak. The repertory of furniture is definitely not large—beds, stools, chairs, cupboards, tables, and chests (Figs. 23-31). Of these, chests are the most numerous and the most clear-cut representatives of the style. The chest consists of several wide, heavy planks nailed together and bound with wrought iron. It is utilitarian, sturdy and heavy; its sole ornament is the hardware. Notice that the ornament is extrinsic, not part of its basic design. A more elaborate chest may be constructed of panels. These may be perfectly plain or they may be embellished with carving. The carving may be of linen fold (Fig. 22) or of typical tracery.

Panel construction is also used for some chairs (Fig. 26, 31) and cupboards. The chairs are frequently high-backed and with straight arms. The whole is constructed of joinery. In chairs and cupboards, the tracery carvings are frequently pierced or à jour. The smallest objects are made as if they were parts of buildings. As the late Gothic reaches the end of its time, the applied tracery disappears, the forms and carving become simpler. Some of the carved ornaments become influenced by Classical forms. Some lighter pieces of

Fig. 23 — Beds of Gothic design (three variants)

Fig. 25 — Cupboard with a jour carved tracery

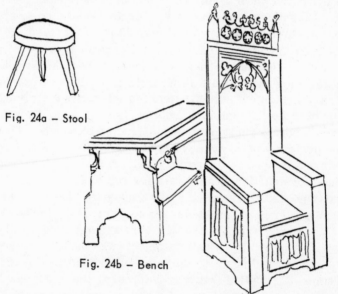

Fig. 24a — Stool

Fig. 24b — Bench

Fig. 26 — Chair joined, carved with linenfold, tracery, and a jour cresting

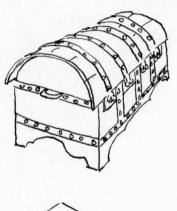

Fig. 27a – Chest of planks
bound with iron as sole
ornament

Fig. 28 – Table of planks
laid on horses

Fig. 27b – Joined, panelled chest carved with
tracery on face, linen fold on end

Fig. 29 – Square post slat back chair – fourteenth to eighteenth century

Fig. 30 – Spindle bark turner's chair, of American type called Brewster chair

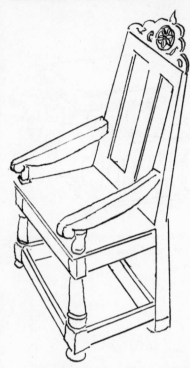

Fig. 31 – Joined and panelled
wainscot (oak wood) chair

furniture, such as chairs
and stools, are made with
mortised or drilled joints
(Figs. 24b, 30). Chair posts
are embellished by turning and
chamfering. Tables are
planks supported on horses,
like a carpenter's saw horses.
(Fig. 28).

There is a third type of
chair in which the members
are mostly turned (Fig. 30).
These, in themselves, because
of the turning, show some
Renaissance characteristics.
Such is the kind of furniture
in use in France and the Low
Countries during the fourteenth and fifteenth centuries,
in England in the sixteenth
and (in country districts) into
the seventeenth century.
It forms the earliest phase
of furniture-making in the
American colonies up to 1660 or even later. The furniture
sets the tone for the style, which is simple, straightforward
and, on the whole, ponderous. The chief instruments used in
the work were the ax, the knife, the drawshave, and the
chisel (in such varieties as were needed for the execution of
the designs).

THE RENAISSANCE STYLE

The Renaissance required little more in the way of furniture than the Late Gothic (Figs. 32-40). The chief difference
was in the ornament and in the greater use of turned pieces.
The Gothic spire and crocket was replaced by an acanthus
leaf. The panel enframement became simpler and the panel

Fig. 32 — Chest or Cassone ornamented with rams' heads,
gadrooning, lions' paw feet, and Classical moldings

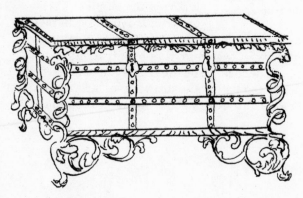

Fig. 33 — Iron-bound chest with ironwork in
classicizing form

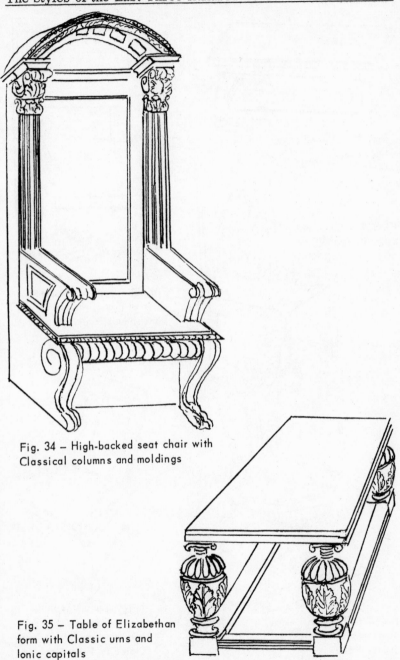

Fig. 34 — High-backed seat chair with
Classical columns and moldings

Fig. 35 — Table of Elizabethan
form with Classic urns and
Ionic capitals

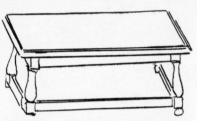

Fig. 36 — Joined bench with vase-turned legs

Fig. 37 — Chair with supports in the form of Tuscan columns

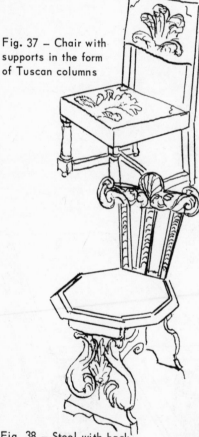

Fig. 39 — Typical Renaissance chair with arms ending in lions' heads, finials in the form of acanthus scrolls

Fig. 38 — Stool with back ornamented with classicizing detail

Fig. 40 — Joined chair in form of stool with back and arm supports assimilated to Tuscan columns

was carved with the late Gothic linen fold. The space left
vacant by the departure of the applied carving in Gothic taste
was soon appropriated by Classical detail. Acanthus leaves,
lion heads, or other Classical ornaments were used on ends
of chair arms, and finials were used on chair backs.

The high-backed seat chair (Fig. 34) of the Medieval period
was duplicated in construction, but equipped with a monumental, architectural, Classical pediment, triangular or seg-
mental as the case might be. S-shaped consoles formed the
arms. The back stiles were in the form of a Classical order,
usually Ionic or Corinthian. The iron-bound chest (Fig. 33)
remained, its hardware wrought in semblance of Classical
forms. Where turning had been used in tables (Fig. 35),
stools (Fig. 36), or the small chairs with low backs upholstered (Fig. 37), the turnings might take the form of Tuscan
Doric columns with smaller columns to support arms. Classical urn and vase shapes were used as supports.

Smaller pieces had analogous forms. Finials, stretchers,
arms, aprons, and side rails furnished a field for carving
and for the use of moldings of Classical form. The ovolo and
cyma moldings were especially favored. Stools began to sprout
backs and these ultimately to sprout arms, thus giving rise
to a new kind of chair (Fig. 38, 40).

The earliest type of chair is foursquare and solid in construction (Fig. 39). This type disappeared from the scene
about the end of the seventeenth century. It was revived with the
return of Medievalism in the third and fourth quarters of the
nineteenth century.

The second form of chair (cf. Fig. 31) resembled the
first except that it was lower, of panel construction, and had
open arms and four legs tied together below with box stretchers.
In this type of chair, the back legs and posts were all of a
piece. The arms were supported by elongations of the front
legs. Seats were square or rectangular.

The third type of chair is the stool with back (Fig. 38). The
legs rake out to make it sturdy. The back rakes backward at
a cocky angle and is frequently held in place by the arms. This
chair is less dignified in appearance than the other types, but
certainly more comfortable. The latter became the ancestor

of most French and Italian chairs, the former of English and American chairs. Construction varies considerably between the two types, but time has brought them close together in appearance.

Supports provided a magnificent field for the carver and gilder, no matter what their form. At first, the carving is only applied to or sunk in the surfaces. Chests and cupboards form an elegant example of such carving. Now they are ornamented with Classical patterns—egg and dart, Lesbian leaf, acanthus leaves—and pagan subject matter. Panels are shaped in the form of semicircular arches. Columns of Classic form are used on cupboards, legs get longer, drawers are added to the upper and lower sections. The ornament is always largely an added feature. Remove Classical ornament, substitute Gothic, and you are back where you started.

There are, however, many changes, one of the most notable of which is in the increased amount of furniture in use. This leads us to another difference and that is the wide variety of forms. As the number of forms increases, the more likely special uses will be found for the different kinds.

The character of High Renaissance furniture shows all of these characteristics: first, complete dominance of Classical decoration (you should note here that if the furniture of the Renaissance bears any relation to Classical furniture, the resemblance is coincidental); second, there is a great variety of types and these vary not only in decoration but also, and most importantly, according to where they were made; third, all pieces made at this time show considerable monumentality; fourth, the decoration is extrinsic, like the iron decoration on the chest—it might as well be pasted on; fifth, there has been a continuous effort to lighten the structure in every way possible. The pieces have dignity, proportion, and sturdiness.

THE BAROQUE STYLE

The Baroque style can be said specifically to be that style in which the Classical elements of design, including the orders, were used for coloristic effect to create patterns of light and shadow without any attempt to use them architecturally, that is to say, structurally. The orders are as unfunctional as if painted. Fronts of buildings are no longer straight but may be elaborately curved in plan, with a number of hexagonal bays or semicircular projections. Pedimented window heads alternate with segmentally arched ones. Plans are irregular and full of surprises.

A new type of colonnade appears. This is based on a column, called the colossal column, which rises through more than one story. Such columns make façades more imposing and enhance the verticality at the expense of Classical design. The element of light and shade is carried out by making use of rusticated masonry and many projecting cornices and moldings, all of which cast shadows and enhance the play of light and dark. The vertical emphasis is carried still further by having each horizontal molding break in and out as it passes over vertical members. Statues are placed above the columns so as to break the horizontal line of the flat roof and create the effect of a series of spires. It is almost as if the Gothic were having its revenge on the Classical style.

The colorism is equally evident in interior walls, which are broken up by paneling. Columns or pilasters flank bays and niches alternately.

It is under the influence of this style that curved designs begin to affect the form and structure of the chair. The "S" curve becomes prominent as a support for the various types of furniture (Fig. 42). In the beginning, the designs are so arranged that the curves are of simple curvature, that is, they curve in only one direction at a time. X-shaped or saltire stretchers appear first as straight stretchers. Then the arms of the X are brought into an S-shaped form. Gradually, the supporting members are set cornerwise in many instances, to give an effect of curvature in two directions. This is called the cabriole leg (Figs. 44-47). It seems to get its name from the leaping goat. Indeed, in this period and in the preceding one, leaping goats and mythical animals as well as human figures (Caryatids and Atlantes or Giants) are used as supports for furniture. In addition to the Classical zoo of fantastic animals, satyrs, masks, shells, acanthus leaves,

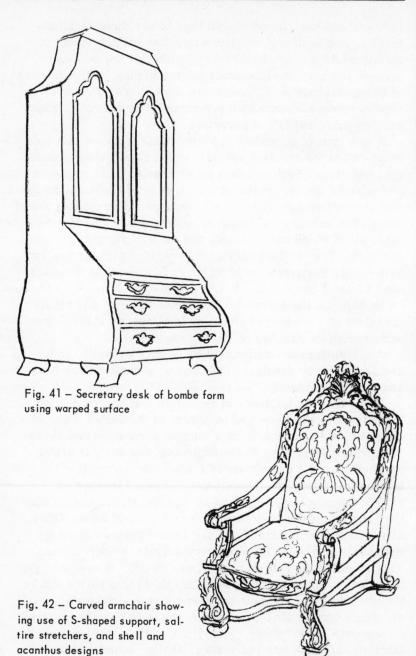

Fig. 41 – Secretary desk of bombe form using warped surface

Fig. 42 – Carved armchair showing use of S-shaped support, saltire stretchers, and shell and acanthus designs

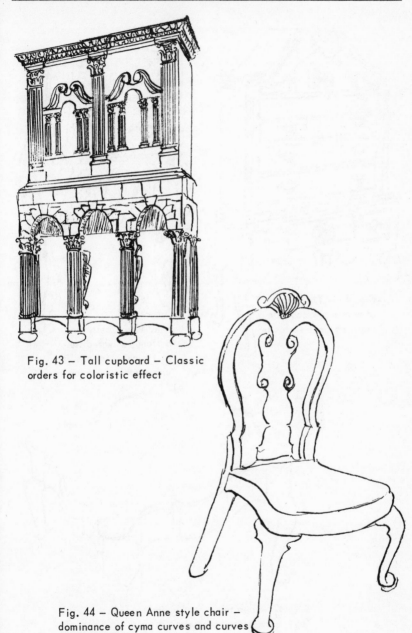

Fig. 43 — Tall cupboard — Classic
orders for coloristic effect

Fig. 44 — Queen Anne style chair —
dominance of cyma curves and curves
in plan

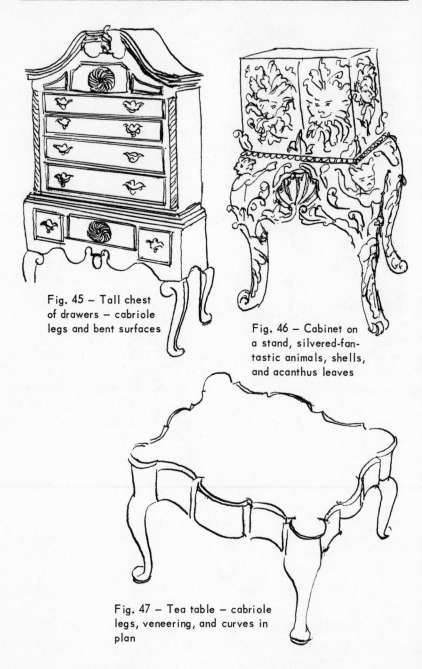

Fig. 45 — Tall chest
of drawers — cabriole
legs and bent surfaces

Fig. 46 — Cabinet on
a stand, silvered-fan-
tastic animals, shells,
and acanthus leaves

Fig. 47 — Tea table — cabriole
legs, veneering, and curves in
plan

rocks—the whole Classical mythology—are conjured up to
serve as ornament (Fig. 46). Reappearing also in these
styles is the occasional use of grotesques as elements of surprise and excitement. Ornament tends to be piled on ornament in one delightful, tumbling confusion (Figs. 42, 43, 46).

By the time the Baroque style has run its course, almost
all the forms of modern furniture have been developed and a
few besides. Not all Baroque furniture is heavily ornamented.
All make a great use of the cyma curve and, in general, the
curve in plan (Fig. 47). Seats of chairs depart from straight
rectangles to trapezoids narrower at the back than in front.
Upholstery is the rule rather than the exception. Legs of
chairs and tables are carved very heavily, as are the skirtings and the backs (Figs. 42, 46).

Another characteristic of the Baroque period at its later
end is that it enjoys warped or bent surfaces, such as bombé
or bulging shapes for various case pieces (Figs. 41, 44, 45,
47). S-shaped fronts to cupboards and chests (Fig. 41) curve
sinuously but monumentally to give the fullest play to the
surface of beautifully figured wood. Veneers, marquetry and
inlay are characteristic. There has been a change in woods
used. Walnut, beech, fruitwoods and, finally, mahogany
replace oak. The Baroque style is always monumental (Fig. 43).
Baroque pieces show an amazing variety in form and design
over this period, and while as time goes on the style gets
less ponderous, it is always bold and impressive, never
fussy or delicate.

In conclusion, we can think of the Baroque style as making
use of Classical details with a familiarity that frequently
verges on contempt. The general effect is not dissimilar to
the complication and variety of Gothic work. It differs from
the Renaissance and Classical work in its colorism, its infinite variety, and its richness. In many respects, the Baroque
has the qualities of a fusion of Classical and Gothic. The
ornament and superficial form remain Classical, the structure
and use are still, in part, Gothic.

THE ROCOCO STYLE

By the end of the sixteenth century, France was becoming the most important and wealthiest power on the continent of Europe. The Renaissance in France was well established and had combined with the Baroque to develop French forms somewhat more restrained than those of Italy and Spain. Under Louis XIV, France tended to supersede Italy as a center of style. By the end of the seventeenth century, the styles of Italy begin to have a French look—a little more exuberant, perhaps, but not inordinately different.

The Baroque style made much use of shells and rocks as part of its ornament. The very name, Rococo, seems to be derived from the French rocaille—(rockwork) and coquille —(shell). Thus, rococo is shell-and-rock work. But that is not all.

The Rococo house—and we think of the style primarily in connection with domestic architecture—is close to being un-adorned on its exterior, except occasionally for the brick and stone work at the corners. Such ornament as may occur is used around the principal openings. It follows Baroque usage, but a tamed and restrained Baroque.

Rococo design seems rather to belong to the inside of a house, for it is too subtle and soft in its forms, too fanciful in its images, to endure, undiminished, the harsh light of day. It has a made-in-the-moonlight look about it. Every line is a flowing line. There are no straight lines observable in most Rococo design. Bisymmetry is avoided in the best Rococo work (Fig. 49). Anything executed under the influence of this style is crawling or infested with carving (Figs. 48-51). But what delightful carving—fanciful, delicate, light, airy, and deceptive—above all deceptive. For never are Rococo things entirely what they seem. All is becoming. The changes seem to go on under your very eyes.

One of the tricks of Rococo fancy is the image of double reference. Feathers that become trees or are trees, flowers that become or are faces, and so on (Figs. 50a, 51a). This is the moment of illusion. Paintings are made to look like real objects and vice versa. The whole of the Rococo is one

Fig. 48 – Chippendale's "ribband back chair," decorated with acanthus leaves, foliated borders, C-scrolls, ribbons

tremendous optical illusion, a <u>trompe l'oeil</u>. All that is evanescent and delicate, bizarre and fantastic, is grist for the mill. Figures from far-off China rub elbows with shepherds and shepherdesses (Figs. 50b, 51b); the gods of antiquity, especially the Amores, play among garlands of flowers. Fairy dragons fight with knights in armor. To subdue them all becomes part of the artist's material. Medieval Gothic tracery is embellished with Classic acanthus leaves in the continual search for what is new, what is novel, what is fantastic (Fig. 50c). Fantasy has a delicate touch, its fabric light as gossamer. It is magic, fairylike. Its palaces and

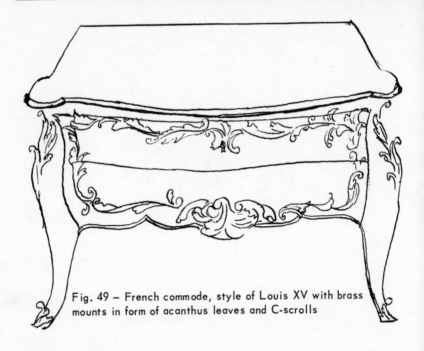

Fig. 49 – French commode, style of Louis XV with brass mounts in form of acanthus leaves and C-scrolls

drawing rooms are fit for Queen Morgan le Faye and then they are gone, like the Fata Morgana. For the age of the Rococo is also the age of reason. It is the age of enlightenment, the age of revolution.

THE FIRST PHASE OF NEO-CLASSICISM

The Classical styles, which seemed to have danced themselves out in the exuberant Baroque and which were not greatly important in the Rococo style, became the sources of the last of the great styles—the Neo-Classic.

When Robert Adam did the continent, he went south to study architecture. Southern Europe, both contemporary and ancient, was his particular interest. Finally, he undertook

Fig. 50 – Rococo orna-
ments – fantastic bird,
C-scrolls lattic work,
dripping water, tree of
double reference, Chinese
figure, Gothic arches, rocks

Fig. 51 – Rococo ornament,
top to bottom: C-scrolls,
dripping water, lattice work,
shepherdess and lamb, foliated
border, bird with wing feathers
developing into acanthus leaves.

a study of the Palace of Diocletian in Spalato (1757), which provided him with that glimpse of Roman private palaces for which he had been searching. The knowledge gained by Adam served as the foundation for his style. The publication of his studies in 1764 acquainted the world with the results of his research, but Adam had already completed the remodeling of Syon House, where the "new style" is very much in evidence. By 1763, he was the chief architect to George III.

It is tempting to attribute the rise of the new style almost entirely to the efforts of Adam, but the ancient cities of Herculaneum and Pompeii were uncovered at about this same time with their wealth of information about ancient domestic architecture and painting. Herculaneum was being systematically excavated from 1738 to 1780. Published material became available in 1757. The excavation of Pompeii began in 1763, so that, by the third quarter of the eighteenth century, there was available not a little material on Roman domestic architecture. The parallelism between the style of Louis XVI and that of the brothers Adam is close and yet too distinct to say that one was the source of the other. Their relation is one we have to discover in the source from which each drew its inspiration.

The Classical orders, when used, are used in the manner for which they were designed—as supports. The proportions are changed from Classical rules. The columns are more attenuated and the superstructure is lightened. The architrave, frieze, and cornice are cut down from a third to a quarter of the total height to a fifth, sixth, and even less. Wall surfaces are left plain. Ornament is concentrated on doors, windows, cornices and chimney pieces. Ceilings get extra ornamentation by being coffered and decorated with paint and molded stucco.

Decoration derived from the Roman Imperial period is one of the important innovations of Neo-Classicism. Thus, painted panels and painted furniture are used (Fig. 61). Fantastic but ordered forms of very slender proportions frame the decoration.

Adam and his contemporaries, having designed more intimate, more delicately chaste Classical interiors than had

Fig. 54 — Upholstered side chair
in style of Louis XVI with rope
turned legs, guilloche border,
acanthus feet

Fig. 52 — Neo-Classic armchair with
legs in the form of a bundle of reeds,
shield-shaped back, and bosses on
arms and legs. Style of Hepplewhite

Fig. 53 — Serving
table in Neo-Classic
style showing fluting
of legs, paterae on
skirting, tapering legs,
spade feet, swags

Fig. 55 — Term (pedestal) for
bust or urn. Hepplewhite. Use
of patera, water leaf, pendant
husk ornament

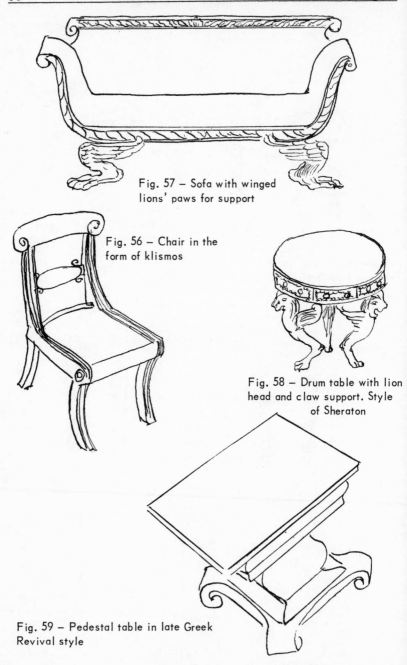

Fig. 57 – Sofa with winged lions' paws for support

Fig. 56 – Chair in the form of klismos

Fig. 58 – Drum table with lion head and claw support. Style of Sheraton

Fig. 59 – Pedestal table in late Greek Revival style

Fig. 60 — Pier table in Greek Revival
form

Fig. 61 — Painted Sheraton
chair

been seen theretofore, did not take kindly to having them spoiled by the introduction of overornamented furniture. Rococo design was about as welcome in the Adam drawing room as a prima donna at a choir rehearsal. Adam, therefore, undertook to design the furnishings that went into his houses. The style of the new Classicism, then, adds a new kind of furniture design to the books.

Pieces are designed with the rugs, carpets, hangings, lights, and the other furniture of the room in mind. Rooms in the Adam style were frequently of odd shapes, with circular or elliptical plans. Tables, sofas, and benches, designed to fit against the walls of such rooms, would fit in only one spot. Adam favored clean, simple decorative motifs, which he used to perfection over and over again. The flute, the water leaf, the husk pattern, paterae, and wreaths were tantamount to a signature (Figs. 52, 53, 55). Adam used inlay and marquetry in the furniture he designed. Abandoning the curved supports, he designed straight legs for chairs, tables, and case pieces (Figs. 52, 53). Sometimes the legs are carved; more often they are inlaid. Backs of chairs are of simple shapes, such as the circle and the oval. It is amazing how the furniture of Louis XVI shows these same elements combined in much the same way to produce an effect that is as clearly French as the other is English (Figs. 52, 54).

The cabinetmakers seeking help in designing pieces in the new taste soon found it in books. Two notable books were published toward the middle of this phase of designing, one by George Hepplewhite in 1789, and the other by Thomas Sheraton in 1791. These two men have lent their names to two versions of the Neo-Classic style in furniture, today called Hepplewhite and Sheraton. Their books served as the chief source of designs for the Neo-Classic style in England and America.

The Neo-Classic style is polished and extremely tasteful, if somewhat thin and cold. The designs tend to emphasize delicacy, intimacy, and special use. The words that best describe this style are exquisite, elegant, delicate, detailed, refined, polished—and cold. This Neo-Classic style is never massive, ponderous, or dull. It suggests a style at its best in boudoirs and drawing rooms—in fact, in any place where

the petticoated half of humanity might be imagined as gracing
the scene and dominating it with its charms.

THE GREEK REVIVAL

One odd thing about furniture styles is that somehow, every
so often, they get involved in politics. The style that ends the
eighteenth and opens the nineteenth century is such a style.
The Greek Revival was the result of political causes that
shared in making it the symbol of political change.

We mentioned earlier that the eighteenth century was the
century of revolution. The first revolution was that of the
American colonies against the British. In 1789 the United
States of America was two years old, if its beginning is dated
by the adoption of the Constitution, or thirteen if we take the
usual 1776 date. The artists and literary figures of Europe
may have been seeking to restore the glory of Greece and the
grandeur of Rome, but the Americans were not seeking Roman
grandeur or Grecian glories—they had them. They were the
heirs of antiquity. The Greeks and Romans were held in
honor second only to God. Rome was a republic, so was the
United States. As the people held the power in Athens, so did
they here. Since, then, we had a Roman government of
Grecian spirit, it seemed to follow that we could pretend to
their pre-eminence in art and literature. Where were the
artists? No one knew, but everyone expected them to appear
momentarily. What form would this art take? Why, it would
assume that form that is as natural to art as breathing is to
man, the very aim and inspiration of every artist—the
Classical form! No one doubted it and so it came to pass.
The Neo-Classicism of the British and French was received
with open arms. The Neo-Classic wasn't Greek, but this did
not matter: it was getting there.

The style of the brothers Adam and the style of Louis XVI
began, in America, to merge into a more or less unified
form called by us the Federal style, since it belongs to that

period when federation was important and the Federalists were politically powerful.

By the time the Federation was well established, the French were having a revolution of their own. If the Roman Republic was the inspiration for America and Republican France, the Roman Empire was the inspiration for Napoleon. The French Empire needed an imperial standard of art and elegance. Pompeii and Herculaneum were mined once more for the forms of art to magnify an emperor. Where do the Greeks come in? Well, the Greeks didn't come in, they were discovered. In his designs for an empire, Napoleon somehow overlooked Greece as he picked up pieces of Europe. But the English, prevented by Napoleon from studying in Italy, went to Greece. During these years accounts, sketches, and stories began to furnish artists and decorators with new forms and a new experience of old forms. The Classic Revival became, like the Romans it emulated, quickly Hellenized.

The Greek Revival differs in one marked fashion from the other styles that have been encountered up to now. This most important characteristic was the attempt to achieve archaeological correctness. The orders were no longer <u>derived</u> from the antique, they were <u>copied</u>. This tendency to go back to the source had a powerful effect on the style of furniture. Up to this time the furniture designer took the form that was fashionable and combined it with fashionable ornaments to get a design that would be fashionable. By the time of the Greek Revival, the designer might consult a book to see exactly what a Grecian chair was like.

More and more publications were being devoted to the past. Greek architecture was available in publications such as Stuart and Revett's <u>Antiquities of Athens</u>. The Hamilton collection of Etruscan vases became available as a sourcebook. Thomas Sheraton used vase paintings as sources in his second book, published after his death, under the title, <u>Designs for Household Furniture</u>.

The strong resemblance his designs bear to the work of the designers of the French Empire cannot be entirely coincidental. Chairs have the form of the Greek klismos (Fig. 56), but are rather richer in carving and in the application of odd details.

Feet are in the form of paws of various animals. Backs, when not upholstered, have a rich variety of unlikely forms that derive from the fanciful ornaments of the third and fourth styles of Pompeiian wall paintings.

Carved caryatids again are called into use as supports and ornaments for tables, desks, cabinets, and sofas (Fig. 60). Lyres and winged lions' paws occur as supports for tables and sofas (Fig. 57). Tables used pedestals rather than legs for support, in the form of a column rising out of a plinth set on four paws. Pedestal tables (Fig. 59) have an advantage over tables with legs: there isn't always a leg in your way when you want to sit down and the skirting doesn't damage your knees. But pedestals with four feet are unstable: if the feet reach out as far as the extent of the top, the table is reasonably steady; but in order to provide stability, the legs stick out too far. The solution to this problem is to make the base sufficiently heavy to lower the center of gravity—resulting in a loss of delicacy. The style tends to be heavy, ponderous and, on the whole, dull (Figs. 56, 57, 59, 60).

Furniture of this second phase of Neo-Classicism starts out simple, charming, at home in the beautiful renditions of the Greek Revival house. As the style grows older, the furniture also becomes more monumental, finally overpowering. It is not at home in less than imperial quarters.

The Greek Revival came to a rather sudden end and left no legacy to other styles. Its failure is not due to the fact that it didn't succeed in its aim, but rather that it succeeded too well. It ends the Classical influence in the Western world as a vital creative force. Once you have scaled Everest, there is no place to go.

THE ECLECTIC STYLES

The Greek Revival demonstrated that the past could be mined for what it was worth. But the immediate past was, on the whole, uncomfortable. Life was changing all over. The world of the banker, businessman, and factory worker was too much with the people. The middle-class world of the 1840's and 50's wanted comfort and quiet, a chance to manage its affairs properly and to get away from it all.

One way of doing this was to pretend it wasn't there. This kind of pretense leads to daydreaming, fairy stories, and tales of ghosts, hobgoblins, and haunted castles.

The Gothic Revival was, as the name implies, an attempt to do the same thing with Gothic forms that had been done so successfully with the Greek. Scholarship uncovered the necessary facts, the designers made use of them, and the success of the revived Gothic was as great as that of the Greek. The work in Gothic, at first hesitant, quickly became scholarly and has left us with such charming edifices as Neuschwanstein and the restorations of Carcasonne, to say nothing of the delightful carpenter Gothic of our own country.

Concurrent with the revival of Gothic architecture was the revival of the Rococo. The flowing lines of the Rococo period, but particularly the Rococo of France and its provinces, were copied and the salient points stressed. The curved lines curve much more, the upholstery is much thicker and softer, the carving is in high relief and more naturalistic, the wood is more in evidence, the pieces heavier. Much of the furniture is machine-made.

The name <u>Victorian</u> will pop into your minds, but the style could equally well be called Louis Philippe, and this is surely another indication of the character of this eclectic period—its international character. Its furniture can be called Victorian and made in London, but it could equally well be made in Grand Rapids or Istanbul.

However, Eclecticism rapidly becomes boring, so, before we know it, we have a series of other revivals. We can lump the whole group of these hunting expeditions into the past under the heading <u>Antiquarianism</u>. Those who were wealthy and powerful began to ransack the world for examples of painting, sculpture, and the like to glorify their names and their houses. Those who were not so wealthy went in for emulation—cheaply. They bought contemporary things that were "superior" in appearance and "better made" at a fraction of the price.

Price was the ruin of many an artistic movement of the
nineteenth century. The need to produce cheaply and the
need of certain designs for handwork were contradictory. The
manufacturers did not know which line to develop. To be safe,
they followed the middle course of taking a little from each
style of the past, with astonishing results. Some designers
took umbrage at such methods and tried to get back to honest
craftsmanship, blaming the manufacturer for what was a fault
of the times. Medievalism was one such brave and futile
attempt, Eastlake's efforts still another. These attempts to
improve design by introducing hand craftsmanship, which few
could afford and fewer would pay for, ended by adding to the
hodgepodge.

In desperation, the designers decided to try all over again.
"Consider the lilies of the field . . . They toil not, neither
do they spin . . . Even Solomon in all his glory was not
arrayed like one of these." Evidently, considering the lily was
taken quite seriously, because the new Naturalism and its
close cousin, Art Nouveau, produced a tremendous number of
lilies—lily electric lamps, lily vases, lily patterns in textiles
and leather goods, lily carvings. The growing lily imparted
its form to the moldings in a room so completely as to give
the impression that they had grown there.

The eclectic nineteenth century has produced the form and
substance through which we view the past. The eclectic approach to art still remains. The characteristics of eclecticism
are, in brief: styles are combined without regard to com-
patibility; basic forms undergo rapid changes according to
fashion; sources reveal themselves in the object; designs are
likely to exist in many versions of increasingly poorer quality;
and they are likely to be international in distribution—no hint
of their nationality is apparent.

We have at last come to the end of what is the most basic
chapter in this book. If you make use of these capsule descriptions of the styles, you will learn something of their
character. Use the pictures for reference and you should
begin to get some feeling for them. The tables in the Appendix
will give you a ready reference to dates and also to different
names for the same thing.

In discussing styles, I have spoken of them largely in terms of furniture. This is because the evolutionary nature of style is clearer in furniture than in other objects, and once you understand it in furniture you can recognize it in other kinds of antiques. To help you decide whether a piece of furniture is really as old as its style seems to say, I shall discuss how furniture is made, of what materials, how put together, and what the telltale marks are that betray the spurious or prove the authenticity of a piece.

Chapter V

FURNITURE

CONSTRUCTION, MATERIALS, AND TOOLS

Once we have placed an object within a style, we know
approximately how old it <u>ought</u> to be. If it is truly old, materials, tools, and workmanship will be consistent with its
style. Both materials and tool marks should support its
claims to antiquity. Perhaps this Louis XV chair is too
delicate, the lines curve too much, the carving is too obvious,
and somehow the chair is too typical. After you have settled
on the style, you are ready to look at the way in which the
piece is finished, searching for something wrong there. In
many cases you will find it. Always remember that workmanship also has style.

Each man using a tool will do so in a different way, depending on many factors, such as his size, weight, and tempera-
ment, as well as his experience and training. Let two men
saw a board. If one man is approximately six feet six and
weighs about 250 pounds, while another is a bare five feet
and tips the scales at 120 pounds, it is impossible for them
to leave the same marks. For the greater height and weight
of the first man will tend to make his saw cuts more vertical
and farther apart than those of the second. If this is true,
how much more variation there will be between the work of
men with different tools and training and different work to
carry out! Inconsistencies between work and style in joinery
and workmanship will be bound to show up in a fake.

To this end, we can examine profitably the joints. The
joints are what hold furniture together. A piece of furniture
is as good as its joinery.

Wood splits easily in the direction of the grain but will not
split across the grain. Just as it comes apart most easily in
the direction of the grain, so, if we get the grain in two
pieces of wood running in the same direction, they are easy to

fasten together with glue, nails, or other fasteners. When we attempt to fasten the wood in such a way that end grain meets a side or end grain, it is difficult to get a good surface for gluing or nailing that will not come apart easily. Therefore, joints were developed for the purpose of holding an end grain to an end or side grain.

Joints Used in Fastening Pieces of
Wood Side Grain to Side Grain

Of these, the simplest is the butt joint (Fig. 62a, b). The

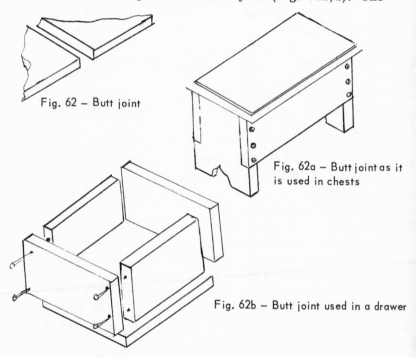

Fig. 62 — Butt joint

Fig. 62a — Butt joint as it is used in chests

Fig. 62b — Butt joint used in a drawer

end is squared in reference to the faces of the piece and the adjacent piece is butted against it. It is used on doors, table leaves, and other movable joints, and nailed and glued block work to turn a corner or make a box. The use of a butt joint for most purposes, except for gluing two boards side to side to make one wide board, is an indication of old, primitive, or crude work. (Fig. 68).

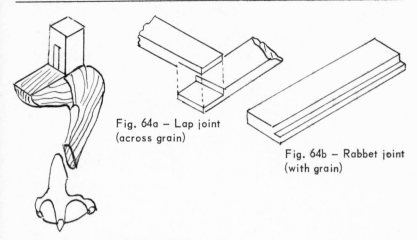

Fig. 64a – Lap joint
(across grain)

Fig. 64b – Rabbet joint
(with grain)

Fig. 63 – Scarf joint used to attach a new
(white) foot to a broken cabriole leg (grained)

Somewhat similar to the butt joint is a scarf or beveled
joint. This joint is used principally to fasten two pieces of
wood together so that the joint does not show. Scarf joints
(Fig. 63) show where repairs have been made, but they were
also used early in special cases, such as in fastening back
legs to the backs of some upholstered chairs.

The next most complicated joint is the rabbet or lap joint
(Fig. 64a, b). It is used in some types of panel construction
and in the backboards of case pieces, designed to stand against
the wall. In the latter use, this joint was seldom glued—the
lap was to keep dust out. This is an early construction not
used on fine furniture much after the earlier part of the
eighteenth century.

Similar to the rabbet but slightly different is the dado or
grooved joint (Fig. 65). It is used to hold panels (Fig. 66a)
and drawer bottoms in place. In conjunction with a tongued
piece, it makes the tongue and groove used for floors and
siding (Fig. 66b). It served as a transition type of joint in
table leaves (Fig. 67) and in the construction of the tops for
tables. Dado and tongue and groove are rarely glued except in
very modern work.

Figures 67, 68, 69 show three types of table joint. Earliest
is the butt, next the tongue and groove, last the rule joint.

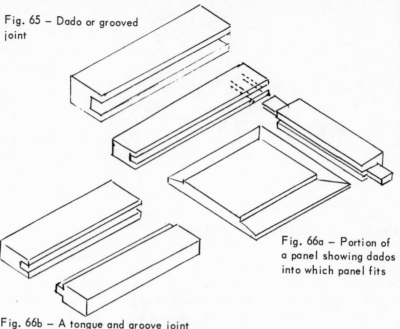

Fig. 65 – Dado or grooved joint

Fig. 66a – Portion of a panel showing dados into which panel fits

Fig. 66b – A tongue and groove joint

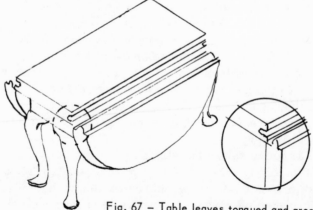

Fig. 67 – Table leaves tongued and grooved, a type of table joint seen on early and simple eighteenth-century tables

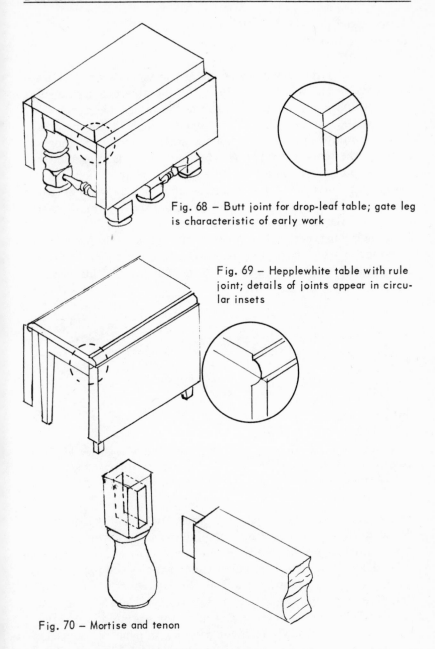

Fig. 68 – Butt joint for drop-leaf table; gate leg is characteristic of early work

Fig. 69 – Hepplewhite table with rule joint; details of joints appear in circular insets

Fig. 70 – Mortise and tenon

Joints Used in Fastening Wood End Grain
to Side or End Grain

The best joint to use where end grain meets side grain is
the mortise and tenon (Fig. 70). The mortise is a rectangular
hole, which is cut in one member of the joint. The tenon is
the squared portion of the other piece, which fits in the hole.
In the old days, pin holes were cut in the mortise and those
through the tenon were placed off center so that when the
tapered pins were driven in, the shoulder of the tenon was
pulled tight up against the other member. They were used for
paneling, chair, table, and bed construction, and in all case
furniture wherever panels were used.

Panel construction is a prominent part of early furniture
making. A panel is a flat piece of wood of such size and thickness that it can fit into a frame (Fig. 71a, b). To this end,

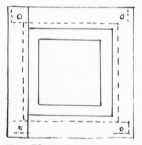

Fig. 71a – Panel as seen
face on. Dotted lines show
mortise, tenons, and dados
invisible from outside

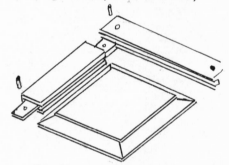

Fig. 71b – Exploded view of panel in
Fig. 71a; one stile and one rail not
shown for sake of clarity

the outside edges of the panel are usually beveled or cham-
fered to fit in a groove run in the horizontal and vertical
pieces that make the frame of the panel. The horizontal pieces
are called rails, the vertical, stiles; hence such paneling is
known as stile and rail. It is usually the stiles in which the
mortises are cut; the tenons are on the ends of the rails.

Panels may be single or multiple; for example, a chest
may have a front made of three panels. In panel work, the
mortise and tenon are generally pegged and seldom glued;

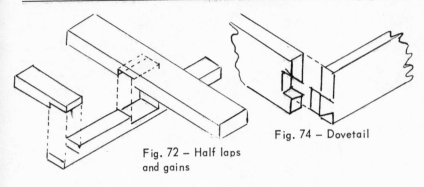

Fig. 72 – Half laps and gains

Fig. 74 – Dovetail

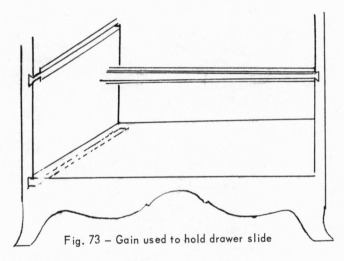

Fig. 73 – Gain used to hold drawer slide

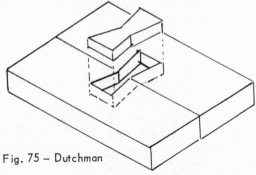

Fig. 75 – Dutchman

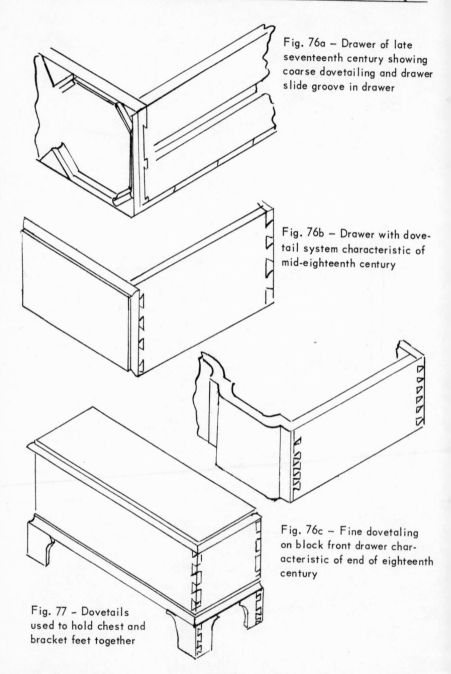

Fig. 76a – Drawer of late seventeenth century showing coarse dovetailing and drawer slide groove in drawer

Fig. 76b – Drawer with dovetail system characteristic of mid-eighteenth century

Fig. 76c – Fine dovetaling on block front drawer characteristic of end of eighteenth century

Fig. 77 – Dovetails used to hold chest and bracket feet together

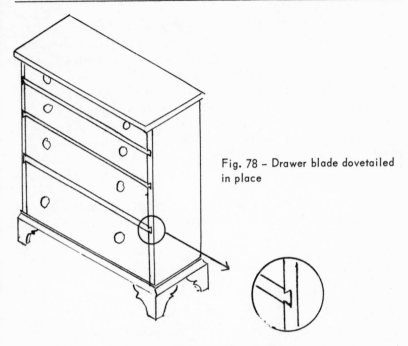

Fig. 78 – Drawer blade dovetailed in place

where glued, they are seldom pegged. The panel is never glued into its dado.

Another method of fastening boards together is by half-lapped joints or gains cut in wood (the gain is much like the dado, although it usually runs across the grain instead of with it). Half-laps (Fig. 72) and gains will not stay together without glue or nails or both. Lapping is used to hold light structures together—to hold on drawer fronts or to hold in place drawer blades, drawer slides, dust panels and, occasionally, the bottoms of drawers (Fig. 73).

Next in strength to the mortise and tenon is the dovetail, a truncated wedge used to hold two pieces of wood together (Fig. 74). Except for the Dutchman (Fig. 75), dovetails are usually multiple and are used most frequently to hold the front of a drawer onto the lining (Fig. 76a, b, c). Dovetailing is coarsest on Late Gothic and Renaissance pieces (many of which are not dovetailed); the finest is encountered in furniture of the 1840's. Dovetailing, then, other things being equal, is a clue to date. Handmade dovetails are all typical of the time and the workman.

Dovetails are used also to fasten the drawer blades (Fig. 78) into the sides in case pieces, to fasten the tops into the sides of tall case pieces, and to fasten the skirting of tables together at the corners where a mortise tenon joint is not used. In chests, dovetails are often found as a more elegant means of fastening than nails or iron bands. Chests so fastened together are early. The dovetails may show on the ends, but not on the face. In this case, the dovetailing is said to be blind. Dovetailing is used to hold the corners of bracket feet together and again is a sign of earliness within the construction (Fig. 77).

A final way of joining two pieces of wood together is by means of a joint called a miter (Fig. 79). A miter is necessary

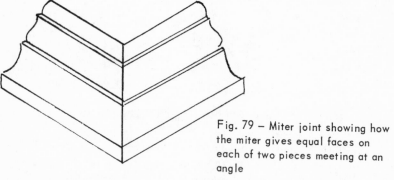

Fig. 79 — Miter joint showing how the miter gives equal faces on each of two pieces meeting at an angle

where two pieces of wood meet at an angle that is most commonly a right angle but is sometimes another angle. The angle of the saw cut is always half of the angle at which the pieces meet. This means that the length along the miter will be the same on each piece of wood, an important consideration in matching moldings. The miter is used where a molding turns a corner or to avoid showing end grain.

A miter is usually strengthened in one of three ways. First, dovetails can be constructed on the inside of the miter (Fig. 80). The joint has the appearance of the miter and the strength of the dovetail. Sometimes a dado is cut in each face of the miter and into this is fitted a piece of wood called a spline or a feather (Fig. 81a, b). Splined miters are not often used in antique furniture, but they are common in modern work.

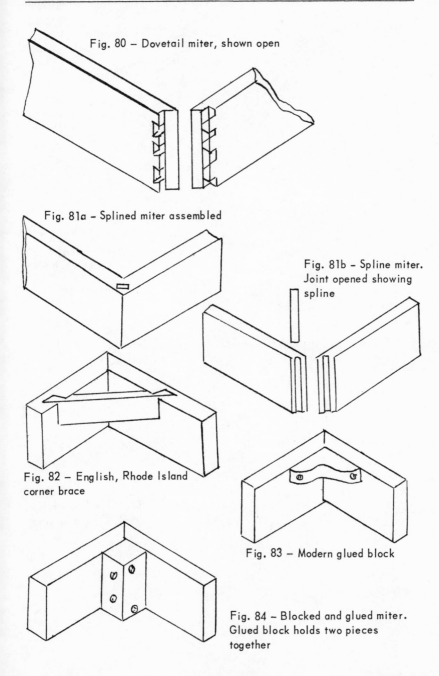

Fig. 80 – Dovetail miter, shown open

Fig. 81a – Splined miter assembled

Fig. 81b – Spline miter. Joint opened showing spline

Fig. 82 – English, Rhode Island corner brace

Fig. 83 – Modern glued block

Fig. 84 – Blocked and glued miter. Glued block holds two pieces together

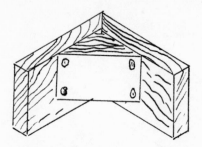

Fig. 85 – Ordinary American corner brace

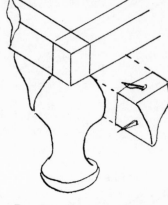

Fig. 86 – Ornamental glued block nailed and glued in place

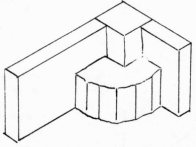

Fig. 87 – "Philadelphia" corner block

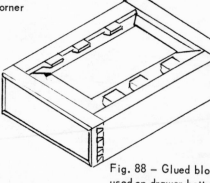

Fig. 88 – Glued blocks used on drawer bottom

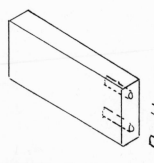

Fig. 89 – Doweled joint

The third and most common type of reinforcement is a block glued to the inside angle of the miter.

This brings us to two other methods of fastening two pieces of wood together. Both make use of extra pieces. One is the dowel and the other the glued block method. The glued block (Fig. 84), although not nearly so strong or dependable as the dovetail or mortise and tenon, is very often found.

Glued blocks were frequently used with mortises and tenons and dovetails to reinforce them. Nails were commonly used with glued blocks. Ornamental glued blocks also fill in the corners between leg and skirting in the Queen Anne, Chippendale, French Baroque, and Rococo work (Fig. 86). In much English and some other Continental work, these blocks were mortised into the legs and nailed into the skirting, in addition to being glued.

Glued blocks were also often used to hold bottoms in drawers (Fig. 88), to hold drawer slides in place, to hold tops of chests and tables in place, and to secure bases onto the tops of case pieces made after 1760. The glued block is still in use but is generally screwed in place.

The English and some other cabinetmakers of Europe preferred to run strips across the corners of the piece inside. These strips are generally glued and often fastened in place across the corners by dovetailing, although they are sometimes nailed (Fig. 82). The grain runs in the direction of the strip. Cabinetmakers in Rhode Island and Baltimore followed English usage. Most American cabinetmakers used a corner block, set so that the grain ran across the corner (Fig. 85). In Philadelphia in the eighteenth century, the corner block was set with the grain running vertically and its interior corners rounded (Fig. 87). This type of corner block spread from Philadelphia to the rest of the country at the close of the eighteenth century.

The second method of using a wooden piece to hold furniture together is the dowel method (Fig. 89). Dowels are cylindrical pieces of wood of various lengths. A hole is drilled in one piece and another in the piece to go against it. The dowel is coated with glue and inserted in the hole on the first piece, then in the second hole. The pieces are clamped together, the excess glue removed and set. Doweled joints are inferior to any other kind because they loosen on shrinking. Doweled joints open up readily, so the important points are also reinforced with nailed or screwed blocks.

Except for turned members such as chair spindles and rungs, table and chair legs or in any furniture where the dowel is turned or put on the rung or spindle at the time of making, dowels were not used on antique furniture. There are some chairs, tables, and case pieces in which the legs are doweled on, but here again the dowel is part of the leg or foot. With these two exceptions, dowels were not used until about 1835-40. Thereafter, they became the rule. Conservative European cabinetmakers carried earlier construction methods into the later periods.

Tools

The study of construction methods also involves the use of tools. New tools can beget new ways of accomplishing old needs, and as easier, faster, or better ways of doing things are discovered, they will displace the harder, slower, or poorer ways. Poorer tools get discarded, and with them the skill to use them. We have evidence that remarkable work was done with stone tools. Yet give them to a modern cabinetmaker and the chances are he would not be able to accomplish a thing with them. Today the carpenter depends heavily on saws, hammer, plane, and chisels in about that order. The joiner in the Late Gothic period depended heavily on ax, adz, knife, drill, and chisels in this order. The ax and adz served as saw and plane for squaring wood and bringing it to a smooth face. With drill and knife, he could cut a mortise and make a tenon. Chisels served for carving.

To saw logs into boards is a difficult operation; it requires a pit and two sawyers. If you can split the wood you save a lot of trouble and work. A plank split out is much better than one sawed out because it follows the grain. The early cabinetmarkers were expert at splitting woods. A riven piece is unmistakable once seen. It has a slightly irregular but shining appearance. A riven surface shows no tool marks of any kind but it is not perfectly <u>smooth</u>.

Woodworking tools are really of three basic types, of which the ones used for pounding, for example, the hammer, do not leave marks upon it. This reduces the basic kinds of cutting tools to two types—those that cut by a knife-like action and those that cut by abrading the surface. An example of the first kind is a knife; of the second, the saw. A knife does not leave a hole or remove any material as it cuts. It merely parts the wood. In parting it, it compresses the fibers slightly in the direction of the cut. The knife cannot enter the wood very far without getting stuck, so knives are used only for splitting thin pieces, for short cuts, and for removing small pieces. A very important use of the knife is for layouts and markings, for instance, mortises and tenons, dovetails, etc. Such lines usually occur on antique furniture even of the finest sorts. The saw, on the other hand, is narrower at the back than at the cutting edge, for the alternate teeth of the saw tilt outward in what is called the set. Since the saw removes little pieces of wood, it doesn't usually get stuck in the wood and can be used for long cuts across or with the grain.

Tools That Cut Like Knives—The ax is very little more than a large and very heavy knife attached to a handle. It is used for felling trees and for splitting wood. It comes in a number of forms; the most common variations are the hatchet and the broad ax. Wood can be split or a log can be squared with it to the point of looking as if it had been sawed and smoothed. This tool can also be used for large-scale ornamentation of timbers or house frames. The ax makes the same kind of mark as a knife, only a little broader slice is removed—up to eight inches and considerably longer.

The marks of the ax, like those of the knife and of splitting, will be found only on the heavy members of the earliest pieces of the Late Gothic and the Early Renaissance. The chip removed by the ax is flat across its breadth and slightly concave along its length. An axed surface is quite smooth to the touch except that it has a slightly wavy surface.

The adz is a tool very like the ax and leaves much the same kind of mark, except that its dimensions are smaller and the surface it leaves is less wavy. Adzes were used by early carpenters to level floors, smooth heavy planks, and do a variety of jobs beyond belief today. The adz replaced the ax work on Renaissance and later furniture. Properly used, an adz can do such an excellent job that its use is very difficult to detect from its marks. The surface it makes is like that of an axed surface except that its unevenness is slighter. The marks of these tools (adz and ax) will all be found on unexposed surfaces (except in the crudest and simplest work). Although these are unfinished they show a dull luster in the right light.

Another cutting tool used in antique work is the spokeshave or drawshave. This is a heavy knife with the blade mounted so that there is a handle at both ends. It was used to round spokes, as is suggested by its name, but it also served to smooth rounded supports, to shape chair splats, to true up squared work of smaller dimensions, and to round legs of tables and chairs. The spokeshave was used to smooth the shaped portion of skirting, cut-out work, and pierced, à jour carving (when it was not too small). A spokeshave could and frequently did take the place of a lathe. It was essential in shaping the legs of furniture of Baroque type.

The mark of the spokeshave resembles that of a plane except that it follows the most irregular contours. The direction of working is always parallel to or angled with the grain. The spokeshave was frequently employed for bringing the edges of heavy planks (used for table tops) to a thin edge along the surface. Like the marks of splitting by ax and adz, the marks of the spokeshave are seen chiefly on interior surfaces.

Chisels were used for a variety of jobs in addition to carving. Chief of these was the making of joints. Although the mortise and tenon can be made with an augur and a knife, it can be made more easily with a chisel. The mark of the chisel is like that of the plane or ax, but of very narrow width. The chisel has always to run in the direction of the grain and cut down across it at a slight angle.

Flat chisels are used chiefly in making joints, and you usually have no opportunity to see their marks. Carving chisels have flat, curved, and variously shaped sections. These are called sweeps or gouges. They vary from semicircular section to V-shaped to almost flat.

The mark of the chisel in carving is very characteristic, since it cuts downward across the grain at the same time that it cuts across it. It leaves a polished surface. Good, skilled carving has this polished look, which is clearly noticeable even under a finish. Carving, of course, may be early or late. You can identify the carved surface by rotating it under the light. Carving was not sanded until into the nineteenth century, so early work will show every tool mark. Tool marks do not too often help much in dating carving, except that modern tool marks are mostly removed with sandpaper. Modern carving will, then, either be too suave and competent in its lack of tool marks or else look as if it had been smoothed with sandpaper, and so lack sharp edges.

A plane is little more than a chisel in a frame. The plane leaves the surface smooth and leaves little evidence of its presence except at the edges of its knife. To avoid this line, the blades of smoothing planes were rounded at the corners. A plane so used leaves only the faintest suggestion of a hollow mark along the surface. These marks usually are too slight to be seen but may sometimes be felt.

Besides smoothing planes, there were grooving planes for making dados, rabbet (rebate) planes for the construction of rabbets, beveling planes, molding planes, and scrub planes. Most of these planes betray their use by slight irregularities in the work. Modern planes leave perfectly smooth surfaces, while the hand plane is likely to jump slightly when it encounters a harder spot in the wood. Hand-planed moldings will be found in all work down to the end of the 1830's; they are likely to be a bit irregular.

Especially important is the mark of the scrub plane. Its large curved blade brought boards to the proper thickness. It was often used across the grain. Its marks consist of a series of parallel, shallow grooves, or flutings, meeting in sharp irregular line. It ceases to be used much after 1800, except in country-made pieces.

Last of all is the scraper, which served to remove irregularities left by the smoothing plane. Its mark was also a slight flute, which can be felt rather than seen on tops of tables and other surfaces. We should not expect to see the scraper in

evidence much before the seventeenth century (except on
refinished pieces).

Tools That Cut by Removing Pieces of Wood—An example
of a tool that cuts by removing little chips of material is the
saw. Saw marks were left only on surfaces not expected to
be seen at all, for example, the dovetail and tenon. The
presence of saw marks is almost sufficient to warrant rejec-
tion.

You should be able to recognize and distinguish between
three kinds of saw marks indicative of machine sawing. The
first of these is the mark of a circular saw. It consists of a
series of curved bands paralleling one another. The marks
of the band saw consist of straight parallel lines perpendicular
to the edge of the board. The old-fashioned up-and-down saw
leaves marks somewhat similar to those of the band saw,
except that the parallel marks are always 3/8 to 1/2 inch apart
and ragged. It is not a conclusive indication of date.

We find the augur used from the earliest times right up to
now. Its most common use was for boring holes for pins or
for mortises. A related tool was a reamer and/or special
flat-bottomed borer for boring tapered holes. The tapered
holes for rungs and chair legs were thus bored. This is, at
least, what is to be expected. A cylindrical hole in this use
should be an object of suspicion.

There is one more group of tools that work in much the
same way as the saws, that is, they cut by removing small
chips. They are rasps and files. Rasps are metal bars of
differing shapes—flat, round, and half-round—which are
covered with little sharp points. These, when rubbed over the
surface of the wood, tear it down very quickly. They were
used in the old days mostly for roughing up a surface to be
glued or to which veneer was to be applied. Files are like
rasps except that they have a regular pattern of teeth caused
by crisscrossed lines milled on the surface. Files are not
usually employed by woodworkers, but their marks are often
met with in old and new work.

The rasp and file leave characteristic marks—a series of
parallel grooves crisscrossing at various angles. Such surfaces almost never appear on old work. Sandpaper usually

indicates subsequent reworking and refinishing. Marks of filing in places where it cannot normally be seen, such as the undersurfaces of aprons of tables, the skirting of chairs, and the inner contours of knees on cabriole legs, are almost certainly an indication of new work.

Fasteners—While the best way of fastening woods together is to use the wood itself, other fasteners are used. Nails are pieces of bronze, brass, iron, or steel that have a head at one end and a point at the other. They are driven into pieces of wood to fasten them together.

The earliest nails are fairly large and heavy. They were made by hand out of chunks of red-hot iron, hammered to a point from all four sides, and after that the head was spread out. Nails of this kind were used on very early furniture. The hammered head identifies them. Nails were used to hold some chests together, to hold backboards on chests, to hold sides of drawers to the face, and to hold the bottoms of drawers in place. Smaller nails without heads were used to fasten applied carving on cupboards and chests of drawers and the half-turnings, moldings, and blocks characteristic of Renaissance and Baroque furniture.

Later (c. 1780), nails were cut out of iron plates by hand. Such nails have the head on one side and taper to a point on two sides only. The similar machine-cut nails of a few years later were introduced into cabinetmaking about 1800. By 1840, the familiar cut nail with a head made by machinery was available. It has a square head and slopes to a point in two directions. Today's common wire nail appeared toward the end of the nineteenth century.

Nails help to date furniture, for they cannot be removed from a hole and reinserted without showing that a change has been made.

Screws are used occasionally in old pieces, not so much to hold the cabinetwork together as to hold escutcheons and metal mounts in place, and in modern work to hold glued blocks in position. Hinges on cabinet doors and on table leaves and desk fronts all employ screws as fasteners. Antique screws were made by hand with an engine for getting the turn and advance even. Some may have been cut with dies.

Old-fashioned screws do not taper and they have no points.
To use them it was necessary first to bore a hole. Screws
were used extensively after 1840 to hold large pieces of furniture together. Before then, the only similar use for a screw
was to hold a top onto a table, bureau, chest of drawers, or
sideboard. Screws, then, are not, like nails, a help in dating
a piece, because their forms have not changed much.

Another use for screws was to hold metal mounts in place.
The metal mounts used in the Renaissance, Baroque, and
Neo-Classic periods are of an order that, in the best work,
approaches the delicacy of sculpture. The bronze or brass was
frequently fire-gilt. While the use of ormolu is very effective
and gives a rich appearance to furniture, it is not really
cabinetmaking. Ormolu mounts, by their style and because
they will fit only the piece for which they were made, can
help us assign dates to the furniture.

Another adjunct for dating furniture is the brass pull with
which it was equipped. The earliest brass pulls are in the
form of heads—sculptured animals, lion heads, etc. Later,
brasses of the seventeenth century were pendent from plates.
They were called teardrop brasses. They were held into
drawer or cupboard by cotter pins, turned over and driven
into the wood. Cotter pins fastened the earliest plate bail
brasses of the period around 1700 to 1725. Posts, bail handles,
and plate brasses were used on ordinary furniture of the mid-
eighteenth century. More elaborate furniture had ormolu
handles of cast brass in foliated floral designs. The furniture
of Early Classic Revival type used plain or embossed gilt
plates, posts, and bail handles. Later, up to 1840, Classic
Revival favored knobs in floral form or lion heads.

On old brasses, posts are irregular, nuts are round and
misshapen. A check of brasses is a very good check on a
piece of furniture that has them. First, examine the brass.
Does it appear old? Examine the nuts and bolts. Do they look
handmade? Take particular notice as to whether there is only
one set of holes for bolts or cotter pins to go through. If
there is, and the brasses appear to be old, they may be the
original brasses. Remove the plate and look for the lighter
silhouette of the original brass on the face of the piece. If the

brasses match the silhouettes, both brass and piece are likely to be original. Brasses have frequently been lost and replaced with old brasses or reproductions of a type to match. A piece with missing hardware may still be worth having. The fact that the hardware is not old does not mean that the piece is new. The fact that the brass is old and the piece seems to be fairly early on other grounds makes an examination of the brass worth while because it may serve as further evidence for the authenticity of the piece.

Woods

The wood out of which furniture is made is often a help in deciding whether the piece is as old as it should be. However, woods by themselves are not intrinsically very valuable when we consider the value of the wood in comparison with the cost of labor. Besides there is the difficulty of distinguishing one wood from another, especially when the wood is old and has had a finish on it, because of the changes in appearance that finish and time bring about. For example, American furniture may be made of oak (at least five different sorts), elm, maple (at least three sorts), ash, beech, birch, cherry, hickory, walnut, larch, spruce, pine (five or six kinds), gum, whitewood, cucumber wood, sycamore, chestnut, red cedar, white cedar, cypress, tropical cedars, mahogany (at least three varieties), poplar, or basswood.

Of these two dozen or so different woods, some are used much more than others. Those more often used are oak, pine, maple, cherry, walnut, and mahogany. Oak, chestnut, and sycamore can, under certain conditions, be confused. So can sycamore, beech, maple birch, and whitewood. Walnut and mahogany and the tropical cedars may look alike.

Woods are classified into two groups—soft and hardwoods. Softwoods are not necessarily soft and hardwoods are not necessarily hard. Thus, the soft basswood (Tilia americana) is a hardwood and the very hard pitch pine (Pinus rigida) is a softwood. Woods are soft if they have cones like pine trees, hard if they do not. The softwoods are usually more resinous than the hardwoods.

Softwoods—Pine is a white to yellow wood, darkening to
brown with age. Some pines are soft and not very resinous,
others are very hard and resinous. Typical of the first is
American white pine (Pinus strobus). The other type is
represented by pitch pine (Pinus rigida) and long-leaved yellow
pine (Pinus palustris). The latter is easily recognized by the
pronounced contrast in color between the summer and winter
growth marks. Pines are generally even-textured, close-
grained woods. Similar to pine but coarser are hemlock
(Tsuga), spruce (Picea) and fir (Abies).

The cypresses, cedars, and yews have wood of similar
appearance, somewhat harder than the pines, but with a less
pronounced grain and often with a deeper yellow color. Red
cedar (Juniperus virginianus) is typically striated, red and
yellow when new, but older cedar has a more uniform color.
It may be mistaken for mahogany, though it is lighter in
weight and softer. In general, softwoods were used for
woodwork, simple furniture, and foundations for gilding or
veneering. They were used as secondary woods in the
eighteenth and nineteenth centuries. American veneered
pieces are usually veneered on pine.

Hardwoods—The hardwoods show much more variety in
color, texture, and figure than the softwoods. In point of
time, the first wood in use was oak. In America, there are
available for timber approximately fifteen species of white
and black oaks. The lumber of the white oaks is finer-grained
and better adapted to cabinetwork. English and European oaks
present much the same appearance except that they are
somewhat finer-grained than their New World counterparts.

Oaks are coarse-textured and do not work easily. When
new, oak ranges in color from a golden yellow (white oaks) to
a tawny color (red brown or black oaks). They change to a
deep honey color to brown to sable with age. Oaks of the New
World tend to deepen in color slowly as compared with
European oaks; consequently, oaks of the seventeenth century
in American furniture are not so dark as in European furniture
of a much later date.

The grain of chestnut is like oak, except that chestnut is
a little finer. Chestnut is lighter in weight and darker in color
than oak.

Sycamore resembles oak but is lighter in color and very much finer in grain. It can be confused with oak and chestnut on the one hand, and with birch, beech, and white walnut on the other.

Walnut has widespread use in furniture. It began to supplant oak during the Renaissance styles in Europe of the sixteenth and in America of the seventeenth century. Walnut varies in color from the dark brown American black walnut (Juglans nigra) to the somewhat more reddish-brown walnut of Europe (Juglans regia). This wood has a fairly uniform open grain containing short, darker hairlines.

A second wood confused with walnut is that of the sweet gum tree (Liquidambar styraciflua), which is roughly of the same color but close-grained. White walnut or butternut resembles walnut's open grain, hardness, strength, and fine lines, but is considerably lighter in color, even when old, then either European or American walnut.

Quite similar to white walnut are birch (Betula) and beech (Fagus ferruginea). Both are less textured, heavier, close-grained woods. Birch tends toward a reddish color, while beech tends toward brown. As they get older, the woods deepen similarly. In American work, birch frequently is used for maple and the reddish varieties are sometimes used for mahogany.

Maple (Acer Saccharinum) is the lightest in color or patina of the woods used regularly in furniture. It usually turns a deep honey color when it ages, and may become deep brown in time. Maple and birch are easily confused; maple and beech may also be confused.

Hickory (Carya) and ash (Fraxinus) resemble both oak and white walnut. They are used mostly as secondary woods.

Finally, there are a few woods that occur often enough in furniture to warrant recognizing them. The first is a group called fruitwoods. Of these, the chief are pear (Pyrus communis) and apple (Pyrus malus). Both are hardwoods that do not split easily, very uniform in texture, and light tan to honey-colored. They can be recognized primarily by the lack of any character in texture.

Cherry (Prunus cerassus) is a fruitwood, but is red in
color and easily identified by the presence of gum pockets or
little dark irregularities in its grain, peculiar to this wood.
These are from 1/2 to one inch long, broaden out to 1/16 of
an inch in width, and then shrink to a hairline.

Woods that are occasionally mistaken for pine, although
they are much harder, and for maple, from which they differ
markedly in color, are whitewood (Liriodendron tulipifera),
cucumber wood (Magnolia acuminata), and poplar (Populus
alba). All have a similar medium hard texture, absence of
any pronounced grain, and a tendency to olive-greenish streaks.
They age to a greenish color.

In addition to native woods there are the exotics, the
most important of which is mahogany (Swietenia mahogani,
macrophylla, humilis). This wood is dark brown to reddish.
It may resemble walnut or cherry. The absence of pockets,
as well as its more varied, finer grain, should help to distinguish it from cherry and walnut. It darkens rather rapidly;
in a few years it becomes quite dark. The tropical cedars
(Cedrela odorata) are nearly indistinguishable from the
mahoganies (except for the smell), which they closely resemble
when new. They were used during the same period and served
much the same purposes.

Rosewood (Dalbergia nigra) is reddish brown, streaked and
mottled or clouded with darker brown or black. The only
other wood resembling it is macassar ebony (Diospyros discolor). There are a few other woods that appear as inlay,
such as white holly (Ilex aquifolium), or in veneering, such as
satinwood (Chloroxylon swietenia). Holly is a white wood used
only in marquetry. Satinwood is used more often to veneer
whole pieces. It is light yellowish in color with a grain that
gives it a silken luster. The wood looks also as if it were
divided into a series of rectangular compartments. Teakwood
(Tectonia grandis) is a light yellow-brown wood, very hard and
durable, that is not much affected by change in the moisture
content of the air. It is primarily a wood of Oriental use.

Any wood will, under certain conditions, develop figure or
fancy grain. Certain effects such as the blotchiness of
quartersawing and the stripes of edge-grain sawing are due to

the way wood is cut. Birch, maple, cherry, mahogany, and poplar are frequently found with curly or fiddleback grains, but such grains occur in all woods. Walnut is likely to produce a burl. Blister occurs in mahogany, poplar, maple, and cherry. In general, fancy figures are used on fancy furniture and frequently are in the form of veneer.

Veneers are thin pieces of fancy wood fastened onto wood that is not so fancy but is stronger and more durable. In Europe, several woods serve as cores, the chief being pine, oak, and the wood appearing on the surface, for example, mahogany under mahogany, walnut under walnut, etc. In America, pine is the most usual wood underlying veneering.

Marquetry is the use of different veneers in combination to create patterns.

Inlay is the setting of a piece of one kind of wood into another to create a pattern. It differs from marquetry in that the wood into which it is set is solid, that is, not made of pieces. Inlay may also be of metals (brass and silver), mother-of-pearl, tortoise shell, and ivory.

Boule work, using tortoise shell and brass in combination to cover the surface of a piece, is probably to be classified as marquetry rather than inlay.

Parquetry is the use of small pieces of wood to make a pattern as in a parquet floor. It is typical of French Rococo.

Woods should match the style, and in general they do (even in new work). For the Late Gothic, oak is the wood; for Renaissance and Baroque walnut along with fruitwoods are added. In America, maple and cherry are used together with walnut. For the Rococo, beech and mahogany become common. Oak is seldom used after the Renaissance styles end. For the Neo-Classic styles, mahogany is the chief wood, but the addition of satinwood sets it off from the previous style. The last wood to be popular and new is rosewood (1830's and 40's).

CHANGES DUE TO LAPSE OF TIME

Whether or not the cabinetmaker always finished a piece before letting it leave his shop is problematical. Furniture of

good workmanship that never seems to have had any finish
turns up occasionally. Finishes as we encounter them are
seldom original, for ordinary wear and tear will damage most
finishes. Care of the best kind, that is, regular dusting and
polishing over the years, will put a finish on the furniture
that was not there in the first place.

A piece of furniture could be finished with wax, oil, varnish, paint, or lacquer (Japan). With only few exceptions,
such as paint, these involved a polished finish. Oil, wax,
varnish, and oil paint amount to the same thing in the long run.
Oil, wax, and varnish are more or less transparent; paint
is not. On exposure to air, finishes dry. This drying is the
result of a chemical change in the varnishes, waxes, and
paints. The change takes place very rapidly in the beginning,
but is a continuous, never-ending process. Since the topmost
layer is in contact with the air, it tends to harden first;
deeper layers harden more slowly.

Polished finishes are very durable but difficult and time-
consuming in the application. For this reason, furniture was
never finished in areas that did not show. The undersides of
table tops, the inner sides of table leaves, the under portions
of chair rungs, skirting, seats, and legs were never finished
even in painted work. The backs of cupboards and chests of
drawers are never finished. No finish was ever applied to the
interior of drawers. Since few refinished pieces will have
been refinished in the areas mentioned above, the presence
of paint in an unaccustomed spot is almost certain to betray
something wrong at that spot.

As a finish dries, it tends to contract. The contraction
results in many very fine cracks in the surface, which catch
dust and soot. Finally, this crazing of the surface, plus the
dirt and grime that accumulate within rather than upon the
finish, cause the finish to lose its transparency and to darken
with time. Ultimately, all furniture finishes made with waxes,
oils, or varnishes tend to become opaque and more or less
uniformly brown. When this finish is removed, as it should be,
traces of the old finish will show in less accessible portions
of the furniture. You should look for these.

Most persons getting an old piece of furniture in its original if somewhat dilapidated condition will set about at once to "take it right down to the wood," when they should stop with the patina or the outermost surface of the antique.

Water-soluble casein-based tempera paints were also used. These finishes wear off and can be partially washed off, but they do not check as do the oil finishes. Spirit varnishes, which were something like shellac, are likely to be crazed to a very large degree. If you are lucky enough to find a piece of old furniture with original finish in good shape, you will know it instantly. Its appearance is unmistakable. Even though it may be the result of repeated treatments with French polish during the nineteenth century, this patina is the most foolproof of all tests for an antique.

Aging of the finish is not the only kind of aging that takes place. The wood itself also ages. One of the main things that happens is that it dries. The loss may be perfectly uniform. Frequently, one portion of the wood loses moisture faster than another, in which case the wood warps, twists, checks, or does all three. In checking, splits develop in the end of the wood and tend to run down its length. Wood shrinks across its grain much more than it shrinks along the grain. This shrinking is so much greater in width than in length that we can assume that there is none in length.

Many case pieces are constructed by being mortised and tenoned into posts at the corners. Since the boards forming the sides were wide, labor was saved by cutting two or three smaller mortises instead of one extremely large mortise. As the wood shrinks, the spaces between the mortises act like wedges and split the sides. In addition, shrinkage causes mortised and tenoned joints to open slightly in time, even—or especially—when pegged. This is a good thing as far as we are concerned. We can, with the aid of a flashlight, see into the joint and compare its color and tool marks with the outside of the piece.

Shrinking will cause breaks in the smooth-flowing lines of the Queen Anne or Chippendale chair. Turned members shrink so that they are no longer circular in cross section. In old work, this elliptical shape is measurable, especially in

circular table tops and large turnings, such as the bulbous
turnings in Early Renaissance pieces. Shrinkage causes
table tops to warp so that the leaves usually are cupped up.

Shrinking also causes little checks in the ends of legs and
table tops. It causes breaks in moldings worked across the
grain, such as are seen in Queen Anne and Chippendale
mirrors. Drawer faces frequently do not quite hit the drawer
blades. Drawer bottoms, especially where they have been
nailed at the back, tend to pull out of the dado at the front of
the drawer. These are the large effects of shrinking.

When wood shrinks because of loss of moisture, its
effect over a cut surface is quite characteristic. The tools
have left the wood smooth, but where they have been run
cross-grained, as in the beveling of the bottoms of drawers
to fit them into the dados in the sides of the drawer, the new
work shows the cut across the grain to be porous. With
shrinking due to age, these cut surfaces take on a soft look
due to closing of the pores, as if the wood were the same
texture throughout, like a piece of cheese. Fresh-cut surfaces never resemble these, no matter how well executed.
The wood of old pieces may be rough or even torn, but it
always presents this cheese-like uniformity of appearance
wherever cuts have been made and where finish has not been
applied. Some of these are the backs of case pieces, the
bottoms of drawers, the insides of chair and table skirts, the
lower sides of chair and table stretchers, inside seat rails,
or undersides of table tops.

Age also changes the color peculiar to the wood itself.
Thus, cherry tends to redden and whitewood to become greener
with age. Varnish tends to darken when exposed to light,
oils to bleach slightly. Surfaces most exposed to light tend
to develop the deepest color. Since these are the surfaces
that are usually finished, they are further altered by the
changes that the finish undergoes. If this finish is paint,
some of the pigment will tend to remain in the pores of the
wood even if the paint has been lost or removed from the surface. If the surfaces have been cleaned and refinished, as is
frequently done, color is insignificant as a clue to age. Stains
can work wonders in this direction. Stains that age wood can

be used successfully if the faker gets the buyer to overlook
the fact that paint or finish has been used where it should not
be.

Since a piece of furniture made by a single maker is made
entirely out of the same wood at the same time, it should
color in the same way in all parts subjected to the same conditions. This expectation provides a very fine way of checking the age of a piece. Look at the unfinished surfaces and
check whether the different pieces coming together match in
color. They should, if they are all of the same wood. This is
especially important in judging whether a table has a new top
or not. It is impossible to put a top from one table on another
and have the lines of exposure match, for where the wood has
been less exposed to light and air, it will have a different
color. You can always find out whether the top is new by
looking for signs of this color line on the inside of the table.
Shrinking of the apron should disclose it, as well as warping
of the top. There should be a general similarity in color, if
not an exact match, even where the woods are not exactly the
same, for the dust and grime they have absorbed tend to bring
them closer together in color. This fact is so well recognized
that fakers rub dirt and grime into the wood to get this effect.
These attempts usually overshoot the mark; there is too much
dirty work.

Finishes tend to darken also. Reds tend to fade or become
brownish; greens, blues and yellows, gray to the same color
or fade, white gets gray. To detect color differences right
away, take a photograph of the piece with black-and-white
film. The camera sees color differently from the way you do,
so that even though you see no color difference, the camera
does. It is very like matching colors by artificial light and
then comparing them in daylight. The effect is startling.

Wear and tear is of two sorts: that occasioned by ordinary
use and that occasioned by extraordinary violence or with
intent. Ordinary wear and tear results from ordinary use.
The simplest kind is the wearing down of exposed surfaces.
This means the flattening of rungs and wearing down of feet.
If a table has stretchers, they may or may not be worn down,
depending on their location. In the case of fly-leg drop-leaf

tables, the fly legs may show wear in the foot and at the top.
The leaves are certain to show the marks of the fly-leg on
the undersurface. These are frequently well-worn, semicircular grooves. Backs of chairs are likely to show wear on
finials and cresting; the back splats or slats may show wear.
The ends of the arms of the chair are frequently worn to a
magnificent polish. The front legs of chairs usually show
wear on the inside surfaces; the back legs are worn off at an
angle on the back, caused by the movement of the chair as the
occupant gets up. Another place where there is a great deal
of wear is on the bottoms of the sides of drawers: the wear
here causes the bottom surface to be curved upward.

These worn surfaces are of two sorts: those that get the
bulk of the wear from handling, such as arms and finials of
chairs, and those that are caused by friction with other surfaces, such as the floor. The first take on a magnificent polish
from the friction of the hands and the oils of the skin. This
is particularly true of surfaces that invite handling such as
carvings, especially in the round.

When the wear is caused by contact with the floor or feet
or with another piece of wood, the surface has a polished
look and is covered with a series of random scratches. Both
the polish and the scratched surface are almost impossible to
duplicate because of the fineness of the one and the randomness of the other.

So much for the wear, now for the tear. People, especially
men, are not content with the way a chair is made. They are
always teetering on the two back legs and racking them around.
For giving a piece of furniture tear, there is hardly anything
like it. Not only do rungs and backs get broken this way, but
they get lost altogether, occasioning replacements and restorations. However, ladies seem to satisfy their destructive urge
by overloading drawers. This breaks drawer sides, knocks
down the drawer slides, and makes a mess of the piece.

Besides the accidental, there is also the intentional damage. If men did not get shorter during the nineteenth century,
the furniture did. The man of the house, with the aid of his
trusty saw, shortened chair and table legs, chests, highboys,
and lowboys, and cut off the tops of tall beds. When he was not

sawing, he was boring holes for rollers. The world was on wheels, why not the furniture? In addition, table tops served as chopping blocks, and drawers held grain to feed the chickens.

All of this brings us to the antique that is so dilapidated that it is in urgent need of repairs or restorations. Repairing does no harm to the antique, provided that in repairing the surface is not reworked in any way. Breaks repaired and joints reglued all fall under the category of repairs and help rather than harm the antique.

Restorations, on the other hand, damage the antique. They are either acceptable or unacceptable. One rule of thumb for acceptable restorations is that they not exceed ten percent of the piece. The restoration of a piece where there are several others to serve as a pattern is a minor restoration; where the pattern has to be invented or imagined, the restoration is major. If one cabriole leg on a table has a damaged foot, the restoration is minor. If the table has lost all four feet, the restoration is major. The same applies to the arms of a chair. One is a minor loss, two is a major one.

To what extent should we accept pieces with restorations? In this day and age, the answer is, to the extent that we have to. Minor restorations can certainly be accepted. You should, if possible, buy such pieces in the rough, that is, in an unrepaired condition, so that you know the extent of the restoration. Pieces with major restorations are to be avoided if possible. I say if possible advisedly, because in many cases the unrestored piece is becoming harder to find.

Double case pieces assembled from parts of others are called marriages. Many persons do not object to owning such a piece but they should at least know how to identify the marriage. One easy way is to pull out all the drawers and look at the edges. If the dovetailing differs, the piece is a marriage. It ought to sell for considerably less than a piece that is not.

In buying a piece of furniture whose value is based on legs and feet, be extremely careful to see whether these have been replaced or restored. Spanish feet may not be original. Examine the connection between the block and the foot below it to see whether there is not some sign of a glued joint. If the foot has been doweled on, the joint will appear on the face; if it has been mortised into the block, the joint will be visible only from below. Joining on cabriole legs is usually in the form of a scarf joint. If you look carefully, you can detect the joint in the middle of the leg. Frequently, in order to avoid having the joints show, new legs are substituted for old ones. This is worse than the patched leg. Such substitutions can be detected by differences in color and workmanship and by the presence of lines where joints have been made for restoration purposes.

The restoration that is worse than any necessitated by wear and tear is the glorification made to enhance the apparent value of the piece. It goes all the way from staining maple to look like mahogany or walnut to rebuilding the piece. Often an original table of simple form is recut to a more elaborate form. Though difficult to see, you can discover this by comparing the shaped surfaces adjacent to those elsewhere on the top. Chances are good that differences in the cut surface will show what has happened. If a plain skirting has been made fancy, style will give it away, for shaped skirtings were deeper than those not shaped. Thus, in the parsimonious and ambiguous curve, you can detect the glorification.

The addition of carving to an uncarved piece will show itself first in its awkwardness and lack of spontaneity; second, in the stinginess of the work; finally, in the amount of space allotted to it. Parts intended to be carved were made heavier than those not so intended. The effect is especially conspicuous in legs of chairs, tables, and case pieces. New carving on an old leg is almost always betrayed by the fact that the outline of the leg itself has been spoiled. A piece is often reconstructed to make it more salable. This may mean cutting it down to smaller dimensions or enlarging it. This can best be discovered by taking the thing in as a whole. The scaling of antique pieces was very carefully planned. Additions or subtractions tend to make the piece look ungainly or incomplete. Careful examination of all joint surfaces for evidence of new work ought to uncover this deception.

FAKES

From glorification to outright faking is but a step. Faking
is an art that is frequently underestimated. The successful
faker is usually proficient in one line of production. But the
faker, whether he is a specialist or a jack-of-all-trades, is
faced with the same problem. No matter how familiar he may
be with the designs of the period in which he works, he finds
that to produce the same effect as in the original is very difficult. After laboriously trying to work out the curves of a
skirting, he finds that they look labored, overdone, incomplete, or meaningless.

The faker is more likely to copy the leg from this piece, the
arm from that, and so design a part at a time, as if he had
assembled one piece out of the parts of several. Thus, the
totality has an ambiguous look about it. The patched-up appearance, the hard, dry, machine-made look, are characteristic of the fake. Most fakers are graduate repairers and
restorers. Their knowledge of antiques is good, their workmanship is extremely careful, as is necessary in repairing and
restoring, and for this reason their work may look hard and
halting when it is entirely new.

There are other shortcomings. One is that incorrect materials will have to be used. The wood for the piece will not
match for the simple reason that it has not come from the
same tree. Modern milling and marketing methods only acci-
dentally provide a cabinetmaker with enough wood from the
same tree to have it match. The marks of the file and rasp
will turn up rather than those of the spokeshave and knife. The
body of the work will be made of dimension stock and all pieces
will measure up to the same thickness. Riven boards, hand-
planed and scrub-planed surfaces will be missing.

The color of age will have to be achieved with stain. It is
easy to use stain on surfaces to be finished, since the finish
will cover it up. Staining unfinished surfaces to look old is
another matter. Various water-soluble dyes may be used for
this purpose, as well as acids and chemicals. Regardless of
the nature of the stain and the care with which it is used, the
wood surface is more porous in one place than another;

consequently, the stain will be darker in one place than another. Wood colored by time alone will not show this variation.

The faker is apt to wear the surface down in places where, under normal conditions, it receives very little wear. Applied wear and tear will lack randomness. It will show up in the symmetrical disposition of wear marks, dents, and scratches. If there are dents on the surface, they often disclose that they were made with the same instrument (a collection of keys on a chain makes a good one). Antiquing, then, discloses itself in its patterning, its abstraction, and overstatement. Several isolated elements are abstracted from nature and worked in isolation. The faked piece shows too much wear and tear here, too little there. Nature is overdone and outdone.

All these things together—the lack of shrinkage effects in the large, and in detail, the presence of stains in places where finish was never used, the too worn surfaces, the inconsistencies in design and color, the nature of the material, and the pretentiousness combined with the hardness in design and the machine-made look—should make it clear that what you see is a fake. Unfortunately, the seller is as well aware as you are of what you are likely to look for. If he can prevent you from seeing what is there to be seen, he will have achieved his purpose of making a sale.

Foreign fakes are harder to detect than native, for it is easier to keep abreast of American faking methods than of Persian or Turkish ones. Differences in climatic conditions, however, tend to make imported antiques come apart. When they do, it is fairly easy to see whether they are new or old, for if an antique piece of furniture breaks, the old wood will show its age, and the fake, its youth. The faker frequently uses old wood, but here he is apt to be defeated by the worms.

Wormholes are always round, which means that their direction is perpendicular to the surface. After penetrating the wood for a very short distance, about the thickness of this paper, the wormhole turns and runs parallel to the surface. Any disturbance of this surface will be sure to do two things— lay open the worm channels and/or cut across them at oblique angles. Now, the faker is certain to insure that his work has wormholes in it. Since the worm turns, the use of a flexible wire as a probe should help you decide whether the wormhole is genuine or faked. Fake wormholes can be bored straight in, shot in with bird shot or made with a drill, which, like the worm, will turn. Not turning will uncover the first two, entering into the wood too far before it turns will disclose the second.

ON BUYING FURNITURE

Before I end this section on furniture, I will offer a few suggestions as to how to buy what you want. The first step consists of looking at the prospective purchase. Don't look at it and think how much it will do for your foyer or your self-esteem—you can think about these things later. Look rather at the piece as a whole. See whether it is a clean piece or not. Has it been repaired or refinished? Ask the dealer about this. Your examination will be facilitated if the piece is in the rough, that is, unrefinished and not repaired. Do not expect it to be cheaper on this account. Pieces are restored, refinished, and repaired not to make them more valuable but to make them more salable or usable.

If close examination supports the conclusions from the style tests (be sure to look for shrinkage, wear and tear, tool marks of proper tools and working methods, wood, color, fasteners), the piece is old. Having seen that it is authentic, decide whether it is a good example of its style. If you are satisfied with the price, buy it and take it away with you. If you can't take all, take some of it, for instance, the drawers to a case piece.

Chapter VI

GLASS

INTRODUCTION

No product of human effort and ingenuity comes closer to rivaling the works of nature than those of the glass furnace. Nothing so emulates the mysterious workings of the plutonic forces of the nether world as the production of glass. If the art of the potter can be likened to the reconstitution in plastic form of the igneous rocks of the earth's crust, the art of the glassmaker can be likened to the creation of ever novel crystals in endless variety. The sparkling gaiety, the brilliance of color, limpidity, richness, and depth of shading are rivaled only by those rare minerals of the earth, the gemstones of the lapidary. Glass has all the attractiveness of these soughtafter stones coupled with a usefulness and aesthetic appeal that place it in a category by itself.

It is not surprising that we find it in tombs of princesses of Ur and Pharaohs of Egypt, along with treasures of gold, silver, and precious stones. Glass itself, that is, its very substance, has been so admired throughout most of its history that it has been used, along with precious stones, for personal adornment. In fact, until the end of the eighteenth century, glass pastes were cut, polished, and used in jewelry in the same pieces with precious and semiprecious stones. A vase made of flawless emerald, an urn of ruby, or a pitcher of sapphire are beyond the reach of the fabled princes of the East or the wealth of the Indian Seas. Yet, as glass, these are within the reach of all of us.

Yesterday, the story was a little different. In ancient times, glass was mentioned in the same terms of respect that were accorded the precious metals, and in many cases was worth considerably more than its weight in gold. Although glass also served utilitarian purposes, its use was reserved mainly for the glorification of God (as in Medieval cathedral

windows) or the aggrandizement of the wealthy and powerful.

The first colonists of Virginia were sent out to establish,
among other things, a glass factory. And yet, of those early
settlers in Jamestown and Plymouth, it is doubtful if many
had ever seen, much less used or owned, a piece of glass
tableware. The collecting of glass, then, is very like the
collecting of fossils, for within its fragile substance is frozen
much of the history of mankind.

Glass consists largely of silica, (quartz or sand), soda, and
lime. The addition of lead oxide made the well-known flint or
present-day crystal glass. The chief difference between glass
and ceramics is the presence of alumina and feldspathic
minerals in ceramic objects and their relative absence in glass,
which makes glass translucent, at the least, and ceramic
objects only rarely so. Glass and pottery also differ in their
preparation and working. First, the ingredients of pottery
are mixed together, whereas the ingredients in glass are
melted together. The heat is applied before the shaping in
the one and upon the completion of it in the other. Clay is
worked while plastic and cold, glass while ductile and hot. For
this reason, the tools used in the working of glass differ
from those used for clay and leave a different impress.

Glass Materials

The appearance of glass depends upon the materials of
which it is made, the purity of these materials, their proportion, and the care with which the melt has been prepared. For
our purposes, glass can be divided into three types on the
basis of materials: soda-lime, flint (lead), and improved
soda-lime or lime glass.

It is fairly safe to say that soda-lime was the only kind of
glass available during the Medieval and Early Renaissance
periods. It can be recognized by its greenish to brown color,
impurities, light weight, and high-pitched nonresonant tone
when struck.

There are two types of soda-lime glass, ordinary soda-
lime and potassium-soda lime. The latter type was known from

the earliest days of its production as crystal because of its
resemblance to rock crystal, and is almost free of any greenish or purplish color. It is clearly transparent and relatively
free from blemishes (bubbles). It is out of such material
that the fine glasswares of the fifteenth and sixteenth centuries
in Italy, Germany, Austria, and Bohemia were made. Potassium-soda-lime glass was made up until the advent of flint
glass in Europe, and certainly through the eighteenth century
in America.

If I were to pick one easily recognized quality of this type
of glass, it would be its lightness in weight. This quality,
together with its brightness, clarity, and imperfections,
should identify it. Imperfections consist of (1) bubbles, which
are not numerous and vary in size within the same piece of
glass; (2) dark-colored spots due to some aggregation of
impurities (these are called sand spots because of their
resemblance to grains of sand); (3) light-colored collections
of opaque material somewhat resembling white paint spots,
called lime spots because of the impression that they are spots
of undissolved or unfused lime; and (4) color, which varies
from green to brown to pink to purple. The colors are not
deep and may result from (1) improperly prepared materials,
which give the glass a greenish to brownish tinge; (2) improperly proportioned materials or too much manganese,
which will give glass a pink to violet tinge, and (3) a dull gray
color, caused by the use of too much decolorizer. The de-
colorizers, particularly manganese dioxide, are frequently
known as glassmaker's soap.

Ordinary soda-lime glass differs from the above in having
many imperfections and in being loaded with bubbles. The
colors are as above but quite deep. We can expect glass of
this type to be older than the first half of the nineteenth century in America, and presumably earlier in Europe. The
series runs backward to the beginnings of glassmaking.

Flint or lead glass is easily distinguished from the foregoing glass by its resonant tone when struck. This is the
recognition test par excellence. No other glass will have those
bell-like tones or such resonance when struck. However,
since there are occasions when, due to the shape or form of

the glass, resonance cannot be used for identification, there
are other tests. The next best of these is clarity. Flint
glass has a high degree of internal reflection and is thus
much more brilliant than soda-lime glass. Finally, relative
heaviness is a good indication that the glass is flint.

The time range of flint glass is not so great as that of
soda-lime glass, nor is its geographical area so large. Flint
glass seems to have come into existence at the end of the
sixteenth century and was probably an Italian invention, although if much of it was made in the Italy of that time, it has
been lost without a trace. Hence, the country credited with
the perfecting of flint glass is England, and its invention is
attributed to George Ravenscroft. But Antonio Neri had written of lead glass as early as the first quarter of the seventeenth century, and Ravenscroft attempted making such glass
only after the publication of the English translation of Neri's
book, and had, in fact, Italian help in its development. Ravenscroft's flint glass was developed toward the third quarter of
the seventeenth century, but its final form was probably not
achieved until the mid-eighteenth. Flint glass later spread to
other countries of Europe, particularly where coal for the
furnaces in which it was made was easy to get, and, of course,
to America of the eighteenth and early nineteenth centuries.
Wherever extra brilliance or ease in cutting glass was desired,
flint glass was made.

The latest type that can concern us as collectors is improved soda-lime glass. It is cheaper to make and use than
flint glass. Whereas the latter may be more than two hundred
years old, improved soda-lime glass is less than a hundred.
It can be attributed to Mr. Leighton of Hobbs Brockunier and
Company in Wheeling, West Virginia. It would be much nicer
for us if it had not been invented until 1900, because it makes
the discrimination of certain kinds of pressed glass difficult.
Improved soda-lime glass has neither the tinkle of old soda-
lime glass nor the resonance of flint glass. It has a dead, dull
sound. As for brilliance and clarity, it is more brilliant than
potassium-soda-lime crystal but less brilliant than flint. Its
brilliance also is of a different order. In flint, the brilliance
lies within the glass and is occasioned by its optical qualities

of high dispersion. For example, a piece of flint glass (pressed or cut) is much more brilliant when we look at the pressed or cut surfaces <u>through</u> the glass than when we merely see the surfaces alone. With improved soda-lime glass, the brilliance is on the surface. Improved soda-lime is lighter than flint but not so light as soda-lime, and even less than potassium-soda-lime glass.

You will recognize lime glass by its hard surface brilliance, medium weight and complete lack of any bell-like tone. It is not very old, but many great rarities in glass were made of it. The place of its first use was the United States, the time the end of the Civil War.

Much fine glass is not clear but colored. Here are some of the colors we may find in glass and the substances used to produce them:

> Green: silver, copper, iron, nickel
> Red: gold, copper (modern is selenium)
> Yellow: uranium, gold, chromium
> Blue: cobalt
> Purple to black: manganese, nickel
> Opal: phosphates, fluorides of calcium
> White: tin, calcium

Arsenic and antimony are used to remove bubbles. As you can see, the range of glass color is virtually unlimited. By combining one colored glass with another, various effects may be obtained. You should note that whereas some elements, for example, uranium and cobalt, provide only one color, others, such as gold, copper and nickel, produce different colors, depending on what else is present in the glass and how it is made. Ferric iron in the glass will make it brown to black and sometimes reddish; ferrous iron gives a green color.

Types of Glass

The processes by which glass is made count as much as its ingredients in determining its appearance and behavior. The three chief processes are blowing, pressing, and molding. Of

these, blowing seems to be the second oldest. We have examples of blown glass that probably date from the third century B.C. However, glass was made long before this. We
have glass beads from the Old Kingdom in Egypt and the tombs
at Ur. Small objects such as alabastra of glass appear quite
early, but whether they were blown in the sense meant here is
problematical. Once the blowing technique and its tools were
discovered, blowing remained the standard and only technique
for the manufacture of glass. So universal did it become that
highly skilled and special processes for the making of feet
and handles for goblets and pitchers, or the making of canes
and beads, which are in no sense blown, are nevertheless
thought of as methods of blowing glass.

How does blowing affect the appearance of glass? In the
first place, all contours of blown glass tend to be soft and
flow one into the other rather than stand out sharply. The
edges of blown glass are slick and smooth. Blown glass is
likely to have hairlines on its surface, which show in reflected
light. Glass ornamented chiefly by blowing is always soft in
outline, never sharp and crisp as in pressed or cut glass. The
ornament is likely to be simple rather than elaborate, although
we do have, in Venetian-type glass, wherever made, the
ultimate in elaborately blown glass.

Molded glass fits in between pressed and blown glass in
appearance, though not necessarily in time. Its molding is
more formal than that of blown glass, but also considerably
less sharp than that of pressed glass. It is, as the name
implies, formed by the use of a mold of some kind in addition
to the use of the glassworker's tools. It differs from pressed
glass in the use made of the mold. First and clearly, the
glass is not pressed into a mold by a plunger. In at least
one type, it is blown into a full-sized mold.

Molded glass has three different kinds of appearance,
depending on which type of molding process was used. Where
the glass is molded by the ancient process, a certain amount
of air gets in between the spun layers of glass, giving it a
somewhat scaly appearance when closely examined. Since
most glass of this type is undergoing decomposition because of
its age and long contact with chemicals in the earth, the outside

surface is flaking off. This almost always results in a brilliant iridescence of the surface. Thus there is no reason to
mistake modern glass for ancient because, in addition to the
scaliness of the piece, there are other evidences of great
age, such as the play of colors.

Glass blown with the aid of a dip mold appears different
from all other kinds. It has an unexpected peculiarity: wherever there is a projection on the outside, there is a corresponding projection on the inside. This trait is earily recognized and
a sure identification of this glass. When the glass is blown into
a full-sized mold, the air tends to follow the glass into the mold,
so that when this process is used for the production of a jug,
bottle, or bowl, to every projection on the outside there corre-
sponds a hollow on the inside. Finally, all molded glass is
distinct from pressed glass in that the impressions are not
sharp, and fins, when they occur, are almost invisible.

The amateur glass collector looking for old glass is more
likely to come home with pressed glass than any other kind,
if indeed he is lucky enough to come home with a piece of
glass much older than he is.

To some extent, the pressing of glass is as old as the
manufacture of glass. Even ancient glass is ornamented
with glass wafers that look as if they had been pressed.
Bottles from the seventeenth century and earlier were ornamented with pressed wafers that bore a man's name, some
other device, and occasionally a date. Much of the tooled
ornamentation in blown glass is, in a sense, pressed. Wheel
and some other stoppers seem to have been pressed early in
the nineteenth century, if not before. These, however, are
solid objects. The pressing of an entire piece of hollow glass
is a relatively new process.

Glass Blowing

The final form of blown glass is imparted to it by a few
simple tools, all of which leave their marks on the glass. The
usual handling tool is the blowpipe. This is a hollow tube most
often made of iron, sometimes of copper or brass, with an
insulated cork or wood collar. Shaping was done with the

procella. There were other iron tools, of which the most important was the pontil. This tool, also called pontee, ponto, or punty, was an iron rod of about the same length as the blowpipe, and was stuck on the base of a piece of glass to hold it during operations performed on the glass subsequent to the actual blowing. Of all the tools used in handling glass, the pontil is the most likely to leave a discoverable mark. The pontil mark is visible on the base of a piece of glass in the form of a considerable roughening of its center. Its presence or absence is often the best test of whether glass is blown or not. On fine glass, the pontil mark was frequently removed by being ground off. The presence of the ground spot shows that the glass was blown. There are some exceptions to this, because some of the early pressed patterns up to c. 1850-60 have pontil marks. One other piece of equipment a glass blower might possess was an iron dip mold with which to impress a preliminary pattern on glass later to be blown.

Many of the glass blower's tools were made of wood, which when charred and wet could work the glass without discoloring it. An example of these is the battledore used to flatten bases of blown objects.

Let's watch a glass blower at work. He has a sturdy chair to sit in during some of the blowing operations, a pail of water to cool tools in, and places to hang the tools within easy reach. He takes up his blowpipe, goes to the pot and gathers up, by rotating the blowpipe, enough sticky glass to make what he wants. He then takes it to the marver and rotates it on the cold surface until the glass is more viscous and nice and round in cross section. During this process, he will blow into it slightly to introduce a bubble of air. It is important that the gather be round and the bubble located exactly in the center, otherwise whatever he makes of it will be lopsided and will very likely burst.

The blowing now begins in earnest. Rotating and blowing, he produces an elongated pear-shaped bubble called a parison. This parison is the start of all subsequent operations. Stems and feet are attached to the base of the shaped parison and given the appropriate toolings. If the foot or stem is hollow or otherwise elaborately ornamented, this work, at least in part, is a separate job, and the semi-finished stem is applied at the appropriate time. Ribbing, fluting, or molding of the work may be done now with added glass and the use of appropriate tools, although it may be done at the start. If the ornamentation is made of extra glass applied at the time of blowing, this is evident in the varying thickness of the walls.

When blowing is complete, the work is attached to the pontil and the glass at the top cut free from the blowpipe. The work can now be shaped, provided with a lip, and tooled to any degree desired by the blower. At this point, objects, requiring handles, such as urns, ewers, and pitchers, have them applied. During the operations, it may be necessary to reheat the glass from time to time. At the end of all operations, the finished piece is picked up with a forked stick or, later, with carrying tongs and returned to the leer or annealing oven where it can cool slowly.

The process described above might be referred to as simple shaping, inasmuch as it applies to only one kind of glass. Other methods of ornamenting glass are also part of the technique of blowing. One simple method is to spangle it. Flakes of mica or glass of other colors are broken up to the fineness desired. The mica flakes are occasionally coated with silver or gold. The gather of glass is rolled in these flakes in much the way that flour or cracker crumbs are placed on fish or croquettes. The spangles may be protected by being covered with another layer of glass. Here the glass is said to be cased; this term applies whenever one kind of glass is covered with a substantial layer of another. Casing is sometimes called overlay. The usual method was to blow the outside layer or layers (since there can be more than one) first. The outer layer was placed in a hot iron cup or crucible and the inner layer blown inside it. The two were then fused and handled as one. Casing was used primarily for decorative effect. Frequently, part of the outer layer or layers was ground away to provide a patterned surface in two or more colors. Each time a cut was made through the case or the overlay, the clear glass shape caused by the cutting was surrounded by a colored ring.

More frequently used than casing was flashing. Here the purpose served as one of economy rather than of art, for a

thin layer of an expensive gold ruby glass could be placed
outside (or inside) a much heavier layer of clear glass. When
completed, the flashed glass object had much the appearance
of one made of a solid piece, and the saving in material was
considerable. Essentially, flashing means giving a gather of
clear glass a quick dip in a colored glass and removing it when
it is thinly coated with the color.

Glass at the proper temperature is unbelievably ductile and
can be drawn into the finest of threads. Where the threads
are of the same color as the body, they can be left as applied
ornamentation or they can be pinched together at regular intervals to make chains, loops, or swirls. Where the glass
threads are different in color from the body, they can be
dragged into loops and pressed into the body of the piece on
the marver. Extra lumps of glass can be applied to the body
and left as blobs of various shapes sticking out, as in some
of the German "cabbage stalk" drinking glasses. On the other
hand, the lump can be applied at the base of the piece, dragged
or drawn up over the base, and tooled or molded into a rich
variety of ribbed and fluted patterns, called variously paneling
and gadrooning, according to the form they take.

Because glass can be drawn into rods and threads with such
ease, it lends itself to the making of forms that resemble the
farmer's giraffe in their total unbelievability. The technique
of preparing a rod is to roll a gather of glass on the marver
until it is perfectly cylindrical and then to stretch it by drawing
it. Such rods can be of any size and complexity. If glass of
different colors is used, rods of different and elaborately
coiled and twisted form can be made. These rods or canes of
spun glass can be used for a variety of purposes, such as making stems for drinking vessels and bowls. When heated in
hollow molds, they can be used to produce vases and dishes of
extremely elaborate patterns.

Most baffling in design are the laticino designs. Here, the
canes are partially fused with a gather of glass and twisted to
form cylinders, one with a slightly larger diameter than the
other. When placed in the iron or clay cup and fused together,
they form a crisscrossing of colored canes with little air
bubbles within the lattice-work. Canes can also be cut off like

so many slices of bread and the slices arranged inside a clay
cup into which a gather of glass is blown. The resulting mosaic
of millefiori glass goes back to Roman times and was and is
exceedingly popular in Venetian-type glass and as background
for paperweights.

Air bubbles are what give glass its form; a portion of the
skin is what makes the vase, pitcher, or goblet. Bubbles
also get into glass by accident. Almost any old glass has
numerous fortuitous bubbles. Small bubbles are sometimes
made on purpose for ornament. In this case, a slightly in-
flated gather is rolled into the shape of a hollow cylinder and
then drawn out into a tube. These glass tubes, after annealing,
can be formed into almost anything.

Gaffers or blowers often had the right to blow things for
themselves from leftover glass after their work was over for
the day. Many of these "end of day" pieces, blown with
artistry and loving care, are equal in elegance and technique
to the ornamental glass blown in glass houses whose principal
output was ornamental tableware. The metal, of course, is
inferior to that made especially for fine tablewares.

Molded Glass

Molded glass has a long history. The blowpipe was not
invented until the middle of the Classical period, but hollow
glass vessels of extremely elaborate form preceded the use of
the blowpipe by perhaps a thousand years. How were they
made? Glass spun out into threads or wound around a modeled
removable core and repeatedly reheated and smoothed with
various tools will ultimately fuse together into a single shape.
Such shapes can be ornamented by dragged threads of different
colored glass as in blown glass, and by other techniques used
for blown glass.

A similar painstaking, extremely skilled, and time-consum-
ing method was to press with constant reheating, a continuous
thread of glass into hollow molds of various forms to get
hollow-ware objects, from drinking glasses to plates, bowls,
oenochoes, and amphorae. All of the early glass before c.
300 B.C. was made in this way. Spun glass was also used by

the ancients for the creation of millefiori forms, which we associate with Venetian glass. These patterned types were worked into urns and vases. Before the birth of Christ, glass was prized in the extreme. It must have been available only to the very powerful. It is not surprising that the later Romans spent millions of sesterces for single pieces of it. This valuable glass is generally referred to as Alexandrian glass. The famous Portland Vase is thought to be an example, although there is plenty of evidence that it was made in Italy at a date much later than the Alexandrian period.

When the blowpipe and its attendant techniques were developed, the earlier, more painstaking methods were gradually abandoned. The blowpipe finally reigned supreme, and the molding process was abandoned forever, sometime during the first or second centuries A.D. Yet patterned glass was never abandoned.

There are two ways in which molds may be employed to give form to blown glass. One type is called a dip mold and was used primarily to give a preliminary pattern to the glass. Although this technique is used today in handblown as opposed to machine-blown glass, it was very likely introduced soon after the invention of the blowpipe, since it depends on the blowpipe for its effective use. In using the dip mold, the blower inserts a partially blown bulb of glass into the mold and expands it until it comes in contact with the patterned surface of the mold. The glass, now carrying a pattern on its surface, may be expanded and manipulated like other blown glass, but the pattern impressed on it remains with it until the end. By using a fluted mold and placing glass rods into each flute, vertical ribs could be obtained. On occasion, the glass blower could pinch these ribs together to create a variety of lozenge or diamond-shaped patterns. This type of molding, usually called pattern molding, is considered a type of blown glass, but it is also a type of molded glass and for that reason is included here.

Glass can also be molded by being blown into full-size molds. There is some evidence that this technique was lavishly used by the Romans. We don't have much Roman glass of this type, but whatever we do have is interesting and puzzling.

In modern times, molded glass has been used for bottles
and flasks on which, for some reason, there was need for a
patterned mold. Flasks and bottles of this order were made in
most European and American factories from the early nineteenth century on. The bottles and flasks were blown in clam-
shell molds, that is, molds whose two halves fitted together
like the shells of a clam.

Pressed Glass

What was new about pressed glass when it first appeared
was that the whole object of completed size and pattern was
pressed, not blown, into a mold. The first such object in the
modern world was made in the summer of 1827. It is credited
to a Mr. Deming Jarves of the Boston and Sandwich Glass
Company. Pressed glass is not confined to United States
production; it was made in most famous European factories
such as Baccarat and St. Louis, to name but two.

The mold for pressed glass had to be a little more sturdy
than that for blown three-mold glass. The gather was deposited
in the mold and a plunger was pressed home, driving the
plastic glass into the mold. Considerable pressure was required because of the viscosity of the glass. The shape of the
plunger varied in accordance with the shape of the thing molded,
but, whatever the shape, one thing is clear: the upper end had
to be larger than the bottom end and there could be no rings
or ridges in the plunger, else it could not be withdrawn.

Since the pressure was greater, the mold marks and the
fins are readily detectable. Many early pieces were removed
from the mold to have feet applied. For some reason such as
this, they were handled with pontil rods and hence show pontil
marks.

You should have no trouble distinguishing pressed glass
from all other kinds. First, it is heavier in thickness and
weight. Second, the mold marks are sharp and clearly to be
seen. Third, the pattern feels sharp. Fourth, there is no
relation between inside and outside contours, thus distinguishing it at once from blown, part-molded and blown three-mold
glass, whose characteristics in this respect are described

above. What the inexperienced person is most likely to confuse
it with is cut glass, but the presence of the mold marks and
the glass surface should give it away at once.

The following explanation should help to distinguish between
early and modern pressed glass (after c. 1860). In early
glass there is a slight wrinkling of the surface, often having
the appearance of a giant fingerprint. There is also the tendency for fine lines to develop on the surface. The appearance
is not very different from that of paint that has "alligatored."
Don't expect this type of surface to stick out like a sore thumb;
when it does, the effect is intended, as in various types of
crackle glass or "Tree of Life" patterns. Less readily noted
are random squiggles in the unpatterned surfaces, which, save
for their color, resemble the silk threads in United States
paper money. They serve the same purpose for us of indicating
the genuineness of the piece in question.

Another characteristic pressed glass may have, and this is
chiefly noticeable in the glass made before 1850, is the disappearing crack or check. Glass is a peculiar material. It is
often described as a super-cooled liquid, for it does not have
a crystallizing point. Instead, and this is what is meant by its
being super-cooled, it doesn't crystallize as it solidifies. As
glass gets cooler and cooler, it gets less and less like a
liquid or more and more viscous or sticky, until it is solid at
temperatures at which one would expect it to crystallize. It is
ready to form separate crystals at room temperature but is
prevented from so doing by its viscosity. This is one reason
why glass so readily shatters when struck. Strains set up in
the glass as it cools are often indicated by "disappearing"
cracks, so-called because they are visible only when seen
from certain angles.

Pressed glass was made over a long period of time and is
still, with variations, being made today. The earliest pressed
glass goes back to the 1830's and the latest collectible goes
down to about 1900. The early type was flint glass up to about
1863-65, when it was supplanted by the improved soda-lime or
lime glass of the post-Civil War period. Early pressed forms
imitated the forms of cut glass with typical cut patterns such
as strawberry diamonds, flutes, punty, and thumb print.

Later, 1835-50, the distinguishing character of pressed glass
is the flowing curves in its pattern and, above all, its stippled
background. This is the so-called lacy glass, whose brilliance
has never since been rivaled. At the end of this period, the
metal had improved to the degree where the stippling was no
longer necessary and was abandoned. Bold high-relief patterns
are characteristic of the fifties, with more detailed low-relief
patterns coming in at the end. By the late 1860's and into the
70's, the glass ceases to have much lead content and therefore
does not ring. The relief is much lower, the pattern finer, and
acid treatment of the surface is introduced in a few patterns,
for instance, Westward Ho!, Three Face and Lion. As time
went on, more and more patterns were introduced, so that
today the dealer or collector has to keep track of about a
thousand patterns, not counting the lacy ones. Since the metal
in many pieces is not very different from that of modern glass,
it is little wonder that there are so many fakes on the market.

ORNAMENTATION AFTER ANNEALING

Engraving

   Glass can be ornamented after it is cooled in a variety of
techniques, each of which changes its appearance. The simplest
is engraving, which can be done in a number of ways. Most
persons know that glass can be easily scratched with a diamond,
as the windowpanes of many an old house attest. Glass is soft
enough to be cut by hardened steel tools as well as by diamonds.
It is most often cut with an abrasive material such as corundum,
which is next to the diamond in hardness.
   Diamond engraving is about the earliest form of engraving
on glass. It became extremely popular in Europe from the end
of the sixteenth to well into the eighteenth century. It was
raised to the level of a fine art by many of the German and
Low Country engravers, and at the same time it was taken up
by amateurs for their amusement.
   Two types of engraving may be distinguished. One is line
engraving, where the effects are created by means of line

shading, much in the nature of any other kind of engraving, but most resembling dry point. The second, somewhat later type is stipple engraving, which creates its effects by the use of small dots or stippling. This much more painstaking method has greater possibilities for handling light and shade. Such engraved glass is exceedingly rare and so extremely hard to find that the figures at which it changes hands are likely to rival the prices paid by Roman collectors for the famed Alexandrian glass.

The next most common method of engraving glass is by the use of the copper wheel. Copper is not hard enough to cut glass, but the wheel is run in a slurry or mudlike mixture of pumice, corundum, or some glass-cutting abrasive, which, rubbing against the glass, grinds out pieces of it. Since the copper wheel is between the engraver and his work, he has to depend on experience, memory, and judgment to cut the pattern. This pattern has therefore to be carefully planned ahead of time not only as to the form, but as to execution. This type of engraving was invented in seventeenth-century Germany (perhaps as a substitute for diamond point engraving).

Since careful planning is necessary, wheel-engraved patterns do not have the flexibility and spontaneity of diamond point engravings, nor are they so detailed. They can vary, however, from a cursory frosting of the surface to fairly deep cutting and even modeling. Wheel engraving can easily be distinguished from diamond point by the thickness of its line, and from etching with acid by the presence of fine parallel lines visible under magnification.

Related to copper engraving is cutting, also usually done on a wheel. One important difference is that the cut surfaces are as a rule polished, which renders them transparent, while the engraved surfaces are rarely so treated. Cutting is less difficult than engraving, for the cutter can at least see what he is doing, even though the pattern is in reverse. Cutting is also deeper. Where the cutter had unlimited time to work, which is to say, where the cost to the patron was of no concern, relief cuttings of depth in the most elaborate form could be made.

Again, the cut-glass technique began in Venice but was elaborately developed elsewhere. Elaborately carved glass became one of the great achievements of Germany during the seventeenth and eighteenth centuries, but glass cutting was popular all over Europe by the end of the eighteenth century. From France at the end of the eighteenth century William Peter Eichbaum, chief glass cutter to Louis XVI, came to America, bringing the art of cut glass to the factories around Pittsburgh, whence spread the art during the nineteenth century. English and Irish cut glass of the late eighteenth and early nineteenth centuries is justly famous. Much American cut glass of the early nineteenth century emulated Bristol and Waterford.

Cut glass could, of course, be made more spectacular and colorful by starting with a cased or overlay glass of more than one color and cutting through the casing to get fancy effects. This is the overlay technique par excellence. When one color besides the base is used, the effect is of a painted glass. When more than one layer of glass is used, the glass pattern of overlay may become extremely elaborate, with the intermediate layer or layers outlining the patterns.

Cameo glass is made of overlay glass; large portions of the outer case are removed by cutting (or by acid) and the remaining islands of the outer portion are carved like cameos with regular carving tools. Overlay glass can also be and frequently is engraved, although this technique in bicolor glass is usually reserved for flashed, stained, and luster-enameled glass, because both staining and luster enamel leave thinner films of color on the glass. As a result these types are more suitable to the shallowness of engraving than is overlay or cased glass.

Glass can also be ornamented when treated with the hydrofluoric acid first discovered at the end of the eighteenth century. This very corrosive acid attacks glass of all kinds and was used especially during the late nineteenth century. Glass to be so etched was protected by engravings printed in acid-resistant material and transferred to the glass in much the same way that ceramic wares were transfer-printed. The reverse of the printed pattern would be etched on the glass. Later the French, in particular, developed the technique of using acid to the degree where the results approximated relief obtainable by cutting and carving glass. In general, the glass ornamented by etching was cheaper and the etching was only on the surface, simulating copper wheel engraving. It was usually applied to luster-enameled or flashed glass.

Enameled Glass

Another way of ornamenting glass after it was finished was with enamels. Enamels are themselves a kind of glass. They are very easily fusible. In fact, the ease with which enamels fuse can be so well controlled by varying the composition slightly that enamel painting is used on both ceramics and glass where it is desirable to place one color next to another.

Decorating with gold is closely allied to, and sometimes identical with, the use of ordinary enamels. At least as far back as late Roman times, glass objects were made in two shells, an inner and outer shell that fitted together exactly. The outer surfaces of the inner shell or the inner surfaces of the outer shell could be decorated with gold, and the two shells were then cemented together. Much Byzantine glass used this technique.

The technique of cementing two glass shells together was rediscovered in Venice and used most extensively in Germany and Bohemia in the late eighteenth and early nineteenth centuries. The use of gold enamels came fairly late in glassmaking, as in ceramic wares, that is, at the end of the eighteenth century. The most widespread use of this technique, however, took place from the last quarter of the nineteenth century until the present.

Of the transparent enamels, the most characteristic are the luster enamels intended to give the appearance of gold ruby glass. These are sometimes applied in patterns to imitate the overlay glass mentioned above, but were used as often to coat the entire piece. Patterns were then engraved or occasionally etched through the enamel.

Stained Glass

Finally, glass could be stained. Most of the stained glass
windows of the eleventh, twelfth, and thirteenth centuries in
Europe are not exactly stained but more nearly painted. However, some substances applied to the glass and heated do, in
effect, stain it. The chief substance is silver nitrate, which
produces a yellow color over clear glass and green and orange
on blue and red glass. Much of the nineteenth-century Bohemian
glass is stained with this yellow stain.

STYLES IN GLASS

Styles in glass follow those of architecture and furniture
and reflect the taste of the various periods. We have very
little glass remaining from the period between the collapse of
the Roman Empire and the rise of the Renaissance, save in
the area we call the Middle East today. The metal of this glass
is neither very white nor very transparent. Its cloudy green-
ishness makes a fine background for elaborate enamel work.
For the time limit under our consideration, about the earliest
types of Western glass are Italian in origin and more or less
closely connected with Venice.

Venetian and Fancy Blown Types

Venetian glass, first, last, and always, was primarily
blown glass and was finished when it came from the leers.
This is not to say that there was no cut, engraved, or enameled
Venetian glass, but that the character of Venetian glass is
really set by the elaborate molding work and the use of colored
metals and air-twist and cane types of glass, that is, molded,
threaded with laticino and filigree ornament, millefiori, and
mosaic glass. The frivolous, elegant airiness of the forms is
immediately apparent even when we set them against Venetian
types made elsewhere. This glass reaches its highest degree
of artistry in the sixteenth and seventeenth centuries when
Venetian glass blowers went from Italy to the rest of Europe to

ply their trade and make their fortunes. Such glass as this is
more or less out of your reach, but Venetian glass has been
made ever since.

Nineteenth-century Venetian glass is technically superior
in elaborateness and metal to the earlier glass, which it
clearly copies. Such glass is available in quantity and is
worth owning, provided you do not think it is earlier than it is.
Venetian glass is extremely light in weight and does not ring
well. When very old, it tinkles slightly, like early crystal.
Late nineteenth-century Venetian glass does not even tinkle.
It is a little less light, sturdier, and much more brilliant,
like the lime glass of the late nineteenth century with which it
is closely related.

German, Austrian, and Low Country Types

The French, Germans, and Austrians all knew how to blow
glass before the rise of Venice, but with the advances in style
and technique of the Venetian glass blowers, they began to
emulate them. The Germans and Austrians took certain ways
of glass blowing or working and developed them, so when we
think of German glass we automatically think of these techniques. They developed the art of engraving not only with
mond points but also with the copper wheel, to the degree that
little seventeenth- and eighteenth-century engraved, cut, or
carved glass is without German influence. Typical of such
work are the carved and engraved covered drinking glasses
or pokals, sometimes of enormous size. Here the metals are,
for the most part, nonflint crystal, that is, potassium-soda-
lime glass. The metal is heavier than that of Venice and does
not often ring with resonance. What is most characteristic
of it is its freedom from serious imperfections. By today's
standards, however, it is very imperfect. The makers of
bottled beverages would not accept metal of this sort today,
yet compared with what preceded it, it was remarkable.

It was in eighteenth-century Bohemia that enameling of
glass was raised to such a peak of perfection that when we
think of enameled glass we are most likely to think of Bohemian
or Czech glass. The styles of enameling ran from the Baroque

elegance of armorial forms to the tight, hard drawing of the
early nineteenth-century Neo-Classic forms. During this
period, the color of the metal changes from pale green to
crystal clear, from slightly cloudy to completely transparent.
Glass at the early end of the sequence is hard to find and much
imitated, but in better metal. At the nearer end, the Neo-
Classic types are more common, although far less common
than they would have been if the area had not suffered so much
damage through war and revolution.

French Influences in Paperweights

The French learned how to make fancy glass from the
Italians along with other Europeans. What stands out as particularly French in glass blowing is the work of the late
eighteenth and particularly of the nineteenth century. What is
French about French glass is the manner in which the techniques were used, but the techniques and designs come, at
least in part, from elsewhere.

Several of the famous glass houses in France, such as
Baccarat and St. Louis, though founded before the end of the
eighteenth century, made their most impressive impact on
glass design during the nineteenth century.

While we must remember that all types of glass were made
in these factories, those most sought after as representative
of the French are the paperweights. Collecting of these <u>tours
de forces</u> has been very popular almost since they were made.
Every type of elaborate preparation goes into the making of a
paperweight, from casting to cane making to cutting the glass.
Glass weights of the nineteenth century from St. Louis or
Baccarat are worth almost their weight in gold—which is quite
considerable, for they are heavy. The metal is frequently
flint or lead glass that may have a <u>laticino</u> or a millefiori base.
Butterflies, roses, and other flowers seem to be imbedded in
the glass. The glass is frequently cased in overlay, not infrequently cut, and of extraordinary brilliance.

In passing, we might note that we received a great deal of
instruction from French glass blowers here in America. The
most notable was Nicholas Lutz, who is known principally to

American collectors as one who brought the art of Venetian glass blowing to America.

English Flint and Cut Flint Glass

English glass is the kind of glass we think of when we think of cut tableware. With it we also think of Irish glass, for they have much the same history. Bristol and Waterford are two places that exported a great deal of glass, especially to America. In part, they set the vogue for cut glass in the late eighteenth and early nineteenth centuries here in America.

Bristol is famous for its translucent white glass (opal), which was made, at least in the beginning, as a kind of substitute for the porcelain of the Orient during the second half of the eighteenth century. Bristol continued to make opal glass well into the nineteenth century.

Another specialty of this glass factory was the production of overlay and of cut glass. Collectible cut glass from Bristol falls into the period before 1830, that of the overlay extends through the nineteenth century. Overlay and thin enameled glass, as well as opal (opaque) glass in a variety of colors, are frequently called Bristol in the trade when there is no reason to suspect they were made anywhere near this factory. In fact, the nonspecific character of this designation indicates chiefly the close association between this factory and glass of certain kinds.

It is to be remembered that Bristol's production is not limited to the types of glass described above, nor was Bristol the sole producer of them. Nevertheless, the term Bristol is attached to the following kinds of glass: (1) the white porcelain-like enamel-decorated glass of the eighteenth and early nineteenth centuries; (2) opaque glass of heavy character in various colors, frequently decorated with enamel; and (3) thin-walled opaque blown glass with elaborate color combinations of nineteenth-century types.

American Types—Blown, Three-Mold, and Pressed

To most Americans, American glass is the most important and, as usual, type for type, the scarcest. American glass

made earlier than the nineteenth century is exceedingly rare,
although glass was made in this country almost from its found-
ing. Certainly one of the first factories, if not the first, in
America was set up for the making of glass of apparently Venetian type. The history of the glass houses at Jamestown is
certainly cloudy so far as documentation goes, but recent
excavations have shown that a glass factory did exist, and the
nature of the product is partly known: window and bottle glass
as it was in early American glass houses through the eighteenth century.

Blown glass developed two traditions. The first, associated
with the factory of Caspar Wistar, is light in weight, fairly
heavy-walled soda-lime glass, in various bottle colors, for
example, deep blue and amber, olive green to almost black.
These were chiefly simple blown forms. Similar forms also
exist in window glass colors, for instance, pale green to aqua.
The glass is heavy in appearance but light in weight. It used
to be attributed to Wistar's factory. Actually, since we know
of the types only through newspaper advertisements and in-
ferences based thereon, it has become usual to call this glass
South Jersey, unless it can be documented to a specific factory.

Collectors of thirty years ago, speaking contemptuously
of Sandwich glass as fine for the five-and-ten-cent store, were
anxious to acquire pieces of Stiegel, Stoddard, and Wistarburg
glass, without knowing very clearly what they were talking
about. Their Stiegel was unprovable, some of it English or
German; Stoddard had nothing whatever to do with the glass
to which the name was applied; and as for Wistarburg, there
wasn't any. The Sandwich glass so condemned was, far from
being a five-and-ten-cent item, fine glass of top quality, which
sold for good prices when it was new.

The second type of American glass is in what is known as
the Stiegel tradition. This glass more nearly follows English
taste and is intended exclusively for table use. Much of it is
clear, some colored. It was molded, thin-walled glass of
some lead content, ornamented with copper wheel engraving or
enamel in the manner of Bohemian glass. Much of both the
engraving and enameling is cursory if not crude. Here again,
although there is good documentary evidence as to the type of

glass produced, there is no one-to-one relation between the type and the factory, so that once again it is usual to generalize the descriptive name to Stiegel-type glass.

Now, while both of these types are different from Continental or English glass in one way or another, they are not sufficiently different to constitute a distinct new type. American innovations in glass blowing exist, and it is these that constitute the character of American glass. There are several of them, each owing its existence to an attempt to get the glass industry out of a financial rut. Two of them, certainly, and perhaps all of them, owe their existence to the mobility of American society. American glass manufacturers in the early days were continually importing skilled workmen from abroad, only to have them abandon their trade as quickly as their contracts terminated to take up with the more profitable and eminently more respectable calling of agriculture. For this and other reasons, labor in America of the eighteenth and nineteenth centuries was always scarce. The more expensive its services, the more Yankee ingenuity went to work to find ways of getting the most possible production from each hour of work—hence, the popularity of the Stiegel type of pattern-molded glass.

By the beginning of the nineteenth century we had a number of glass houses making use of molds in one way or another, so it was not surprising that when a financial crisis overtook the glass industry at the end of the War of 1812-14, the glass manufacturers took to the use of molds in a large way. The result was the first innovation—the production of blown three-mold glass, wherein the glass was blown into full-sized molds. While we have to be cautious in these matters, it seems to be a type or glass peculiar to the United States and limited in time as well as in place. It differs from blown molded bottles in three respects. First, it is frequently, although not exclusively, blown in clear white glass. Second, it consists of many articles for table use. Third, the molds in which it was made were in three instead of two parts. The glass was frequently of bottle or window quality and often of the dark brown or black glass type, but also of green, aqua, or amber color, not by design but by accident. The blurred character of the impression and the dull fins, as well as the lightness in weight of the pieces, help distinguish them from pressed pieces. How old is such glass? The answer is problematic. American blown three-mold glass probably dates from c. 1816-50, European and American blown flasks and bottles (two-mold) perhaps from a generation before.

The second innovation is the pressing of glass. Early writers on the subject have been reluctant to ascribe this invention to Americans for the reason that the evidence is confused. However, the fact remains that, although small objects such as stoppers, salts, small ornaments, and parts such as feet and ornamental bases may have been pressed abroad previously, the pressing of an entire hollow object, like a bowl or tumbler, in one operation, was an American innovation.

The third innovation was the development of fancy glass of a very specific sort. This is generally called art glass, which, on the whole, is a good name for it.

The vases don't hold flowers, the bowls are impractical, the tumblers and stemware seem designed for fragility and easy spilling. Fancy art glass makes its appeal through this very uselessness of its forms as well as the lovely range of color and texture. Peachblow glass of several sorts, Burmese, amberina, satin glass and iridescent glass—all are part of American inventiveness in the matter of glass chemistry and new manufacturing techniques.

This is not to say that Americans dominated this field. Much art glass was produced abroad. Some of it, however, like Webb and Company's Burmese, was produced under patent agreements with American firms. Cameo glass seems to have been the chief art glass of Europe. I doubt that much of it was made here, due to the high cost of American labor. Cameo glass had to be carved by hand, and handwork is one of the things we don't expect to find in late nineteenth-century America. Thus, most Cameo glass is of English or French origin. Aside from this, the development of most other types is indeed American.

American cut glass of the late nineteenth and early twentieth centuries is in a sense an innovation. Cut glass had always existed, but the so-called brilliant cut glass had its origin here. The wide, deep cut glass in a variety of geometric patterns (although it has an English and Middle European background) is a type of glass that is associated more closely with America of the last quarter of the nineteenth century and the first decade of the twentieth than with any other country, although, at the peak of its popularity, I doubt that there existed a single factory in Europe devoted to ornamental wares that was not making it.

EVIDENCES OF THE PASSAGE OF TIME

We have come to the end of the description of antique glass. All the things that have been discussed concerning its materials, manufacturing methods, ornamentation, and style are clues to its age. Other clues to the age of glass derive from the "slings and arrows of outrageous fortune"—in short, the strains and changes arising from the effects of the passage of time.

Glass a hundred years old will be colored ever so slightly greenish or pinkish, with the chances of its being pink somewhat better than of its being green. New glass will be neither green nor pink. Glass that has been exposed to the elements will, for various reasons, show color changes to a much greater degree. Exposure to sunlight tends to color it purple.

Beyond this, however, weathering does something else. As glass is exposed to the elements, various layers begin to separate from the main body of the glass. The layers are of varying thickness and thus cause a play of color on the surface. This iridescence is at its most pronounced in glass that has been buried in the ground for some time, as is the case with ancient Greek, Roman, and Egyptian glass, in which the wonderful glow of changing color is always admired. It also exists in all glass that has been around for more than fifty years.

This iridescence has to be looked for carefully, and care should be taken not to confuse it with the iridescence of a film of oil from your hands or grease from the atmosphere. When these precautions are taken, it is one of the best tests for deciding the age of glass, since, other things being equal, the older the glass, the more intense the iridescence. Other things are, of course, not equal, and the iridescence varies according to the glass. It is greatest in coarse, dark, ordinary soda-lime glass, less in potassium-soda-lime glass. The conditions under which the glass is kept will intensify or lessen the process to a degree. Dampness, contact with organic matter—all tend to intensify it. If you want to get the glass colored in a hurry, bury it in a manure pile. Fortunately for most of us who collect, this hastening process will give itself away by the character of the iridescence produced, which has the hard, overdone intensity characteristic of all hasty jobs. Further, it easily rubs off, revealing new, sound glass.

The separation of layers in glass can proceed to the point where the glass is constantly flaking off. On the exterior surfaces (since the exfoliation produces a brilliant play of colors) no one objects too much. When it occurs on interior surfaces, however, it gives them a cloudy or dirty look. Such glass is said to be sick, and certainly looks it. Glass sickness can affect any kind of glass, but favors decanters because of the continued presence of wine in them. The curious effect of water or any liquid on such glass is to dispel the cloudiness when the container is filled, but it returns when the liquid dries out.

Finally, there is wear and tear. Glass gets scratched from time to time, and the sum of these scratches is the product of its age. These scratches have two characteristics that separate them from those put there to deceive. The first is their complete randomness. The surface between scratches is likely to be highly polished. Secondly, they occur only on contact surfaces; if they extend beyond these, the piece needs re-examination on all counts.

While scratches are the most obvious sign of wear and tear, they are not the only ones. Somewhat akin to the scratches is the loss of luster on parts frequently handled or subjected to extra wear, such as the feet of dishes and the handles of pitchers, knobs on drinking glasses, and finials of covered pieces. Somewhat similar in origin but different in appearance is a polished surface where extra wear has taken place. In point of time, it takes a piece of glass longer to become polished than it does to get roughened; consequently, polish will point to

greater age than loss of luster. Polish also occurs on pieces
that were roughened on purpose when new. Satin-finished
pieces and ground surfaces on the bases of paperweights have
frequently been polished smooth in places. Related to this
polish is the loss of roughness in coarse-ground or stippled
surfaces. These marks of the passage of time should all
occur together.

FAKES

Glass of almost every type discussed here has been imitated.
There are a few exceptions to the rule. One is that glass like
iridescent Favrille, which costs so much to produce, has not
become high enough in price to attract the faker. Glass that
currently sells for very little, such as carnival glass (contemporary with Tiffany), does not bring enough to warrant
faking. With these exceptions, all other types of glass have
been, are being, or are going to be faked.

How are we going to distinguish the fake from the original?
Certainly one thing that will distinguish later imitations from
originals is lack of age. All the signs of wear and tear referred to above will be absent; or the faker is likely to have
overdone the application of wear so that it is never in exactly
the right places. Most particularly, it is not random. The
scratches on a fake will show patterning as to predominant
size, direction, and type.

A less obvious but far more reliable characteristic of faking will be inconsistency. This can occur in relation to tools
used in combination with the metal, or the metal itself will
contain ingredients affecting its appearance which are incon-
sistent with the date of the glass. For example, a typical piece
of late eighteenth-century American glass ornamented with or
made of opaque white glass would illustrate this type of inconsistency, since opaque white glass, so far as America is
concerned, is a product of the second half of the nineteenth
century.

Blown glass fakes are the most difficult to detect, because
hand-blown glass will have all the character of hand blowing.

The wavy surfaces, typical blown techniques and pontil marks,
so avidly sought by beginning collectors, will all be there.
What we have to check for carefully is the relation between the
form and the metal. Here we find that most modern imitations
of early blown pieces are heavier and that the changes in color
of the metal itself are consistently different. The later metal
is more perfect, freer of bubbles and other imperfections.
An exception is Mexican and similar blown glass from other
parts of the world, but here the bubbles give the glass a frothy
appearance that suggests the lightness in weight that you experience whenever you pick up the glass. These characteristics
are accompanied by both a hardness in design due to either
frozen traditionalism or conscious copying, and a carelessness
in execution.

Harder to spot than inconsistency in blown glass is the
subtle degrading of style, especially in simple pieces. Nevertheless, it exists. Copies lack spontaneity. They are always
faltering, even when they are most technically deft. Reproductions of any sort always have hard lines. Throughout this
work and elsewhere, you will be reading about the hard, un-
certain lines of copies. This is easy to demonstrate.

Write half a dozen words on a sheet of paper in your ordinary
handwriting. Now, set out to copy these half-dozen words
exactly. This means as to height, spacing, and form, not
only of every letter, but every stroke! Before you have completed one word, you will see the enormous difficulty of forging your own handiwork. Compare the two groups of words and
notice that the difficulty of doing synthetically what was once
natural is reflected in the copy. This is what is meant by the
hardness of the copy.

There are other things to consider too. The copyist does
not know the formula for the original piece, which would vary
from melt to melt in the same factory, especially in older
factories. Secondly, the old workman was an innovator; each
new piece was a new challenge. Such is the nature of handwork.
For this reason, the forms of old glass have a sense of inevi-
tability about them; copies somehow bulge too much here or not
enough there. While all of these differences are very slight,
they exist and show up immediately, especially if we compare

a copy with the original or with an authentic piece of roughly the same sort.

There is one last characteristic that imitations of antique glass may have. It is often said that if you're going to steal, it's better to steal a million dollars than a thousand. Consequently, the faker is likely to feel that the work of making, antiquing, and marketing a blown glass piece might just as well go into faking an expensive one. Thus he is tempted to pile rarity on rarity, with the result that an elaborate design is likely to turn up in a rare form in an unusual color. Such a temptation is hard to resist.

While all of the above applies generally to all kinds of glass, it applies even more to simple blown pieces like early German, American, and English glass, than to elaborate Venetian or Bohemian glass.

In cut glass, especially carved pieces, faking occurs, but here we have a better chance of comparing copy with original because the style is higher. Modern carved and cut glass of any elaborateness is so fantastically expensive that in this category, while fakes do exist, they are not going to upset the applecart so much because of the difficulty of executing a passable fraud for less than the original would cost. Here the effort to cut corners may be evident in the use of molds for all but the final cutting and polishing. An examination of the interior surface will likely give this technique away, since there will be slight hollows opposite bulges on the exterior, from expansion resulting from the air that follows the glass into the mold. An examination of the object in polarized light would also reveal different stress patterns. For glass approximately three hundred years old, examination by ultraviolet light would provide some clue as to age, although this is not so reliable as a test for style and what your fingers and hands will tell you.

Fakes in engraved blown (or pressed) glass are not difficult to detect, for the reasons given above. Here, I might caution you, is an excellent area for the demi-fake or the glorification of an earlier piece. Obviously, there are more simple pieces about than engraved ones, so that if an unscrupulous individual wishes to upgrade an authentic piece, he may try to do so by engraving it. As some risk is involved and the piece may be damaged in the process, greater care must be taken. This, and the fact that the engraving technique may vary, help to give away the fraud.

To lessen the risk, the glass may be etched rather than engraved. The difference is easily established with the aid of a magnifying glass. Although hydrofluoric acid was a late eighteenth-century discovery, it was rarely used on glass before the late nineteenth century, so etching on glass of earlier date is a giveaway. Styles of engraving have changed, and the elaborate early copper wheel engraving is different from the modern to the degree that you should have little trouble discovering it. Modern engraving is more perfect in technique and more cursory in application than that of earlier periods. Most that I have seen is clumsy and simply doesn't look right.

Enameled glass is very popular as of this moment—I am speaking of glass made now. To distinguish between a fake and a nineteenth-century recapitulation of an earlier style is not difficult. We can separate nineteenth-century glass from the modern fake by its metal, which will be almost perfect. The modern faker attempts to use metal that will look old and he usually does not know when he has gotten it to look old enough. The nineteenth century's fondness for overstating its formal relationships in design (for example, its Rococo is too Rococo) helps us, as does its love of gold and choice of color. Nineteenth-century color combinations are less startling, but, most particularly, they are more sullied and somber than the earlier colors.

Enamel is softer than glass and shows the wear and tear of handling to a greater degree. Again, all that can be said of weathering of glass is true also of enamels. Once again, style is the best indication of age. High style in design is often accompanied by inferior materials; for example glass, metal, and enamel are combined with loving care in execution. Modern work has magnificent materials, used in designs lacking the consistency as well as the careful execution of eighteenth-century work, while it exhibits simultaneously an almost meretricious perfectionism.

Applying new enamel to old glass is a risky business but can be and is done. Since enough heat is required to mature the enamels, the surface changes characteristic of old glass may be reversed in the firing process. At the same time, some changes may occur in the metal itself. Thus, you have clear inconsistencies between the color changes in the metal, due to greater than normal weathering and the no weathering of the enamel.

TESTS OF AGE

It is worth while considering some of the obvious tests to be applied to glass to determine its age. One thing important to remember is that if it can be established that the glass is over 150 years old, any greater age that it may have, determined on the basis of style, is also virtually established, because faking and making imitations of earlier glass were then rarer than the objects they copied.

The first important criterion of age is imperfections. These take the form of imperfections in the metal—bubbles, sand and lime spots, streaks and folds. Then there are imperfections in design. The glass lacks the sweep and certainty of machine work. Compare a circle drawn by hand and one with a compass.

There is also imperfection in handling. That is, a goblet does not always stand without rocking or the bowl (frequently handsomely engraved) is a little lopsided. These warpings may have occurred in the annealing oven or in the making. A fourth type of imperfection occurs in actual execution. Panels of glass may not all come out the same size, there may be irregularity in the fluting, the bowl may be slightly off center, and the same may apply to the foot.

Another objective test is the character of signs of wear. Glass should display the amount of wear appropriate to its age, its metal, and use. Lead glass is softer, hence we should expect more wear in less time than in other types of glass. On the other hand, soda-lime seems to weather faster than lead glass, so this has to be taken into consideration too.

Materials change the rate of weathering, wearing, and color changes. Obviously, color changes will be more evident in clear than in colored glass, but occasionally, even here, one can discover in some of the pale uranium yellows, for example, slight fading due to the graying of the yellow by a change in the character of the iron and manganese in the glass.

Pressed glass, especially of the early types, shows its own peculiar kinds of change as noted above. These characteristics are most conspicuous in the earliest pieces, and the greater the amount of other changes due to wear, the more easily are they seen. In the case of pressed glass, we should remember that around 1865 there was a shift from flint or lead glass to lime glass, which gives us a good dividing line for dating pressed glass on the basis of metal.

The greatest clue to age in glass is its style, and here we must have recourse to dated examples in publications. Within the limits of the nature of glass, it will be either Late Gothic, Renaissance, Baroque, Rococo, Neo-Classic, Greek Revival, Rococo Revival, Naturalistic, or Art Nouveau. Some Baroque and Rococo glass will be flint, and only the late Gothic Revival and modern glass will be lime. Earlier than flint will be soda-lime. As flint gives way to lime glass, the Rococo Revival and Antiquarian forms of glass are upon us. Naturally, flint glass is still used in optical goods and lead is still used in fine crystal, so much collectible late glass will be flint. However, not much early soda-lime, except for glass of Mexican type, was made after the discovery of lime glass.

COLLECTING GLASS

How should you go about collecting glass? You should consider your wants in the light of the likelihood of fulfilling them. It will be somewhat more difficult to get together a collection of Roman glass than American art glass, although the cost need not be far different.

One thing you should wonder about is to what extent you should try to collect Venetian, English, Irish, or Bohemian glass as opposed to the glass of our own country. The taste of

the collector should be the guide. It is well, however, to know
the pitfalls of the one as compared with those of the other.
There is more fancy European glass about than there is
American, especially when we consider earlier and earlier
glass. There are also a great many late nineteenth-century
versions of seventeenth-century glass of European type. By
the late nineteenth century, collecting glass had become
fashionable abroad, and hence earlier fashions were revived.
Not much of the glass is exactly fake, because it betrays its
nineteenth-century character in various ways. It is, nevertheless, easier to be deceived in the matter of age of European
than American glass.

American glass is one of the most popular and, on the basis
of available authenticity, the handiest place to start a glass
collection. All metals and glass-blowing techniques are available to the collector of American glass. The difficulty in this
field is that almost every type of American glass has been reproduced ad nauseam over a period of at least forty years.
Thus each purchase is fraught with danger. But this applies
equally well to glass from Europe. American blown glass will
have to be distinguished from modern Mexican glass, which it
resembles closely.

Blown and molded glass and blown three-mold glass will
usually be found in the hands of specialists, with all the increase
in price that we pay to the specialist for his specialty. Here
your chief difficulty, aside from overpaying for the right kind
of glass, will be to avoid Czechoslovakian reproductions of
bottles and three-mold glass. These reproductions are thirty
years or so old and have lost some of their new appearance.
They usually give themselves away by their unusual colors and
hard outlines.

In the case of pressed glass, the earlier patterns are not so
extensively reproduced as the somewhat later pattern-glass
pieces. Reproductions have been limited, but as the supply
decreases they are certain to increase. Beware, especially,
of colored forms; unusual colors should be suspect.

Although the later pressed or pattern glass represents more
of a problem, it is easily avoided to the degree that one sticks
to the patterns popular in the 1850's and earlier. Later pattern

glass requires all kinds of checking to make sure it is not fake, for the metal is of modern type. A careful search for imperfections in the metal in the case of the old and in the modeling in the case of the new usually separates the authentic from the fake.

Enameled glass presents all the usual problems plus the possibility that, although the glass may be old, the enamel may not be. If the enameled glass is of Bohemian type, I should concentrate on the quality of the enameling and whether it agrees with the style of the piece.

Cut glass is not hard to distinguish if you take the trouble to examine both cut and uncut surfaces to see whether the glass was cut from blown or pressed blanks. Beyond that, the style of cutting in both German and Irish glass determine the age of the piece pretty fairly because the excellence of the cutting is a good clue to separating today's fake from the period piece of yesterday. It is well to note here that the eagerly sought-after cameo glass of the late nineteenth century fits this description.

Engraved glass presents no special problem except that the engraving may be new. Here comparison should be made between the style of engraving expected and that actually present. Overlay and art glass imitations are plentiful. The overlay will give a beginning collector so much trouble that it is not worth bothering with. The art glass imitations currently available, except in nineteenth-century Venetian types, are so obvious that only a little experience is required to make the distinction.

Steps in Examination

You are now ready to go through the steps in the examination of a piece of glass. I think it ought to be clear that you must be able to handle the piece to find out all there is in it.

First, look at the glass where it sits and study its contours, surface reflections, translucency, and style. See where the style should place it in terms of metal, weight, and imperfections. Try to get a good idea of the color of the metal (modern colors are different from old ones). If the glass is clear, see whether it is tinged with green, purple, pink, blue, or gray.

Nine-tenths of what you look at will cease to interest you further.

If you are still interested, ask the owner if you may handle it. Its weight will tell you a lot about the glass. Turn it around carefully in your hand. If it is feasible to do so, see what kind of ring the glass has. The chances are that if it has the ring of good flint glass, the owner will have already demonstrated it when he handed it to you. In any case, see whether the glass is brilliant or dull, and whether it has the internal brilliance of flint or the high exterior luster of lime glass due to fire polishing.

The examination up to this point should have given you clues as to the style, the amount of weathering, the metal, and the method by which it was made. You can be reasonably sure if it is flint, but where it is possible and where the dealer allows it, you could clinch things with a spot test. Feeling the slick, worked surface of blown glass tells you many things about the glass, but at this point your main purpose should be to look for iridescence, its location and degree. Old hand-blown pieces will likely have spots that are soft in contour but others that are sharp, especially the pontil mark. Feel also gives some notion as to the delicacy of the glass (Venetian glass of the sixteenth and seventeenth centuries feels much more delicate than glass of the same type of the nineteenth century).

In the case of pressed glass, the feel of the glass is an extremely important clue of age. The lacy glass is always sharp on all surfaces, and whatever fins exist at seams and edges are sharp enough to cut. Later pressed glass is more perfect in feel, and smoother to the touch, but impressions are always sharp enough to distinguish from modern surfaces, which never have this kind of sharpness. Modern pressed glass always feels flatter and more blurred at all points.

By this time you will have a pretty good idea of about how long the glass has been around. This is the time to look for wear and tear on various surfaces. Examine contact surfaces first. A magnifying glass may be necessary, for some contact surfaces are quite small. Scratches must be random. If the underlying surface is rough or unpolished, there is reason for suspicion. If a pattern is discoverable, the whole piece should be re-examined. Other surfaces should show a small amount of wear and tear compatible with that on the contact surface. If there is a wide discrepancy between the amount of wear on the contact surface and the loss of luster on other surfaces, it is again cause for reconsideration.

You are now ready to make your decision. If all the characteristics agree with the style, the chances are that the piece is what it appears to be; if they do not correspond, something is wrong. If the owner has made no comment, now is the time to ask him what it is. Hear him out to the end, ask him to date the piece, and ask any other pertinent questions. It would probably be a good idea to ask him a few impertinent questions, too, such as "What do you think you have there, a gold mine?" or "Come now, do you expect me to believe that tripe? Anyone can see that's Czech." A few remarks like this will let the dealer know he is dealing with an expert who will not be fooled. If the dealer hasn't thrown you out of his shop, you can ask him to comment further on the piece. Will he put this in writing? His reaction may be a clue to what he really thinks of the piece.

Although it seems like calling attention to the obvious, this is a good time to talk about condition. In your examination, don't fail to be on the lookout for nicks, cracks, and mended breaks. Watch out for sick glass. Condition has little to do with the antiquity of a piece or its aesthetic value, but it has everything to do with the price. A glass cup plate that would easily bring $700 in proof condition is not going to be worth much if it looks as if the Mad Hatter had been munching on it. Cracks in glass are serious; in time, they will work their way through the glass and break it. Scuff marks, scratches, and minor chips also cut down the value, but in some cases you may have to put up with them. Put up with them but don't pay for them.

Chapter VII

CERAMICS

Ceramic wares have long been prized as collectibles. Most are handsome, some are scarce. The great problem they present to collector and student is their bewildering variety of shape, texture, and glaze.

While numerous fakes are waiting to catch you, most of you will not be fooled as much by these as by wares that were never intended to deceive anyone. The chief problem of a beginning collector lies in identifying a piece and thus avoiding buying new pieces in the belief that they are antique. Since many genuine old pieces are without mark, the identification is based on ceramic body, manufacturing process, type, style, decoration, and type of glaze.

You should remember that while many of the wares you will be offered will be supplied with identities by the seller, the correctness of these identifications depends on what the seller happens to know. Most of what you will find is of the nineteenth century, and you should not forget that this is a century of eclecticism. Wares of every early sort discussed here will be found. Some are worth owning, others are not.

Nineteenth century ceramic imitations differ from earlier wares by being better technically. The most beautifully executed of the eighteenth-century wares will show some technical imperfections of the body (pock marks), glaze, firing, and execution. Moldings are not always perfect; the corresponding parts do not always match perfectly. Even the most nearly perfectly potted wares from the royal factories of Europe show variations from true perfection. But these irregularities are combined with the most carefully executed decoration and brushwork. Similar nineteenth-century wares, by contrast, although technically excellent, never show such care. The decoration is coarse and summary by eighteenth-century standards. Forms tend to be exaggerated, colors harsher and stronger.

Most modern forgeries of porcelain are made of hard paste. Attempts at making soft paste are betrayed by the poor quality of the body. In addition, the forger has to simulate the effects of the passage of time.

Although breakable, ceramic objects do not deteriorate as a result of any inherent defect. Slow deterioration takes a long time before any effect is apparent. Thus the chief effect of age is wear. This will vary in accordance with the use. A figurine gets much less handling than a plate. Making allowances for these differences, wear is a function of time; the older the piece, the greater the wear. Wear consists of dull areas on the often handled portions: the glaze may even be worn off in spots; and there will be cuts and scratches on exposed surfaces like the base or the foot. The important fact about wear arising from use is its nonuniformity. Scratches put on a surface on purpose will lack randomness; scratches acquired by accident will show their accidental nature.

The weight of a piece is also a clue to its age. Most early ceramic wares are lighter than their modern forms by about twenty-five percent. This is not true of hard paste porcelains. There the situation is reversed: old specimens are heavier than newer ones and the walls are thicker.

The styles of ceramic objects reflect the styles of the times in which they were made. But styles are altered by materials available, and in this matter there were great differences from time to time. In the finished product, the ceramic body tells us which manufacturing process was used along with what materials. We must first look at the materials and thence go on to consider manufacturing methods.

CERAMIC MATERIALS

Things of wood and/or metal are made of materials created by nature. The material out of which ceramic wares are made has to be created by man. The solid earth underneath our feet is made up of a vast and intricate network of oxygen atoms held together with the help of silicon and aluminum atoms. The rocks, basalts, granites, schists, and gneisses are all made

of various silicates (feldspar) and silica (quartz). Granite is
only as resistant as its weakest component. As the feldspar
weathers, the granite decays. We recognize the debris as
clay. When this clay is fired into a ceramic ware, we are in
a sense reconstituting the rock.

The clay minerals allow almost endless substitutions of
different chemicals, and with each substitution the constitution
of the product changes. That is why there are so many names
for the products of the kiln. Pottery, earthenware, stoneware,
porcelain, soft paste, hard paste, and ironstone are some of
them. Not only does the raw material differ, but the methods
of preparing it, the firing temperature, the methods of decorating it, and the glazes and enamels employed change its character and appearance to an extraordinary degree. Consider a
brick, a flower pot, a Greek vase, and a terra cotta figurine.
All are of the same material, but the appearances differ from
the coarse, irregular texture of brick to the exquisitely fine
one of terra cotta.

Clays vary in appearance, but they differ much more in
their behavior during the potting and firing. The chief ingredients of clay are alumina, feldspar, and silica. Iron, manganese, calcium, and a host of other substances are apt to be
present as impurities. The alumina provides the body of the
clay. The feldspar and silica give vitreosity; calcium and
sodium help to provide fluxes to aid in the fusing of feldspar
and silica. The alumina is best represented by kaolin. Porcelain clays have large amounts of kaolin, low-firing redwares
have smaller amounts.

No matter what its use, there are certain qualities clay
must have. The first of these is porosity; if the clay is not
porous, it will not dry. A wet clay cannot be fired. The second
quality is plasticity. If it is not plastic, it cannot be shaped.
Some clays, most especially the clays used for making soft
paste and bone china, are so deficient in this characteristic
that they have to be supported through the first firing. It is
said that some of the French soft pastes were so crumbly (due
to the admixture of glass and calcium) that the potters had to
resort to mixing soap with the clay in order to work it at all.
A third quality a clay must have is the ability to vitrify in the

kiln without losing its shape. In order to do this, the clay must consist of one substance that dries and holds its shape while another fuses the infusible particles together. The part that holds the shape is the clay mineral proper, the alumina. The fusible element is chiefly feldspar.

A clay containing these qualities can be worked and fired. To insure that each clay has them, they are added in proper amounts at the time the clay is levigated (ground). Clays may contain chemical as well as mechanical impurities. These are avoided by selecting clays that are naturally pure. The major effect of impurities is to make the clay opaque and red to black in color, and they may sometimes lower the firing temperature. It is a good general rule that clays that burn to a fine white require a very high fire.

Clays are washed by being passed down through settling tanks and through sieves of varying fineness; this removes the gross impurities and grades them according to particle size. The clay is finally caught in sheets of cloth that do not allow it to pass through. It is then placed in a mill where it is further ground to get all the ingredients to the same state of fineness and thoroughly mixed. Otherwise, the wares will not come through the processing as they should.

MANUFACTURING METHODS

The clays are now ready to be prepared for working. Clays have to be wedged for most work. Insufficiently wedged pieces may break in the firing. Wedging consists of breaking the clay up into small pieces and slamming the pieces together again. The clay is now ready to use.

To make the clay into a pot or jug, a variety of techniques may be used. The most primitive is simply to take the lump of clay and work it either with coils or some other method to get a smooth, round shape of the proper size and contour. This method is not in use except by primitive people.

The most spectacular shaping is done on the potter's wheel. Here the clay is placed on a slowly turning table and rotated. The pressure of the potter's fingers and hands causes the vessel

to grow and the clay to flow into the final shape. To be able
to throw a vase of any shape on the potter's wheel, to have
the clay completely under the control of one's fingertips at
all times so that the final form is a creation, not an accident,
is a rare skill.

The fact that a piece is hand-thrown can frequently be
determined from the marks of the potter's fingers seen or
felt as spiral grooves on the inside of the jar. Where the
inside is as visible as the outside, as in shallow bowls, these
marks are removed. They are no proof of antiquity, but show
that the pottery is wheel made. The nature of the clay limits
the size of a piece we can throw at a time. Larger pieces will
have to be made in several sections.

Before we leave the potter's wheel we should point out that
the finished contours of wheel-thrown pots are made after the
clay has dried to a leather-hard state. It will now hold its
shape, does not break easily on handling, can be cemented
together with a mixture of clay and water called "slip," and
can be brought to its final form by turning.

Another shaping method is to roll the prepared clay out
into sheets of uniform thickness and then cut out patterns and
work it as if it were sheet metal. In this way, you can get
square, hexagonal, octagonal, and polygonal vases whose
faces meet each other at sharp, unplastic angles. These very
attractive forms were made early by the Chinese, those
masters of the plastic form.

Clay can also be pressed into molds. You can thus make the
same shape over and over again without limit (till the mold
wears out) allowing mass production of the object. It is about
the only way some shapes can be made. More magnificent and
artistic work, especially where duplicates are needed, can be
achieved by this method than any other. It is especially suited
to such unplastic material as the soft pastes. Work pressed
into molds shows occasional dents made by fingers on the
inside of the piece, thus revealing the method used.

Molds can be made of clay, fired but not glazed, or more
often of plaster of Paris. Since clay shrinks on drying and the
porous surface of the fired clay drinks up the water from the
wet clay, it was soon found that stirring up clay in water to

make a slip, and then pouring the mixture into a mold, deposits a film of clay evenly over the inside of the mold. Its thickness depends on the length of time the slip is left in the mold.

Figurines can be made in the same way, or they can be modeled as individual pieces (of which there are no duplicates). Most of the time an in-between process was used. Since the mold had to be made in parts (in order to get it free of the model and the work), the parts were cast separately and assembled by repairers. The body, head, arms, and legs to be put together with slip could be assembled in any of a number of positions, each producing a different figure.

When the ware is removed from the molds, seam marks and imperfections such as bubble marks are removed or filled with slip and smoothed over, handles are cast separately and applied with slip, details that did not come out in the casting are added or corrected. Finally, it is set in a drying room. When thoroughly dry, it is fired. Fine ware is usually placed in saggers (boxes of fire clay) for firing. Soft pastes have to be supported on flint in the saggers.

Fired ware is called biscuit or bisque and is the part of a glazed piece we mean by ceramic body. Most ceramic wares are decorated at this point with glazes, which must fit the kind of body to which they are applied. If the glaze and body expand at a different rate, the glaze will crack and may fall off. Some glazes will not melt or mature even at the temperature at which the body will melt. Thus redwares were generally glazed with low-melting lead glazes. A clear lead glaze is the most lustrous. Glazes may be colored with various minerals to get other effects.

Pottery is often decorated with underglaze colors. These have to be colors that will resist fire. Underglaze decoration on redware can be the oxides of iron, cobalt, copper, and manganese. With salt glaze, which is the glaze used on stoneware, only cobalt or manganese will stand the high temperatures. Salt (sodium chloride) is thrown into the kiln at the peak of the fire. The salt vapor together with the silica in the clay form a kind of glass on the surface. Salt glazes are always pebbly, like the surface of an orange. Feldspathic glazes of varying

fusibility were used on white earthenware and porcelain.
Underglaze colors were blue, black, and copper red.

While the glazes of hard pastes are bright, they are
exceeded in brilliance by the lead and lower-firing glazes
used on redware, creamware, and soft paste. The Oriental
glazes have a slightly pebbly surface similar to, but less
pronounced than, the salt glazes. This offers a handy means
of differentiating between Oriental and Occidental porcelains,
which have a glossier glaze. The soft and hard pastes were
usually glazed with feldspathic glazes. Salt was sometimes
used on the soft pastes.

The palette of underglaze colors was somewhat limited
and that of the glazes was not much richer. Painting with
colored glazes had its difficulties, since the colors might run
together in firing. Thus, for rich and varied colors, enamels
were used. These lie upon the glaze, a fact that can be both
seen and felt. We find them applied to virtually any ceramic
surface.

While the foot of soft pastes is glazed, in hard pastes it
is not. With the hard pastes there is no clear line where the
glaze leaves off and the body starts. On soft pastes and, in
fact, all other wares, there is a distinct line where the one
stops and the other begins.

The glazes on hard pastes do not show crazing unless it is
part of the design. Soft pastes and other wares of any age
almost always show a fine network of cracks (seldom obvious,
you have to look for them). Glazes age chemically, too.
When the glaze is young, it consists of a thin glasslike coating.
As the glaze ages, this coating becomes iridescent when the
surface is seen by reflected light. While this phenomenon is
much more pronounced in the lead and tin glazes on redwares
and the tin slips of faïence, it is also visible on all glazes if
you look for it. It is easiest seen where either the body or
the glaze is dark. However, it can always be detected if you
look. The older the piece, the greater the iridescence.

Many modern methods of pottery-making differ from the
old. Slip casting is much the same except that molds may be
agitated in casting, not so much care is taken to remove
seams and other imperfections, and decorations are summarily

painted but are most often made by underglaze or overglaze chromolithographic transfers. Work is not pressed by hand into the mold but shoved in by means of a "jollier." The mold is placed on a turntable, a wad of clay is tossed onto the mold, and a lever with a contoured form, as of the back of the dish, is brought against it. All such devices tend to give modern wares a hard, machine-made look.

IDENTIFYING CERAMIC WARE

In identifying ceramic ware, marks are significant. If the marks are genuine, they help you to place the piece, and if they are not, they may call your attention to a fraud. Unfortunately, most wares are innocent of any marks. It is here that the ceramic body will help you place the ware. While a person with much experience may be able to pick up a piece of chinaware and say, "Oh, yes, this is a piece of early St. Cloud," you will do well if you place it in the right category of body, for instance, soft paste. This does not look like much of an accomplishment, but it is, because once the ware has been identified as to type, all other types are automatically eliminated.

As with all antiques, style is the best indicator of age. In ceramics, the tendency to continue outmoded styles and to copy previous wares is the same as in other materials. Continuations of the style are, to all intents and purposes, the same as the style. Pieces that are frank copies usually copy only the decoration. Further, form and decoration are likely to be obviously overdone and insufficient attention is given to details. Modern forgeries, since they are intended to deceive, will be equipped with marks. These are often a clue to the fake, for they will sometimes indicate dates that are impossible. The forgery looks too good. It is likely to be very dry and hard in its lines. It will often have the wrong ceramic body, especially where the body is long out of fashion, such as the redware bodies of old luster or faïence or most of the soft pastes.

Before going on to the discussion of ceramic bodies, there is one thing about the development of style in ceramic ware that should be considered: the radical variation in decorative forms according to time and place. Thus shapes of ceramic objects give clues as to date.

****

Since there is no general agreement on the classification of wares by experts on the subject, there is every reason to simplify the classification into easy grouping. Ceramic wares vary in accordance with three or four variables, which can be listed as levigation (the degree of fineness of the clay particles), firing temperature, presence or absence of the ferromanganese minerals, and the general composition of the clay. From these, we can make nine categories of ceramic bodies, each distinct from the other, as follows: (1) redware; (2) terra cotta; (3) coarse stoneware; (4) creamware; (5) white earthenware; (6) white stoneware and fine stoneware of other colors; (7) glass frit soft paste; (8) bone and steatite soft paste; and (9) hard paste porcelain. These nine types of body can be arranged into three groups, as follows: (1) coarse wares, containing redware, terra cotta, and coarse stoneware; (2) fine opaque wares, containing creamware, white earthenware, and white stoneware; and (3) fine translucent wares, containing glass frit soft paste, steatitic and bone paste, and hard paste porcelain.

The firing temperature increases generally from the coarse wares to the fine translucent wares, and it increases within each group from the redware to coarse stoneware, from creamware to white stoneware, and from glass frit soft paste to hard paste. The firing temperature determines the texture, durability, and porosity of the ceramic bodies at the same time that it controls and limits the decorative possibilities of the ware. The higher the fire, the harder the ware. This hardness serves as a check on the authenticity of the wares. For example, Meissen patterns, even from the beginning, were copied in many different places on all kinds of ceramic bodies.

For locating the wares, I use a tick-tack-toe box with nine squares numbered one to three vertically and four, five,

six, etc. (see page 163). Do not think of these boxes with
tight boundary walls; think of them only as regions where we
can set up various types of wares. Most of the observable
characteristics of one group merge into those of its nearest
neighbor except in two cases. A piece of ceramic ware either
will or will not hold water; it will or will not allow light to
pass through it.

I shall now take up each of these nine categories, describe
its look, feel, and texture, and list some of its representative
wares.

Redware

Redware includes all low-firing ceramic wares made from
ordinary clay. They are coarse-grained, very porous, soft,
and low-firing. They break and chip easily with a fracture
resembling that of a brick, a stone, or a piece of cement.
Almost every piece with any pretensions to age has minute
chips, especially on its undersurfaces. You can make these
chips as big as you wish simply by using a magnifying glass.
A tiny chip thus magnified will show all the characteristics of
a large break.

The predominant color of redware is due to the presence
of iron oxide in the clay. However, it may vary from a rosy
buff to red, brown, and even black. Redware is opaque no
matter how thin it is. Antique wares in this class include all
primitive pottery from the Stone Age of Europe down to the
seventeenth century, and all pottery of the Near East to about
the same time. More specifically, redwares include slipware,
sgraffito, majolica, most delft, a large portion of faïence,
and many lusterwares.

Many of the English and American lead-glazed wares are
straightforward, simple pieces, unpretentiously potted and
glazed. The plate, bowl, milk pan, milk pitcher, jug, pie
plate, batter pitcher, and mug are redware's chief shapes.
The glaze will be crackled due to age. In many cases, pieces
show conspicuous iridescence. Both English and American
types are highly collectible. The English wares go back to the
seventeenth century, the American to the eighteenth, with

most of them concentrated in the nineteenth century. American types are fairly reasonable, the English much rarer and therefore more expensive.

More elaborate are the slip-decorated redwares of America and Great Britain. These were ornamented with slip before firing. The decorations, elaborated with slip, are of several sorts producing varied effects. The slip may be molded and used as applied decoration. There are many American wares of this type that you can collect without worrying too much about fakes or reproductions.

In another type, the slip, mixed to the consistency of pancake batter, was poured out on the ware to make decorative forms and sometimes pictures. The technique is difficult, as a moment's hesitation will produce a puddle. The slip is usually of light color and the patterns calligraphic but simple. English and American examples are still available—and at reasonable prices, when you consider their age and decorative charm.

Another technique is to run different-colored slips on the surface of the green (unfired) ware and drag them together with a comb to produce a marbleized effect. These combed types are also of English and American manufacture and are early and rare. There isn't much likelihood of faking either.

A very important type of slipware is sgraffito. In this class, after the green ware has been dipped into slip of a contrasting color, it is engraved through the slip to the clay body, producing a colored outline or areas of color. The whole is usually covered with a lead glaze. Originating in Medieval southern Europe, these wares were popular in southern Germany in the late seventeenth and early eighteenth centuries. The Pennsylvania wares of this type are extremely sought after and bring high prices. Age counts for less than provenance, since many of the European sgraffito types are earlier. So be on your guard against such European wares. The telltale scuffing of redwares, crackle, and iridescence of the glaze are clues to age.

Differing from the clay-slip wares, the tin-slip redwares include majolica, faïence, and delft. The process is the same. The ware is coated with a heavy tin slip and painting is done on

this powdery ground. The colors are iron reds and yellows,
manganese purple (or black), blue of cobalt, and green of
copper. The glaze applied is usually lead; sometimes no glaze
other than the tin is used. Majolica wares of Italy are out of
reach. The faïence of France is almost so, but the delftwares
of Holland and England of the eighteenth century are available
at modest prices considering their scarcity.

Clues to authentic pieces are a fairly coarse redware or
terra cotta body shading from gray to buff to brown. The tin
slip is likely to have pinholes or bubbles in the glaze. Edges
show scuffing of the area where glaze has chipped off. The
chief source of trouble here is to forget that the body should be
terra cotta or redware. Most spurious pieces are made with
a white body.

Terra Cotta

Terra cotta is a term often applied to unglazed redware.
Since most terra cotta is of finer texture, harder surface,
more uniform in shape and finer in modeling than redwares,
there is a distinction between it and redware. Furthermore,
terra cotta can be and is frequently glazed. Terra cotta breaks
with an irregular fracture. Glazes can be thinner on terra
cotta than on redware due to the fineness of the body. The
range of colors is roughly the same as for redwares. The
terra cottas include figurines, most of the ancient Greek and
Roman ceramic wares, much lusterware, and the latest
faïence and delftwares.

Redwares merging into the terra cottas frequently served
as the body for lusterwares. These are the tin-enameled
lusterwares, a typical kind being the so-called Hispano-
Moresque. They are old and valued enough so that there are
forgeries around. If you should find such pieces, you will
discover that both fake and original will look old. To distinguish
one from the other, you should study the style, body, and
marks of age together. You are not likely to see much of
this ware, and the little you may see will be very expensive.

The chief lusterware you are likely to find is not of this
type at all; it is the gold and silver lusterware of England.

The base should be redware, the glaze thin, and in the gold-
lustered wares (usually called copper luster), mottled. Reproductions are usually on white earthenware and are about
twenty-five percent heavier than the originals. Lightness of
weight, mottling of the surface, and iridescence (different
from the metallic sheen of the luster) are characteristic. The
glaze is worn off the contact surfaces, which are very smooth.
Details are very clear and precisely scaled. There are no
blurred or neglected areas. At the same time, there are
those little irregularities characteristic of handwork, no matter how skilled or careful. These run from c. 1780 to 1840.
The colors are copper, pink, purple, silver, and canary.
The silver luster was platinum, the others gold.

Coarse Stoneware

This stoneware is coarse like redware, but very much
harder. It sometimes breaks with a conchoidal (shell-shaped)
fracture like glass. More often, the type of break is the same
as in redware and terra cotta. Most stoneware is nonporous.
Although it is high-fired, it is not translucent. In color, it
varies from gray to buff. Much of the Rhenish stonewares of
this type as well as all American and a small number of English
stonewares are almost invariably glazed with salt. Their
number is not great.

The German Rhenish wares are the earliest, the scarcest,
the most collected, and the hardest to find. The American
wares, save for exceptional types, have been disregarded by
writers on ceramics because they are late and utilitarian; but
they are usually handsome, the texture is good, and the decoration is appealing. The usual decorations are either painted in
underglaze cobalt blue or incised with slip-molded portions.
Some few stonewares with rose, green, and other colors of
glaze do occur, but they are very rare. The ordinary stonewares of the late eighteenth and early nineteenth centuries are
well worth owning and still cost very little; for under fifty
dollars you can buy outstanding pieces. Many are marked.

Creamware

The name creamware comes from the color of the body, which varies from a deep cream to yellow. It is much finer in texture than any of the wares discussed so far. It has a much more delicate appearance, thinner walls, finer molding, and a more finished look. It belongs to the seventeenth and particularly to the eighteenth century and later. Creamwares can be easily scratched with a knife. They are porous and, like the redwares, they break with an earthy fracture.

While there are many creamwares made in different places that are collectible, what we usually mean by the term is eighteenth- and early nineteenth-century English and nineteenth-century American creamware. Typical of the early creamware of England is the Whieldon tortoise shell. This is a molded creamware, highly glazed and covered with spatterings of metal oxides in brown, green, and yellow. The forms are Rococo, the decoration skillfully worked, finely modeled and scaled. It is this fine scaling combined with the Rococo style that distinguishes Whieldon of the eighteenth century from the rather overstyled and much heavier majolica of the late nineteenth century. Whieldon wares are obtainable, but the prices are high.

Equally sought after are Wedgwood's Queensware and its imitations. These also are elaborately modeled, and they have a thin, colorless, but very highly lustrous glaze, almost like the sticky look of a molasses apple. Leeds and Bristol variations of this type of creamware have a softer, slightly greenish or bluish glaze, often quite deep in hollows and grooves. The chief characteristics are the sticky glaze, the very fine modeling, the basket-woven patterns, lightness in weight, and light cream color. Crazing of the glaze, random scratches on contact surfaces as well as the difficult-to-see iridescence help to establish the age of the pieces. Creamwares may be decorated with polychrome designs or transfer decorations in underglaze black. Typical of the latter are Liverpool pitchers, some of which were decorated with portraits of American national heroes.

A characteristic nineteenth-century American variety is Rockingham glazed ware. The name is derived from the brown glazed, mottled ware produced at Swinton on the estate of the Marquis of Rockingham. Both are spotted and mottled with brown metallic oxides in the glaze. The Bennington, Vermont factory added other oxides to produce a variation called flint-ware, which added green and blue to the brown and yellow. Other factories that produced such wares were at East Liver-pool, Ohio, at Trenton and Jersey City, New Jersey, and at Baltimore, Maryland. All these are desirable, interesting, and collectible. The wares of Bennington are so famous that the name has been given to all American Rockingham. It is safe to say that Bennington is only Bennington when so marked.

White Earthenware

By far the greatest quantity of modern china is known as white earthenware. It is distinguished from other soft wares by its white color. In fracture, hardness, and porosity, it resembles creamware. Color varies from pure hard white to light yellowish. Thus, it merges by imperceptible degrees on the one hand into the creamwares, which are somewhat softer, and, in the other direction, into the much harder stonewares.

White earthenware, for the most part, is fairly late. The body of some eighteenth-century French faïence was of white earthenware. The wares of most importance to us are English of the late eighteenth and early nineteenth centuries. Worth noting are the rose-colored Sunderland lusterwares, where the gold luster is placed upon a white ground instead of the red body of terra cotta or redware. Related to these is Pratt ware, modeled in relief with hunting dogs and human figures, decorated with luster and colored glazes. Strawberry ware of the nineteenth century, sometimes with luster decoration, is another variety. Some Leeds wares were also made on white earthenware as well as on creamware. Staffordshire figurines are of the same body. Early figurines tend to be solid, later ones hollow, with vent holes in the backs.

Extremely sought after is the Gaudy Dutch and Gaudy Welsh ware. These are decorated with the Imari colors of dark blue, red, green, and (in Gaudy Welsh) gold. Several patterns using roses are also named: one in ocher red called King's rose, another in rosy pink known as the Adams' rose. These all belong to the early years of the nineteenth century and have the same characteristic forms. All are carefully made and quite light in weight.

Made of the same body are the transfer-decorated Staffordshire wares of the nineteenth century. Most are unmarked, and with the exception of those with historical American subjects, little is know of makers or dates. There are two types, both decorated in blue underglaze transfer. The first seems to be earlier, its shapes closely resembling the early Gaudy Dutch. It uses a somewhat pale blue, whereas the Staffordshire of the 1830's has a much deeper blue. The most valuable of the latter are decorated with American historical views. This whole group has been very well studied for a number of years. Average prices for average plates run about twenty-five to thirty-five dollars. Occasionally, pieces can be had for much less.

Such few forgeries as there are differ in color, the blue (all seem to be in blue) tending to a purplish rather than bluish tinge, and they are heavier in weight and form. In addition they will show either no signs of wear or the handiwork of the faker. As usual, the style of engraving on the older ones is more careful; the same goes for the potting. This care is combined, as usual, with slight technical imperfections such as the marks of the stilts used to support the work in the glaze firing, observable on the back rims of the plates. This ware is more than worth while collecting.

Finally, there is the ironstone china. Ironstone is heavier than the other white earthenware mentioned, and the name refers to the harder, more vitreous body. The decorations are similar to those on other white earthenware. To be noted are Imari-type decorations in polygonal plates, cups, and other tableware, and handsome polychrome Chinoiserie decorations. Typical also are the flowing blue wares of the 1840's in which the printed patterns seem to have partly melted into the glaze.

Another favorite type of ironstone pottery is sprigged ware, which is ornamented with little sprigs of cast slip applied here

and there, usually colored blue or lavender and occasionally
lustered. Such decoration was also used on other white earthenware as well as on soft paste. For some reason—probably
because some of this ware was originally sold under the name
Old Chelsea—it has been regularly called Chelsea. It is attractive, but is most emphatically not Chelsea, old or young.

Toward the end of the nineteenth century in America and
Great Britain, a number of molded wares in the form of
leaves, flowers, seashells, and vegetables, decorated with
enamel colors, were marketed under the name Etruscan
majolica. These have no relation to Italian majolica either
in form or decoration. They are avidly collected for their
attractiveness and have brought high prices for many years.
Griffin, Smith and Hill of Pennsylvania, made large quantities
of this ware, which, because it is American, is more important as a collectible item than the English varieties.

White Stoneware

White stonewares were made in Germany before they were
made anywhere else, and the typical Känne and Schnäbelkruge
Siegburg were very early. The most familiar to us are the
stonewares of England. They were produced first toward the
end of the seventeenth century when white clay became available
there.

English stonewares are certainly worth collecting and have
been favorites with collectors. This is but an echo of the
popularity they had when they were new. It is hardly possible
to dig in the vicinity of any eighteenth-century site without
uncovering fragments of this ware. They are usually salt-
glazed and molded in all sorts of Rococo forms, usually white,
and often decorated with a wide range of enamel colors. They
are of medium rarity and expensive; you cannot expect to pick
them up for less than fifty dollars apiece.

Fakes are not a particular problem. You can, however, get
confused by failing to distinguish them from nineteenth-century
wares of similar type. The latter have a glaze that resembles
the salt-glaze orange-peel surface. But they are much heavier
and thicker; consequently small modeled details tend to get

lost in the glaze. The glaze is, perhaps for this reason, called smear glaze. The late jugs are smeared not only with white glaze but glazes of various shades of greenish and bluish grays. You should recognize them because of their more perfect body and much heavier handling of Rococo details. It is well to recognize this difference; otherwise your salt-glaze collection is likely to be smear-glazed.

Related to the white salt-glazed stonewares are the red and black stonewares. These are more often made in ornamental than in utilitarian forms. They show strong Oriental influence and are usually unglazed, although frequently ornamented with enamel colors. These are contemporary with white salt glaze and thus are Rococo in style.

In the later eighteenth century, Wedgwood, by meticulous preparation of the ceramic body and even more painstaking work in all the potting processes, raised this type of stoneware to a fine art, calling the red stoneware antico rosso and the black basalt. Wedgwood is usually marked and the form of the mark indicates the date. The perfection of Wedgwood's eighteenth-century wares is so clear that once you see and appreciate it, you will never forget it. The best place to see it is in a museum, so take yourself there and study the wares closely.

Glass Frit Soft Paste

The soft pastes developed in the West were always attempts to rival the porcelains of China. The glass frit type of porcelain was as early as any used. Its chief characteristic is that it has little pinholes or sometimes larger light spots that are visible in strong light. Much of the French soft paste, in particular Mennecy, St. Cloud, Rouen, and Vincennes, as well as early Sèvres, is of glass frit type. These are very delicate and behave like glass, ready and willing to break at sudden shock or with quick changes of temperature. Glass frit soft pastes are mouth-watering for any collector. Their textures are so wonderful to look at that the ceramic body itself, apart from any decoration save its glaze, is a delight. Their creamy whiteness is one of their most impressive charms.

The ware came into being almost with the Rococo style. The factories started out to rival the wares from China and Meissen, but stopped by the wayside to develop a kind of material as delicate, as evanescent and, unfortunately, as fragile as the style to which it belongs. The wares of the fine French factories differ among themselves as to styles of decoration, glaze, and body color, but after 1768 all except Sèvres are of the same general kind of soft paste. All are extremely rare and have been faked over a long period of time.

Fakes show up primarily on the basis of style. Rococo pieces are delicately fragile in design and conception, fakes tend to be pretentious and stuffy. These soft pastes show little or no crazing of the glaze, but do show the usual effects of time and wear. They are well faked and expensive, so beware!

The glass frit soft pastes of England have also been extensively imitated. The early Chelsea wares are quite thick and the translucence and famous moons do not show except against a strong light. The bone ash porcelains, such as Bow, Lowestoft, and Chelsea Derby, possess a much more readily visible translucence, mottled by little flecks of lighter color. Once again, the ware will have to be authenticated, primarily by its ingenious and fanciful Rococo painting and delicacy of workmanship. One characteristic of Lowestoft is a tendency for the underglaze blue to run.

Steatite and Bone Soft Paste

The second type of soft paste was more durable. It contained bone ash or steatite and sometimes both. Since many of the glass frit pastes also contain considerable amounts of calcium, the first type merges into the second. When steatite or soapstone is added to the body in place of the glass frit, it becomes tougher and more durable, but the chief characteristic the addition imparts to the ceramic body is the color of the translucence. As the amount of steatite changes with the addition of bone ash and lime, the translucence will vary from pale green to straw color and to olive or brown. Bone ash added to the ceramic body also increases its translucency. In the more perfected and later examples of the nineteenth century such as Spode, the body is exceedingly translucent and glaringly white.

The steatitic porcelains are headed by Worcester ware.
They are unmistakable in their deep pea-green translucency,
due apparently to the attempt to mask the natural yellowish
color with an admixture of blue or green minerals (cobalt or
copper). Caughley used the same paste to a large degree, but
the translucence is of yellow or brownish hue, as is the Worcester after c. 1780. Worcester wares have been imitated in
various ways, but the green translucency is usually missing.
Worcester can be identified by its shapes, translucency, and
style. The ware runs through a number of styles, particularly
the Rococo of the middle of the eighteenth century, followed by
the Neo-Classic and the Greek Revival.

Worcester pieces are strongly influenced by Meissen and
the Oriental wares of China and Japan. Dr. Wall Worcester
(1751-83) uses blue underglaze transfer decoration in Chinese
patterns, as well as enamel colors in imitation of similar
subject matter. Japanese figures and imari colors, as well
as Neo-Classic decoration, are characteristic of the Chamberlain and Barr and Flight periods.

This is the place to include a brief account of Wedgwood's
Jasperware. This is a semiporcelain containing, among other
things, baryta. It is very slightly translucent, and is stained
various colors—blue, lavender, yellow, brownish-green, and
black. The molded medallions and other ornaments left white
were sprigged on by the well-known process. Early Wedgwood
to 1795 will be distinguished by the careful, very exact work
in each detail.

Parian ware is another variety of white bone ash china,
almost always unglazed on the outside, invented by Copeland.
The name Parian was given to this ware under the impression
that it was like Parian marble, which it resembles not in the
slightest. A similar ware was made under that name at
Bennington, Vermont by the United States Pottery Company.
It was mostly blue and white or all white. Another similar
ware was made at Trenton, New Jersey.

There are many imitations contemporary with Bennington
Parian undistinguishable from Bennington except by the mark.
Bennington is the most sought after but must be marked.

Belleek china, although collected by numbers of people, is very late for collectible china. It is easily recognized, if unmarked, by its thinness, lightness, and nacreous luster.

Hard Pastes

The last group of ceramic ware includes the true porcelains. That these should be any truer than any other type is a matter of definition, as if creating useful or beautiful objects were some kind of game. The odd thing is that in this game the rules are made by those who do not play after the game is over and the players are gone.

However, the hard paste porcelains are in a class by themselves. They are translucent, except for the very heavy pieces. In fact, this translucency was thought to be the sine qua non of porcelain or china, as it was called for the obvious reason that it was developed in the country whose name it bears. It is the hardest, highest-fired, and most durable of all the ceramic bodies. The chief ingredient is kaolin, the other ingredient petuntse. It provides at once the vitreosity and translucency of porcelain. The Chinese refer to petuntse as the flesh, to kaolin as the bone, of China. Hard paste is evenly translucent, white to grayish to olive green. At its finest, it has the quality and texture of jade. Its translucency is, on the whole, less than that of the soft pastes. It is harder; good hard paste will not scratch with a knife except with difficulty. It is heavier than soft paste and will hold water even when unglazed. It breaks with a conchoidal fracture, as does glass. The soft pastes do not hold water when unglazed and break rather more in the way that creamwares break.

The soft pastes are frequently referred to as synthetic and the hard pastes as natural porcelains, the implication being that the soft pastes are unnatural and somehow inferior. While it is true that the soft pastes were made in an effort to imitate the ceramic wares of China, the relation ends there; for the soft pastes are actually different substances and look it. If they lack the durability of the hard pastes, they make up for it in the charm of their texture and color as well as their infinite variety, which age has not withered nor custom staled.

Almost all Oriental porcelains are hard pastes. This Oriental ware is easy to recognize by its color, which is slightly bluish or grayish, and by its glaze, which is not exactly glassy. If you look at the glaze with a magnifying glass, you will see that it has a pebbled texture resembling orange peel, although it is much finer.

Recognizing Oriental wares is easy, but dating them is something else again. The early pre-nineteenth-century Chinese porcelains will be recognizable by their hard, fine, white body, which differs from the coarse, yellowish body of the nineteenth century wares and the more glasslike body of modern ones. Of the Oriental wares, the ones you will most likely meet are those the Chinese made for export, or Oriental export china. It was called India China after the East India Company, which brought it to Europe and America. It somehow got mixed up with the soft paste ware of Lowestoft in the minds of collectors and dealers; as a result, it is usually called Lowestoft, in spite of the fact that it was made in China and is hard paste.

This ware is very much in demand and brings fair prices. Those with arms of the states or similar historic types are most sought after. Several other very desirable types are the armorial (containing a crest) blue-banded, ermine cloak (because of the cloak in the design), lovebird, Nankeen, and Fitzhugh. Perhaps the scarcest are those decorated with black-enamel drawings derived from engraving, called Jesuit types. Proof of age is contained in the fine, dense quality of the porcelain, its weight (imitations are likely to be lighter), and the care and skill that went into its modeling.

Collectible, although later, is the famous blue and white Canton china of the nineteenth century. The more famous wares of Chinese origin (Ming and Ching dynasty, which produced the export porcelain) are mostly out of the market and very difficult to distinguish from forgeries. The earliest Oriental export wares (India China, Chinese Lowestoft or Lowestoft) run back to 1700; the Canton porcelains stop at about 1840.

Related to the hard pastes of China are those of Japan, especially the Kakiemon and Imari wares, decorated principally in Oriental red, blue, and gold. You will not find them

very often, especially in their export form, as the bulk of the
wares was made when Japan was not dealing with the West. A
few may have been made up to 1850 or thereabouts.

The first true European hard paste, developed at Meissen
by Böttiger, was not as bluish as the Chinese hard paste.
Meissen came on the scene in the first decade of the eighteenth
century when the favored style was Baroque. After the factory
had been in existence for a short while, the Rococo style
became fashionable in Europe, and Meissen porcelain seemed
made for it.

The forms and decorations are too various to describe in
detail, but three or four characteristic types can be mentioned.
Meissen made a great deal of use of Chinoiserie and Japanese
forms and decorations. In addition, the following are especially
to be noted: the painting of landscapes in monochrome, the
use of figures from contemporary life, and naturalistic native
flowers (Deutsche Blümen).

Collecting Meissen or any of the hard paste porcelains of
the royal porcelain manufactures of Europe is beset with
difficulties. The first of these is in distinguishing the work of
the famous from the less important factories whose products,
although equally antique, did not and do not command the same
prices. Worse is the fact that the extraordinarily high prices
paid have made the forging of these wares profitable. Worst
of all, in the days when porcelain factories depended on the
patronage of penurious nouveaux riches, they resorted to
copying their own earlier wares. A careful comparison of the
pastes will eliminate this type of reproduction, while the
machine-made look shows up more modern ones; but the best
way to discriminate between the originals and fakes is to look
for the difference between the eighteenth-century Rococo and the
nineteenth-century Rococo Revival.

Of Meissen-like body and similar appearance are the porcelains of Vienna, Berlin, Nymphenburg, and a number of
smaller German and Austrian factories. The hard pastes of
Sèvres came at the end of French porcelain development, but
did receive some of the care and expense of preparation that
went into that work. Sèvres hard paste is a little finer and
more delicate than the early Meissen paste. The nineteenth-

century factories at Limoges produced a large number of hard pastes, but these were made after the great heyday of porcelain. They are dull and undistinguished; they follow the revivals of taste that swept through the nineteenth century—when they do not copy earlier French or other Continental wares. But then, they are scarcely antique.

The last ware included in this list is American. The Tucker china of Philadelphia is a hard paste porcelain, pieces of which occasionally come up for sale. You can best describe it as a kind of Sèvres produced in America. The body has been variously described as hard paste and as bone china. The few pieces I have seen appear to be hard paste.

COLLECTING CERAMICS

How are you going to buy and collect ceramic wares? The best way is to get representative sample pieces in as wide a variety as possible. Limit your field of activities to one thing—hard paste, redware, anything that suits your fancy. Look for antiqueness rather than quantity. Buy a piece at a time. Then chase the piece through the books until you find out for certain what it is. Look at similar examples in museums and shops. Most of all, study your piece until you have extracted all that you can get from it. Then you are ready to buy another.

First-rate antique ceramic pieces can be bought for from two or three dollars on up to any price you care to pay. If you remember to be sure that your choice clearly represents its style, time, and place, and to some degree its maker, you will have a good piece of whatever material, nationality, or epoch. Get your pieces in good condition; a cracked or damaged piece has lost most of its value. Damages to pottery are much more serious than damages to furniture. They cannot really be repaired. If you are very eager to own a specimen of a given ware and you can get only a damaged piece, you will have to be content with that. But, on the whole, chips, cracks, and breaks injure the piece exceedingly. A proof piece is the best to own.

CHART OF CERAMIC BODIES

Hardness, firing, temperature → increasing.

I	IV	VII
<u>Redware</u>	<u>Creamware</u>	<u>Glass Frit Soft Paste</u>
Ancient pottery	Bennington	Chelsea
Indian pottery	Bristol	Mennecy
Majolica, Delft	Leeds	Rouen
Marbled and combed wares	Liverpool ware	Sèvres (soft paste)
Sgraffito ware	Queensware	St. Cloud
Slip-decorated ware	Rockingham	Vincennes
Tin slip ware	Tortoise shell ware	
II	**V**	**VIII**
<u>Terra cotta</u>	<u>White Earthenware</u>	<u>Steatite and Bone Soft</u>
Figurines	Etruscan majolica	<u>Pastes</u>
English gold luster ware	Gaudy Dutch; Gaudy Welsh	Belleek
Hispano-Moresque	Historical Staffordshire	Bone china
Tanagra (Greek)	Ironstone china	Caughley (Salopian)
	King's rose; Adam's rose	Dr. Wall Worcester
	Leeds	English Lowestoft
	Prattware	Jasperware (Baryta)
	Staffordshire figurines	Parian
	Strawberry ware	
	Sunderland luster	
III	**VI**	**IX**
<u>Coarse Stoneware</u>	<u>White Stoneware</u>	<u>Hard Paste</u>
American and English	Antico rosso	Canton
coarse stone ware	Basalt	China trade porcelain
Rhenish stoneware	Fine stoneware	Chinese Lowestoft
	Red and black stoneware	Japanese export porcelain
	Salt glaze ware	Limoges
	Smear glaze stone	Meissen
		Oriental porcelain
		Sèvres

Wares below double line are nonporous (except a few coarse stonewares). Wares to the right of the vertical double line are translucent.

N.B. Some opaque soft, white earthenwares and creamwares are occasionally referred to as soft pastes. In this chart, soft pastes are translucent.

Most pieces show wear and tear. Some of this can be
overlooked. An example is the scuffing of delft and faïence.
Crazing of glazes is another sort of damage due to time that
we can overlook.

Now, a word of advice about the mechanics of actually
purchasing old china. Look the piece over carefully before
touching it, to get all you can out of the design and glaze.
Form a tentative opinion of its age on the basis of its decoration. Try to guess its ceramic body. Pick up the piece.
Heft it to get an idea of whether its weight exceeds, equals,
or falls short of your expectations. With the exception of
hard paste porcelains, all ware ought to feel quite light. Now,
see whether the ware is translucent or not. You should not
neglect this detail. Turn it over and look for a mark (the
mark of a country eliminates the object from consideration as
an antique).

Try to discover some area where the glaze is missing or
scuffed. If necessary, resort to a magnifying glass. Look
for signs of wear in all likely places. If decoration, weight,
ceramic body, mark (if any),and signs of wear all appear to
lead in the same direction, the piece is genuine. The ability
of the object to excite you with finely drawn and modeled
shapes, spontaneity, and originality of drawing will differen-
tiate an original from a copy.

Chapter VIII

METALS

Metals are man-made substances to the degree that, with the exception of the noble metals, none of them are found as such in nature; they are hidden away in rocks and minerals. Thus, gold, silver, and copper were probably discovered over and over again by each new race of men emerging from the Stone Age, either as bright and shining baubles or as a queer kind of rock that could be shaped by pounding. Where, when, and how man discovered that metals could be melted, hammered, and alloyed is not too clear. The metallurgist appeared before the historian. When we first meet him in the pages of history, he is already mature.

Some types of metal are quite new, others are very old, but for the antiquary there are only about seven sorts that he will expect to collect. Of these, three are pure metals (gold, silver, copper) and three are alloys (bronze, brass, pewter). The seventh (plated ware) is a combination of two metals, one forming a shell for the other.

At the outset, we should remember that most metals in use are alloys and that our notion of their purity is conditioned. The sterling silver and pure gold of tableware and jewelry are alloys, although most of us do not think of them as such. Both contain as much if not more copper than good plate pewter, which is never considered anything but an alloy. Thus the purity of the metals is only conventional.

SILVER

Antiques made of silver are among the very few that have, in addition to their value as antiques, a certain intrinsic value due to the material of which they are made. This factor has helped to preserve the silver articles that, had they been of some other material, would have been discarded. Silver is

also a monetary metal, and coinage at one time was set up on
a silver standard. Since coins are merely chunks of silver of
a given weight, stamped with a device identifying them by
place of origin and guaranteeing their weight, an object of
silver of given weight was frequently looked upon by its owners
as so much money.

In fact, a great deal of antique silver was made of coins,
so its assay will vary to some extent from the assay of sterling
silver (925 parts of silver per 1000). The coinage of the United
States is 900 fine, meaning that one-tenth of the weight is base
metal. The words pure coin that occur as a stamp on much
American silver of the nineteenth century mean that the silver
is 900 fine rather than 925 fine (sterling). It may or may not
have been made of coins. Certainly the practice of collecting
silver coins with the express purpose of having them made
into silver was quite popular at this time.

Since English coinage is sterling, silver made from English
coins is ipso facto sterling. In other parts of the world, the
assay of silver was not so high. German (800 fine) and Dutch
silver in particular may contain less silver than either English
or American.

Working Methods

Silver was worked in several ways, of which the most
important are hammering and casting. Silver is very malleable
and ductile. In this characteristic it ranks next to gold. Hammering a metal both compresses and shakes it up, thus tending
to make it harder and more brittle. After it has been hammered for a while, it must be annealed to prevent its becoming
too brittle. The process of hammering, annealing, and re-
hammering is called raising. This is the method used for
making hollow ware—plates, teapots, and the like. The metal
is stretched over a variety of stakes made of polished steel,
or squeezed together by putting fine creases in the outside to
reduce the diameter.

In repoussé the work is fluted or modeled by being hammered into a wax medium with dies of the contour for the
modeling. Silver can also be decorated by chasing, stamping,

and engraving. If the silver object is of fairly simple form, it may be raised from one flat sheet. More often it is raised in several pieces and these are assembled by soldering. Separately chased and repoussé borders could be soldered on.

Occasionally, the silver is shaped by casting. This would be particularly true of metal mounts, feet, knobs, tray borders, and the like. The casting process is usually of the lost wax type. The models are made of wax and filled with clay or sand. Wax rods are attached to the completed model and the receptacle of wax (for channeling the metal to the mold). The wax model is then surrounded with casting sand or some similar medium, the mold is heated, and the wax poured out. Molten silver is poured into the mold. When the metal has cooled, the mold is broken open, the rods cut off, and the clay shaken out from inside. Where many similar pieces are to be cast, the lost wax process is abandoned and the cast pieces are made in part molds.

Hammering, planishing, chasing, engraving, bending, soldering, and casting are all hand processes, and the operators must be highly skilled if the results are to be good. Since the tight control of the guild hall upheld the quality of all ancient work, we should not expect to see old silver that is carelessly made. In spite of care and skill, however, all old silver has the irregularities or imperfections as well as the spontaneity characteristic of handwork before the machine age.

Style, as is usual with all antiques, is the best guide. Remember, silver passes through the same style sequences as other antiques, and we thus have Late Gothic, Renaissance, Baroque, Neo-Classic, and Classic Revival silver. In style, silver objects are at once more conservative and more advanced than most other collectibles. The first appearance of a stylistic form, the Rococo, for example, may occur in the silver of a place where the other decorative items are still dominated by Baroque or even Renaissance forms. At the same time, it is in silver that Rococo forms have the longest life. The same is true of other styles.

Hallmarks

Another way to recognize the age of silver is by its marks,
for all respectable silver, wherever made, was marked.
Since the form of the marks was dictated by the guild hall,
they are called hallmarks. They are all similar in their purpose, and silver usually contains four marks, each separately
struck. The first is the place mark, which locates the hall—
for example, the leopard mask stands for London, the harp
Dublin, the thistle Edinburgh. The second is usually the
quality mark—for example, the lion passant of London.

The third mark is that of the year in which the silver was
made. In English silver this is indicated by a letter of the
alphabet, which was changed each year.

The fourth mark is the mark of the maker. In England and
many other places, this is a separate mark, consisting of the
maker's initials. In addition to these four marks, others occur.
The chief mark of this order is the head of the ruling monarch
on English silver after 1784.

French hallmarks consisted of crowned ornamental initial
letters and were changed every year. The letters were lower
case from 1461 to 1620, after which capitals were used. As
each initial is different according to the fancy of the maker,
they serve as makers' marks also. French silver also has
charge and discharge marks to show that the tax per ounce
was paid. The charge was placed on the blank before raising
and the discharge was struck on the finished piece, which was
checked for weight after it was made. Thus, the quality mark
on French silver is threefold. The sequence is the maker's
mark, then the stamp of value. French standards were the
highest in Europe, 950/1,000 fine.

German silver marks varied greatly from town to town and
were not standardized until 1888. At that time silver, to be
eligible for hallmarks, had to have not less than 500 to 800
parts of silver per 1,000. The mark was a crescent moon
followed by the number indicating the degree of fineness. German silver thus hallmarked has on it the royal crown, the
moon symbol, the mark showing the fineness of the silver in
parts per 1,000, and the mark of the city in which the silver

was assayed. In checking German silver for date and location, it is best to identify the town first, then the quality, maker, and date.

American silver—except that of Baltimore for a brief period—1814-30 is not hallmarked. American silver, then, usually has only the maker's mark. The earliest marks consist of the maker's initials in a geometric frame. Toward the middle of the eighteenth century, the second name was written in full. Thereafter, this was standard practice. Some time early in the nineteenth century, place marks began to be included.

Hallmarks can be and have been faked. In countries where silver is still hallmarked, it is a serious offense, but this does not hinder an American from using fake hallmarks.

Clues to Age

In silver as in other things, style is the chief clue to age. The style must be consistent. This is not always obvious, granting the traditionalism in silver forms. Nevertheless, there is a strong difference between Queen Anne silver made today and that made in the reign of the good queen.

Silver that has been polished by hand for two or three hundred years acquires a surface that is characteristic. In addition, antique silver has many imperfections in material and execution, the inevitable result of handwork.

Glorifying Silver

Silver can be faked by changing the hallmark, by substituting an earlier for a later date or the name of a more famous for a less famous maker. Famous makers' marks or special hallmarks are often sawed from spoons or other pieces and set into new or less valuable silver. Silver can be fancified by adding handles to a handleless piece, converting a tea caddy into a teapot, elaborating a simple into a more ornate form. Occasionally a piece is glorified by removing a portion of it.

Each of these techniques can be shown up in one way or another. Where new silver has been added to old, or where the hallmark from one piece has been transferred to another, the two pieces are found to tarnish at different rates.

Old surfaces will show any attempt to rework them because the outer surface of the old piece tends to crystallize and harden. This crystallized surface tends to break up in reworking and will show up under close examination. Secondly, the methods of old work tended to imbed near-microscopic pieces of impurities in the surface. This old surface is unmistakable if examined under a glass. It shows a number of angular, irregular pits at random intervals.

In addition, the surface of silver that has been around for a while has two sorts of scratches on it, one random and accidental as the result of use, and the other patterned and purposeful from cleaning and polishing. The first sort is easily identified, but distinguishing the latter from the marks left by the faker in his attempts to simulate wear and tear is more difficult, for we cannot test the antiquity of this wear and tear by comparing its location with that of the contact surfaces as in the case of china and glass, because silver is polished all over.

Nevertheless, there are differences between old and new. Certainly one of them is the wear on various parts of the surface in relation to other parts. Projecting parts will be subject to more wear than those that do not project, but the difference is not so great as you might think, because of the need for constant polishing. It should, therefore, be an occasion for reconsideration if the silver, well worn everywhere, has nice, sharp hallmarks.

In the long run, three clues will generally establish the age of silver. There is the style. This has three aspects— design, proportion, and ornamentation. Style is always accompanied by two other characteristics: that of the metal with its imperfections and that of the workmanship.

The second clue is the rate of tarnishing, which should be more or less even. This affects the color of the silver. Old silver is always a little different in tone from modern silver. This seems to be because of the scratches—too small to be

seen—which hold small amounts of silver sulphides on their
edges. In time, the sulphides are converted into oxides, which
are both more stable and harder. The presence of this patina
through which the silver can be seen—polishing keeps it thin
enough—protects it from the more rapidly acting sulphides in
the air. Thus it slows down the rate of tarnish.

The third clue to age is the condition of the surface. Polishing exerts a slight pressure on the silver. This repeated pressure tends to work-harden the surface, rendering it both more
brittle and much harder. Often examination of the surface of
old silver with a glass will show a réseau of fine crazing in
places where the contours change rapidly. The surface of old
silver is unmistakable once you have made its acquaintance.
It has a soft luster in comparison with the brilliant, hard luster
of more modern work. It also has a richer look, as if the surface had more depth, almost as if it had a pile like velvet.

Familiarize yourself with this old look. Then, buy some
elderly hallmarked silver, c. 1830, of types not worth faking,
e.g., spoons. A careful study of the color, texture, workmanship, and patina will be a pretty good approach to learning
what old silver looks like.

The next step would be to buy some silver from a reputable
shop. The procedure in this evaluative process is the same as
others. Examine the piece carefully without handling; then
handle it, looking first for style, then for other clues. Finally,
look at hallmarks and for signs of wear. Remember again
that the easiest qualities for you to see and understand will
also be the easiest for the faker to imitate, and he will rely on
just such qualities to catch you.

Sheffield Plate

Another type of silverware almost as much sought after as
old silver is Sheffield. We are here concerned with a process
that is limited in time. Such plate is not being made now, nor
has it been made for over a century.

Essentially, the process consisted in taking a large amount
of copper and coating it with a small amount of silver—precisely what is done in modern silver-plating, but the method

was unique. The copper was formed into an ingot of suitable size and the silver into a sheet somewhat thicker than most silver today. The surface of the ingot and that of the sheet were cleaned, fluxed with borax, and wired together under pressure. The whole assembly was next put into a furnace and brought to a bright red heat just before melting. As soon as the silver was fused to the copper, the assembly was removed from the fire. The silver-coated ingot was next hammered or rolled into a sheet, mostly copper with a thin layer of silver on top. From these sheets, various articles were made.

Many of the hollow ware pieces were assembled like sheet metal, from patterns, thus cutting down somewhat on the work of raising. All repoussé work, as well as chasing, was done as in regular silver work. Handles, feet, and ornaments were made of fine repoussé in the plate, or sometimes in sterling silver, weighted with lead or pewter and soldered on. Where both sides of an article had to be silver, the work was made double and the silver drawn over the edges to conceal the join. Occasionally some ornaments made of sterling silver were cast and attached. Such solid silver parts frequently bear hallmarks. Those bearing hallmarks of Sheffield would date only after the opening of an assay office in Sheffield—about the third quarter of the eighteenth century.

Styles and Clues to Age

Since the manufacture of plated ware at Sheffield covers the period from about 1745 to 1845, it follows the styles popular in that period. Thus we have some Sheffield in Rococo, more in the Neo-Classic styles of the late eighteenth century, and the preponderance in the Classical Revival styles of the first half of the nineteenth century.

Because the manufacture of this type of plated ware fits so nicely into a century and has a clear beginning as well as an end, Sheffield is collectible throughout the whole period of its manufacture. We can expect repoussé where objects are ordinarily cast, for instance, in feet and finials. We can also expect to find evidences of the joining where the copper has worn off. In some cases, where dovetail joins have been made,

there will be here less and there more silver than on the rest
of the piece. Thus the construction can be seen clearly. A
hundred years or so of cleaning will have worn through the
plate in places, especially on the edges. It is here that the
sandwich-like appearance provides a clear indication of age.
Some Sheffield is marked with the maker's name and/or with
a cipher of a manufacturer. If the cipher is supported by
evidence of the construction features mentioned above, the
piece is almost certainly old.

Fakes

The highly skilled handwork of the Old Sheffield process is
too expensive to imitate. Consequently, the faker uses the
next best method. This is to copy in copper an old Sheffield
pattern and electroplate it with silver, rub off silver here and
there so that the copper bleeds or shows, as in much genuine
Sheffield plate. You can distinguish between electroplated and
old ware by the presence in the latter of solid silver shields
for engraving and the occasional sterling mounts and borders,
and by the fact that since the old plate surface is an alloy, that
is, sterling instead of pure silver, it is not so quick to tarnish.
Shields can be made evident by blowing on the silver. The
moisture from the breath evaporates more quickly on the shield
than on the rest of the piece, thus outlining it. In addition, an
electroplated surface has a granular or pebbled look and lacks
the irregular, angular marks on the surface that it should have
as a result of hammering. Any hammer marks on the new
ware are obliterated by the electroplating process.

Electroplating

With electroplating, the whole object could be made of
copper or some other metal or alloy, the completed copper
articles placed in a bath, and electricity could do the work
formerly done by many skilled hands. The cost of production
would thus come down, and no one would notice much difference
in appearance. Sheffield was one of the chief centers of
production of the new as it had been of the old plate. But

electroplating was not a secret process. Sheffield thus became only one among many centers.

In the beginning, the forms of electroplate were the same as those of the old plate, but as time went on, they changed. In Sheffield and elsewhere in England, plating continued to be on copper. Since this type of plate is unaccountably called Sheffield, even if it was made in Birmingham, Alabama, a certain amount of confusion exists, to the delight of the faker and the despair of the collector. The American custom of plating on white metal is better. Good white metal is more costly than copper and shows less wear and tear when the plate wears off. It is thus that the electroplate on copper called Sheffield is frequently mistaken for the old Sheffield, with which it has nothing in common but the copper base. A cursory examination with a magnifying glass will show at once the characteristic pebbled surface of electroplated ware.

Electroplated silver is definitely not collectible, except where the silver plate is an integral part of some object that is antique in its own right. An example would be an art glass cake basket with electroplated silver mounts.

Before leaving the subject of plated silver, there is one caution I would like to give: never have Sheffield replated. It ruins it forever. Try to get it in good shape, with no copper visible. If you don't like to see the copper, don't collect Sheffield; leave it for those to whom the ware appeals for its interesting process, its magnificent workmanship, and its antiquity.

PEWTER

Next in importance to silver, from the antiquarian point of view, is pewter. This metal, which existed possibly from Classical times and perhaps even before, is an alloy like silver. The basic metal is tin, combined with a variety of other metals of which the chief are, in order of their importance, copper, antimony, bismuth, lead, silver and, perhaps, zinc. Because of the dull gray, leaden appearance of uncared-for pewter, there is a persistent notion among most persons that a large proportion of lead is used in the making of pewter. This idea is further heightened by accounts in books wherein pewter is described as a lead-tin alloy. However, most works fail to include any mention of lead in the formula. There is one exception and this is ley metal (often not called pewter), which does contain a fairly high percentage of lead—up to about twenty percent. Good plate pewter contains lead only by accident and only as an impurity.

Pewter assays seem to be <u>sui generis</u> for each piece tested. From this standpoint, it is rather foolish to be dogmatic about the exact make-up of pewter. The amount of tin varies between eighty and ninety-five percent, of copper between twenty and five percent, with varying amounts of antimony and occasionally bismuth (called tin glass in some old accounts). Where antimony is used with copper, the proportions are roughly two of antimony to one of copper, the two together making up about one-tenth of the alloy.

Main Distinguishable Types

In spite of the foregoing, we can distinguish several types of pewter. Ley metal, which contains considerable amounts of lead, tarnishes or darkens more rapidly than ordinary pewter and has a darker look than good plate pewter, which when well cleaned and polished, has a silvery look similar to aluminum.

Like plate pewter, but perhaps a little darker and softer, is the <u>Anglische Zinn</u> of Germany and Switzerland and the Low Countries. This metal, marked with the canting angel and scales device, is evidence of the high quality and repute of English tin and pewter ware. Whether collectors don't approve of cleaning it as often as English and American collectors do theirs, I am unable to guess. The fact is that quantities of this pewter are often covered with a black to brownish gunmetal tarnish, often referred to as a patina, which its lovers seem loath to remove.

The fourth type of pewter is britannia, which looks very like good plate pewter except that the surfaces appear to be harder, as indeed they are.

It is the tin in pewter that gives it its peculiar weaknesses. It can be easily cut with a knife and can be bent with the fingers. It is attacked readily by gasses present in the air, and in the presence of cold and dampness becomes brittle and crumbles.

Manufacturing Techniques

Since pewter melts so readily and at such low temperatures, casting is the method of manufacture. The ware was cast in gun-metal molds, although some of the elaborately modeled Continental pieces may have been and probably were cast in some other way. Thus a pewterer would have to have quite an elaborate set of molds—of flagons, beakers, porringers, basins, tankards, pitchers, ewers, and plates, in a wide variety of shapes and sizes. The chances are that very few pewterers had all the molds for making even these simple forms; probably molds were borrowed and swapped back and forth as need arose.

At the height of the pewterer's art in the sixteenth and seventeenth centuries, pewterers were allowed to market only their own wares, because of the tightly controlled guilds.

London pewter was required by the rules of the guild to be hammer-finished in some parts; certainly the bellies of plates and bowls were so finished. This was not necessarily the rule in Continental Europe nor in America, where hammer-finished pieces are so much the exception that it is often thought that they do not exist.

Some pieces were further ornamented by chasing and occasionally decorated with repoussé. Since hammering quickly hardens pewter to the breaking point and annealing is difficult, elaborate repoussé on pewter is not general. Repoussé effects were mostly achieved by casting. Most of this elaborate work is to be found in Continental European pewter of the fifteenth, sixteenth, and seventeenth centuries. Pewter collectible for the average person falls rather into the declining period of the art. The great rarities of pewterers' art in Europe have long since been gathered into great public and private collections. What remains is of a simpler order. Its charm derives from

its warm, dull luster and simple contours, a fact that has made
it a favorite with still life painters from the fifteenth century
onward. This luster is at its best in simple forms, and these
are fortunately still available for us to collect.

Pieces of odd shapes such as teapots, soup tureens,
tankards, and beakers, as well as baluster-shaped objects,
had to be made in sections (since otherwise they could not be
unmolded). Handles were soldered and riveted in place. Some
porringer handles were drawn out from the piece rather than
soldered on. In fact, use of solder in this connection was not
permitted by the guild. It is out of these simple components
that the wealth of forms of pewter is created. Compared with
silver and even brass and copper, the forms of pewter show
less variety and flexibility. Pewter has much greater stability
in its response to changing styles than any of the other metals.

The last thing done in the making of pewter was the application of the pewterer's touch. For the collector of pewter of
any time and place, the touch is of the essence. The touch is
the mark of the pewterer and, while these marks can be faked,
they are, nevertheless, the hallmarks of good pewter. Yours
should never be without them.

Britannia Ware

The manufacture of britannia employed a few processes
not used for pewter. In the first place, britannia metal is not
at all different from the best plate pewter except in respect to
its fabrication. It was made into ingots, which were either
rolled into sheets or used for casting into small ornaments.
The sheets were tougher and harder than pewter. These
could be worked in a manner similar to the working of other
thin metals such as tinned ironware. The thin sheets were also
stamped in dies by a method that we refer to today as drop
stamping. The stamped portions were assembled and soldered
together, ornamented where necessary by adding separately
cast pieces, soft-soldered on.

A second method was to cast the object in one piece or in
piece molds made of brass or bronze. The third method is
very much in use today for making cheap articles of aluminum,

brass, copper, and other metals. This is the technique known
as spinning. Spun pieces are of necessity simpler in form than
those made by the other processes, but more elaborate shapes
are built up of spun pieces. The spun wares all have circular
cross sections. They may be decorated with some repoussé
chasing or engraving, but this is most certainly a great rarity
in the spun types.

Britannia, as befits a tougher, more machine-made ware,
is marked differently than pewter. First, it contains the full
name of the concern making it, and second, the letters are
sunk in the ware as fine lines, where the letters on pewter are
in relief against a sunken ground. A third way in which britannia marks differ from those on pewter or silver (except for
plated) is that the letters and other devices appear as if stamped
all at once from a single stamp that included the whole inscription. When new, pewter and britannia looked considerably
different. Pewter had the grayish, dull cast characteristic
only of itself, while britannia had the much higher luster of
silver and Sheffield plate. Time has somewhat blurred the
original differences in appearance, so that britannia can be
confused with pewter. One difference is easily told, or rather
heard. Of two pieces of the same size and shape, the pewter
one has a dull, leaden sound when struck, and the britannia
has a distinctly metallic sound.

Here are the important differences between the two metals.
Britannia is much more resonant than pewter; it is tougher
and it will polish to a higher luster. Also, the shapes are
likely to be later in date than those of pewter. Britannia is,
on the whole, more pretentious than pewter, but less desirable
because the quality of close connection with its time and place
is not so high as in pewter. Britannia was worked over frequently and often decorated with chasing. Pewter is not often
so decorated.

Working Methods as Clues to Age

The dating of pewter will be by two methods. The first is
the shape. Shapes are fairly stable and pretty well fixed in
time. The earliest forms are forthright and straightforward.

The later are more frivolous and have less the air of permanence. Once the pewter has been tentatively dated on the basis of form, a check should be made of the touch. If the touch and shape agree with each other more or less (give or take a few years), you will have reduced your problem to two alternatives: either you have a good piece of old pewter or a good fake. The trick is to separate the one from the other.

In the making of pewter, the rough castings were turned down to a final finish. In this turning, the marks of the turner's tools, however skillfully managed, formed a spiral helix over the surface of the work. Such marks are always visible when light from a broad source, such as a window, is reflected from the piece. Rotation of the piece will show these surfaces as planes where the reflection stops abruptly. Years of polishing fail to remove them, although their character may be somewhat obscured by the series of minor dents and bumps that time has given the piece.

On English pewter you can expect to see hammer-finished surfaces on parts of some of the pieces, notably plates, as this was required by law. Continental and American pewter usually do not have these hammered surfaces. Where they occur in old work, they are of a slightly different shape and form from modern hammer marks and again show only slightly in the proper light. Many times the unevenness in design, form, and appearance are more evident to the fingers than to the eye.

Wear and Tear

Wear shows most clearly on the feet and handles and wherever the piece was subject to wear. This wear results in loss of metal, which can sometimes be substantial. Secondly, there are scratches and/or cuts. These are most frequently seen on the insides of plates, platters, and bowls. Any plate that was used at all has them. The cuts are characteristically random, of different widths, breadths, lengths, and direction. There is never any discernible pattern.

In addition to the damage due to physical causes, pewter is also subject to chemical damage. It is corrupted by acids present in foods, as well as by alkalis and salts. It is this surface (best noted with a magnifying glass) that gives old pewter its typical appearance. Pewter bends and warps very easily; consequently, most old pewter has a number of slight bumps and hollows, more readily felt than seen. A still further characteristic of age in pewter is the tendency of tin to change to a gray powder. Pewter is sure to do this if it is kept below 40° Fahrenheit for any great length of time. This leads to uneven pitting and checks on the surface.

Finally, the surface of pewter, whether polished or not, has a film of oxidation lying on it. When this film is not removed occasionally by polishing, the grayness becomes black and the pewter is covered by a heavy brown to black film, extremely difficult to remove. With or without the film, pewter when old has a grayish to brownish dull luster made duller by the pits, cuts, scratches, and bumps. This sum total is the patina of age. A little experience as well as study applied to its recognition will give an almost foolproof method of distinguishing the new from the old.

Fakes

The fakes found in pewter will be more frequent as the price goes up. For this reason, you are likely to find more fakes of seventeenth- than eighteenth-century pewter and still more fakes of sixteenth-century pewter.

While a great deal of faking goes on in connection with pewter, britannia ware is still insufficiently sought after to warrant faking to any large degree, although it is possible that some persons may be adding marks to unmarked pieces and otherwise glorifying them (a rare mark may be forged or sawed from some badly damaged piece and added to a later one). As this is more difficult to do for pewter than for silver, it is less often practiced.

It is almost axiomatic to say that, in originals, elegance and opulence of workmanship always take precedence over elaborateness of form. Thus, the skill and workmanship lavished upon an antique piece of pewter is always more than we would think necessary from the results. For example, when

we encounter elaborately stamped _repoussé_ pieces, the workmanship has all the quality of sculpture in its wealth of carefully executed details. A fake made in such a style is sure to
reveal itself in fumbling workmanship. That is, the design
is carried out in a rotelike way without delicate transitions or
incisive details. Thus, the higher the style and the more
elegant the piece, the more opportunities there are for the
faker to make a mistake.

There is another way of duplicating old pewter, and this is
to make a cast of an original and work from this cast to make
a new mold. No cast, however, can exactly duplicate the
original surface. Actually, casts almost always require reworking to remove the fins. The moment the faker attempts
to rework the cast, he jumps from the frying pan into the fire,
for new work is even more likely to be obvious on a cast of an
old piece (there is less metal in it than there should be) than
on new work done entirely from scratch. If the cast of the
original touch is retained, it will very likely be fuzzy and
show wear in unlikely places. If a new touch is used, a magnifying glass will disclose the newness of the work—and here
again, careful checking will reveal differences between an
authentic touch and the suspected one.

Steps in Examination

First, look at the piece carefully without handling it. Make
a mental note as to what kind of mark it should have and
approximate its age and country. Style is really of pre-
eminent importance for judging its age.

Examine it carefully for cuts, pits, and minor dents. Use
your fingers for this. Does it seem as heavy as you thought
it ought to be? Look for cuts and deep scratches. Are they
random in nature? Reconsider the form. Make sure that it
has the right amount of wear and scratches in the right places
to go with its form. The shape will tell you whether to expect
one, two, three, or four hundred years of wear, tear, and
exposure to the elements. Check the state of the patina. Black,
leaden-looking pieces may not be so old as much brighter
ones. Uniform deep grayness with no areas of bright metal

and few scratches bespeak modern pieces. The typical patina
of well-cared-for old pieces is a dull silvery-looking metal
with numerous signs of wear and tear. Pay particular attention to a hard look in the lines of the piece. Tap it gently.
Pewter both sounds and looks dull.

Finally, turn over the piece and look for a touch. If none
is present, check whether it fits your first concept of time
and place. If the touch does not match the style, try to see
why. If you can find no good reason for the lack of agreement,
don't buy it.

TINNED SHEET IRON

A metal long used for a wide variety of useful and ornamental objects was tinned sheet iron. This is usually referred
to in American and English works as tinware, and in French as
tôle. Tinware, as I shall call it henceforth, was used for all
kinds of utilitarian articles, from butter churns and milk
pans to coal hods and woodboxes.

Painted and Unpainted Tinware

We can, I believe, best study these wares by dividing them
into two groups and considering each separately. The first
group will consist of things made primarily to serve useful
ends and only secondarily intended to be ornamental. Here
the primitive arts of making useful things beautiful in one way
or another come to the fore. I shall arbitrarily keep in this
group a certain number of things that were primarily ornamental
but were made in the same way as the useful articles, and like
them were innocent of any paint or japan.

The second group includes all items to which some painted
decoration was applied. This ware was intended to be ornamental and was bought for that purpose.

For much painted tinware, the condition has no effect on
the salability. In fact, in many cases, a piece with its
decoration intact will bring less money than a similar piece
with not only its decoration but the tin coating gone as well.

That these rusty remnants should be so sought after in today's market is curious but understandable when the reasons are considered. (See below.)

Working Methods

Sheet iron is much more difficult than copper and silver to work into complicated shapes by raising and hammering, and cannot be cast like pewter. Its tin coating prevents annealing. Also the handworker started out not with the basic raw materials but with the tinned iron already manufactured. Because of the limitations imposed on him by the nature of his material, shaping (raising) was kept to a minimum, and all of his work was done by means of cutting, bending, soldering, and shaping with a few simple machines such as slip rollers and bar folders. His other tools, such as hammers, drills, punches, seamers, riveters, groovers, and stakes are all suitable for use on other metals as well.

Generally, most articles made of tin are derived from simple geometric forms that can be cut out flat and bent into shape. The basic forms are cones, pyramids, cylinders, cubes, and parallelepipeds, singly or in combination.

I can mention only a very few of the collectible forms. There are lanterns, pierced or fitted with horn or glass windows. There are dishes, pans, measures, lamps, candle molds, and candlesticks of all simple sorts. There are sconces and other lighting fixtures in bewildering array. Sometimes they include wood or other metal where tin alone would be too difficult to shape. There is much variety in the lighting department, all very much sought after by collectors because of the great difficulty encountered in finding lighting equipment that is old and suitable for use with early furniture.

Because of this, tinware is constantly faked, and the faking is magnificent. Most of it has exactly the proper amount of wear in exactly the proper places. Such forgeries are, of course, made by the old methods. They are in general, however, not made of the older material. Much of the time, the imitation is made of lighter tin and will feel appreciably lighter when lifted. Secondly, the tin coating on the older ware was a dipped coating and is slightly thicker than modern tin.

Obviously, tinware exposed to the elements from ninety to two hundred years is going to show wear and tear. First, the tin will dull and darken. Frequently it wears thin on exposed surfaces, where the iron shows through as a darker metal with less luster than the tin. Soldered seams and joints show up as bright lines. Unfortunately, all of these effects can be achieved very readily with judicious use of muriatic acid.

This looks as if we are helpless to cope with this particular kind of fraud. I must admit that discrimination here is extremely difficult. There are, however, some methods that will work if carefully and diligently applied. First, examine the work carefully for scratches. It is obvious that, for a piece to have any age at all, it should have quite a number of scratches on it, with or without randomness. A piece of tinware minimally eighty to ninety years old without any scratches is an impossibility.

Scratches that go with wear and tear will have different ages, that is, the edges of all scratches will not be alike. Some will have the clear, sharp edge of newness, others will underlie corrosion and tarnish. If all or most of the scratches lie atop the tarnish, the piece should be suspect. Those that seem to lie in or under the tarnish will repay further examination. If they are the result of the passage of time, the film of tarnish will be evenly distributed over them as it is over the rest of the surface.

On the other hand, if the tarnish has been the result of antiquing over the scratch, the edge of the scratch will show this in two ways. First, the tarnish will be heavier on the sides, and the bottom of the scratch will have an eroded or eaten appearance (when seen with a magnifying glass), which suggests use of acids.

The tin layer also has its own characteristics in respect to the way it ages. The first is surface hardening. The tin becomes brittle and dull on the outside. Compare this tin luster with the luster on pewter. Careful checking with a glass should show some surface checks in the dull tin. In those areas where the tin is corroded and the iron has oxidized, the surface of the tin will show little blisters when we examine the edges where the iron and tin meet with a glass. In many cases where

the tin has worn off rather than corroded off, the metal should
show both bright tin and bright iron lying together. Areas of
wear will be those most subject to wear, for instance, handles
and feet.

A still further way to check on all these features is to look
at areas not seen from outside and thus likely to be overlooked
by the faker. There should not be many scratches in these
hard-to-see spots, but there should be a great deal of corrosion. In some cases, small flakes may have fallen off to
reveal rusted spots below them. Such corrosion is difficult to
fake with the means now available (though as fakes using new
methods are constantly turning up, it may be possible for this
type of faking to be successfully carried out as well).

There is also a positive side to work from, and this lies in
the appreciation of stylistic differences. In the first place, a
piece from the eighteenth century ought, indeed, to look like
it. The tinker not only repaired and retinned the kettle and
saucepan, but was a master of all kinds of ingenious tricks to
get elaborate effects by simple means.

One of the great charms of this old tinware is that it always
impresses us with its ingenuity. Each piece has the immediacy
of a quick solution to a new problem. Each has a uniqueness
not to be found in any other field of activity except perhaps
the fine arts. Therefore, the more the piece at hand has a
familiar look, the more thoroughly it should be suspect. The
aesthetics of tinware is surprise and ingenuity.

I have throughout this discussion concerned myself almost
entirely with what is called country tin. There will be found
in addition, especially as we get to the end dates of collecti-
bility, a number of pieces that have somewhat the same general appearance (as to age and weathering), but that are the
products of factories. They are sometimes picked up unwit-
tingly by both dealer and collector. Weight and hard modern
lines and design should give them away at once.

Painted Tinware—Tôle

When tinware is decorated, we can fix dates from the style
of the painting. Paintings on trays can run from those with an

extraordinarily high degree of excellence to the run-of-the-mill kind almost mechanically turned out. The painting of the earlier trays was so well done, especially on the so-called beer trays (round or oval trays with stand-up edges), that they rival the work of artists of note, especially where the subjects—genre, landscape, hunting scenes—bear comparison.

This excellence of work has given rise to stories that many of these trays were the minor works of major artists, who in times of financial difficulty undertook to decorate their inn-keepers' trays in settlement of their bills. This is difficult to accept save for rare instances.

The scenic trays with their rural settings and the hunting scenes are easily recognizable by the coloring, drawing, and painting as well as details, as belonging to the late eighteenth century. In style, they resemble the works of the greater painters of the same time, such as Reynolds and Gainsborough (for figure treatment) and Constable (for landscapes). The similarity is due to the fashions in painting at the end of the century and not in any way to a connection between the two groups of painters.

The decoration on many of the highest-style trays consists of nothing but parcel gilt. Such trays, especially those in orientalizing style (Chinoiserie) may belong to the eighteenth century. This is the type of decoration we find on early Chippendale Gothic (elaborate trays of double ogee form), lace edge trays, some beer trays, and gallery trays. The delicacy of treatment and the care of execution should make it possible to distinguish between the fine detailed work of the Rococo period and the more heavy-handed work of the Rococo Revival.

At about the end of the eighteenth century, the vogue for Rococo design and its dramatic fantasies in light and shade disappeared. At this point, the popularity of swags, flat painted garlands, and small flowers in scattered sprays provide clues to dates. This type of decoration is seen on lace edge and gallery trays of the close of the eighteenth century. More frequently, lace-edged trays are decorated with brightly painted bouquets and scattered flowers on a tortoise shell ground.

More typical of the new styles is the Classical subject in parcel gilt on a black ground. By this time, the form of the tray begins to change and we see lace-edge and gallery trays gradually giving way to sloping-sided, octagonal ones. This type of tray continues in popularity to the early forties of the nineteenth century. Many have parcel gilt borders and plain centers.

At the end of the lace edge period, the use of bronze powders came in. At first, these took the place of gold leaf in parcel gilt work and were modeled freehand on a varnished ground. Somewhat later, the stencil came into use. With the stencils came the rectangular tray with rounded corners and with or without hand holes. These trays were very popular up into the seventies of the nineteenth century and are found with almost every kind of decoration except the lace edge type. Early trays use multiple stencils, later trays one-piece stencils.

A few additional points may be made about the relation of construction to dates. First, most trays were made of considerably heavier-gauge metal than is used today. Secondly, they usually have hand-wired edges (the handwork shows itself in the unevenness of the wired edge). Those with rounded edges show evidence of hand bending or raising in the curved portions. This is readily seen on undecorated pieces, more readily felt on those with decoration. Such Chippendale trays and trays with Rococo borders as you may find are likely to belong to the middle of the nineteenth century. Some few may go back to the mid-eighteenth century.

With the exception of Rococo types, the earliest trays are those with pierced borders on round or oval trays. These seem to have been popular chiefly in the fourth quarter of the eighteenth century. The oval or rounded pierced edges of these trays are one with the body, that is, the border is not a separate piece fastened on. The usual shapes are circular or elliptical, and occasionally rectangular. Circular trays with stand-up rims and hand holes may in some cases go back as far as the last decade of the eighteenth century. The little octagonal trays with straight rims and hand holes may go back to as early as 1800. Rectangular trays with hand holes, curved edges, and rounded corners may be as early as 1810 or as late as 1880.

The bulk of the fancy trays belongs to the mid-nineteenth century.

Many objects other than trays were decorated with japanning. The great bulk were products of the iron works of Pontypool, Birmingham, and other places situated close to iron mines. The tendency is to ascribe most of such work (when it is not obviously French) to Pontypool. Whether America produced tinware in quantity as early as Pontypool is among the things yet to be demonstrated. Some American work is dated and labeled from the 1870's. I have seen a couple of published trays of this date—in this case, stenciled.

One kind of tinware we did produce in quantity was that sold throughout the country districts during the nineteenth century. The typical shape of tray was octagonal, frequently with a seam down the center. This tinware was often decorated with one thin coat of japan, upon which were laid with simple brush strokes gay patterns in reds, yellows, greens, blues, and whites. Most of the objects painted in this manner have a folk art character, although they are not folk art. Most of the flowers, fruit, and leaves can be so called only by courtesy, so little resemblance do they bear to nature. These simple pieces almost never made use of gold or silver leaf or of gold bronzes until stencils became prevalent, around the second quarter of the nineteenth century. Then they are most often single rather than multiple stencils, at which point the stage is set for the decline of the work, sometimes after the Civil War.

So scarce is our information that the question of dating decorated tinware—high style as well as country tin—is not really settled, except in a general way. It would seem, however, that the production of painted tinware became important with the onset of the second half of the eighteenth century (although it may have been introduced earlier, along with the fashion of japanned furniture, which begins some eighty or ninety years previously). Certainly few can be found that date much before the beginning of the nineteenth. The criteria for dating these designs are one hundred percent stylistic, and these are about the only grounds we have. The sequence from Baroque and Rococo chiaroscuro to flat, plein air Classical

Revival treatment is perfectly clear. Subsequent development from hand-painted to freehand bronze work (as opposed to gold leaf or parcel gilding) succeeds the elaborate work of the earlier eighteenth century to pass on ultimately to the stenciled tinware of the nineteenth century.

Restorations

For peculiar reasons there is little incentive for the intentional fake. A number of years ago (about two generations) certain persons began to collect hand-painted and stenciled furniture for the sake of its japan work. At that time people were still living who had been trained in the late techniques of japanning. The need for restoration of an occasional damaged piece brought interested parties together, so that gradually there was a revival of the old techniques. One of the pioneers in this field was Mrs. Esther Stevens Brazer, whose book, Early American Decoration, discusses in precise detail how to duplicate all of the effects of early painting. Mrs. Brazer also conducted classes in the actual execution of projects.

Her students formed a so-called guild to disseminate the true techniques of Early American decoration. These techniques are modifications of older techniques in the light of modern materials and the facilities available to the amateur. The students now are quite numerous, and their enthusiasm has made the demand for old tinware very heavy. Consequently, the prices for tinware in need of restoration equal and often exceed those paid for those needing no redecoration.

Since there is this tremendous vogue, especially among the petticoated half of humanity, for redoing old tinware, we have to be on our guard against these restorations. The first check is style. This can usually be discovered through the hardness of the new drawing. Secondly, the colors are apt to be a little too subdued because of antiquing. Further, an examination of the back of a redone tray is likely to show a finish different from that left by the heat-cured japan. The surface does not have that enamel-like look.

Effects of the passage of time are primarily changes in the condition of the japan. Some of the aging effects of old varnishes used in japanning, even though baked, are evident. One is crazing of the surface. This may vary from a very fine network of cracks visible only under certain conditions of light to a rough surface resembling scaly paint. Varnish becomes less transparent and the colors underlying it fade. There are the results of wear and tear such as worn spots on contact surfaces and around edges, or any other spots where the trays can be handled. Frequently, the tin coating deteriorates and flakes off here and there.

Once any or all of the above-described effects of aging are found on a tray, you can be sure that it is old. How old it is will depend on its decoration. Therefore, in examining a painted tray, you have but to look carefully for signs of age, particularly for the crazing of the finish, and you are all set.

COPPER AND BRASS

Probably no metals collected give the antiquarian more trouble than copper and brass. Copper is one of the few pure metals used for making serviceable articles. Naturally, the copper used for old wares is not likely to be as pure as more modern copper. Brass is an alloy of copper and zinc.

As we go backward in time, we find that brass and bronze become more difficult to distinguish. By the time we reach antiquity, it is problematic whether or not brass was known. The chances are pretty fair that brass was occasionally made by accident, either by mistake for bronze, or in the process of extracting copper from its ores. But it is not until the end of the Medieval period that brass is used much. At this time we find it more in Northern than in Southern Europe.

Over the last three hundred years, brass was used not only for monumental works, plaques, tomb ornaments, and church furniture, but also for such household articles as caldrons, kettles, candlesticks, mortars, pestles, trays, fenders, firedogs, and furniture mounts (its place here occasionally taken by firegilt bronze or ormolu). It is with these latter uses that we are concerned.

Over most of the period from which we can collect it, brass was available in sheets and for casting. The sheets were hand-hammered until the latter part of the eighteenth century. After this time, sheet brass was the product of rolling mills rather than handwork. This change from one form of production to another did not take place overnight, so that hand-hammered sheets continued to be made long after the mills were in use.

The brass in which the collector is interested falls into the group containing from ninety-five to sixty-three percent copper, the group of so-called alpha brasses.

Brass was used in sheets and hammered by the raising processes, with frequent annealing into much the same forms as silverware and copperware. It is tough and works well in this fashion. On the other hand, brass also casts well, and a great amount of brass is and was cast. The methods of casting vary from place to place and time to time. The great bulk of early cast brass is sand-cast and finished by varied methods. Brass and bronze were frequently fire-gilt.

Judging Age

When we come to discriminate between new and old copper, brass, and bronze, we find that we have a great deal of trouble. It is next to impossible to prove that a given brass object is old. However, we can frequently demonstrate that the brass is new. First, there is the matter of work. Machine work is easily detectable in its perfection of form and in its materials, both as to assay and in the marks of machine tools seen under magnification. New hand-worked brass is a little more difficult to detect, but again there are ways of differentiating between it and older metal. Old brass has a distinctly different color from newer brass; it looks less brassy. This is due to the accumulation of oxides on and in the surfaces of even well-polished pieces. Surfaces not easily accessible to polishing will frequently become greenish, due to an accumulation of basic copper carbonate. The surface below the carbonate is red copper oxide, which will again be found on top of the dark sulphide and/or black copper oxide; these are unstable compared with the green basic carbonate.

Most brass will not, of course, be green, or even red.
However, if you look for stylistic qualifications along with the
old dull surface containing little pits, which are the results
of older manufacturing processes, you will be following the
right mode of attack. The lack of proper pickling methods in
the annealing of the brass tends to imbed little specks of copper
oxides in the surface. Areas worn off from use are also
worth looking for.

Inasmuch as brass was cast as often as it was hammered,
the casting process gives some indication of its age. Most cast
pieces, from candlesticks to brass firedogs, were cast hollow in small sections, fastened together with solder, and
often supported on wrought-iron cores. The assembly from
small parts is a fair indication of age. Late castings are in
one piece, much sharper in their impressions, and have a
more machine-made look.

Working Methods as Clues to Age

Another very clear indication of style and date is the combination of beautiful detailed handiwork with minor imperfections, such as slightly uneven shapes, objects out of round
and with minor variations in contours. Many pans and utensils
of copper and brass will show construction details. These
include soldered seams and dovetail joints, for example, the
cylindrical sections of kettles and pots, lanterns and warming
pans may be fastened together by means of dovetail joints.
The bottoms of similar vessels are frequently so fastened on.
These were joined together and hammered flat when the metal
was heated to a state just below melting, and so they are in
effect welded together. Such joints normally do not show, but
can be brought out by carefully rubbing the surface with a
block of wood wrapped in felt, because there is a slight tendency for the dovetails to stand up a little above the rest of the
surface.

In the long run, you have to fall back on the style of working, the style of the object, and the general appearance of the
surface. Thus, the best way to learn about the appearance of
old brass is to study it in museums until you are familiar with

the look of pieces of a given style. You can get yourself a
study collection of brass and copper by concentrating on pieces
of little value but of sufficient age and style to supply a date.
Such pieces would be pots, pans, and simple mortars. Large
kettles are readily available at reasonable prices; fenders,
candlesticks, and firedogs come higher. Lanterns and other
objects should be purchased only after you become experienced.

Chapter IX

THE CARE AND PRESERVATION

OF ANTIQUES

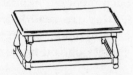

Although antiques are pretty sturdy, their scarcity speaks eloquently of the hazards to which they have been exposed. They are still exposed to damage, unless you make some effort to protect them. Much damage is peculiar to the antique, although it must be touched off by some outside agent. Metals corrode, wood rots. Damage can also result from carelessness and ignorance in cleaning or from attempting to protect or restore the antique. It is here that many an antique is ruined, frequently beyond salvaging.

FURNITURE

The finish of furniture may be scratched and marred. The wood may be stained, eaten by worms, warped, checked, or broken. It may become unglued. Doors and drawers may stick. With the exception of damage from breaking, worms, and scratching of finish, all the other ailments in furniture are caused by the interaction of wood with its environment.

Warping

All of us are familiar with the way doors stick in damp weather, or how the cracks between the floor boards in old houses are much wider in winter than in summer. All of these are caused by the exchange of moisture between the wood and the surrounding air.

Antiques were made of lumber of high moisture content, but since the air to which they were exposed had about the same amount of moisture, any further losses would be slow. Today, our houses are so dry in the winter that the loss of water goes on more rapidly; but in the summer, with doors and windows open, and with high humidity, the furniture picks up moisture.

If one side of a board has more moisture in it than the other, the board will curl or warp. Boards always curve toward the dry side. A knowledge of the cause of the trouble suggests both a cure and a prevention. If the convex side of the warped surface is dried, the warp should be cured. An old warp will have put permanent bends in some fibers, but if the warp is slightly overcorrected, the fibers will be bent the other way and this may finally straighten the board.

To prevent this from occurring again, keep the moisture content of the room at a constant level. With air conditioning, this can be achieved. Next best is to try humidifying the room in winter. Cupboards, sideboards, chests of drawers, and the like can be humidified by placing a source of moisture inside the piece. If the warp is concave outward, the humidity can be decreased by using silica gel or some other moisture-absorbing substance inside. If the warp is concave inward, it is necessary to dehumidify the room.

Chemical changes in the wood alter its color and the character of the gums or resins that all woods contain to some degree. The chief of these is oxidation, which, as it causes the gum molecules to link together, reduces volume and causes further shrinkage in the fibers. Such changes are irreversible. The best preventive is to coat the surface by polishing or waxing the surface carefully, to reduce this cause of trouble to a minimum.

With unexposed surfaces, the problem is more difficult. We could finish these surfaces the way it is done with modern pieces. Unfortunately, it is just these surfaces that we want to leave untouched, to show the authenticity of the piece. There is a way out of this difficulty, and that is to coat most unexposed portions, leaving some areas of the original surface untouched. The best preservative is probably raw linseed oil, to be renewed from time to time.

Sagging and Twisting

The cause of sagging is the continuous pull of gravity on an object supported at its ends into a catenary curve or curve of equal weight. The typical result of this sort of thing in a piece of furniture can be seen in the sag of cupboard shelves, drawer bottoms, table tops, desk flaps, and bed rails.

The cure for this type of warp is quite simple in theory: just turn the piece of wood over. In practice, very few things can be just turned over. As for the parts that cannot be reversed without doing violence to the antique, these can be removed temporarily, reversed, and loaded with weights. This will effect a cure in most instances.

Twisting, the second type of mechanical damage, is caused by stresses on a piece of wood set up by some change in the dimensions of a piece of furniture. When two pieces are fastened together in such a way that the grains are not parallel, shrinkage will cause bowing. This often happens in veneered pieces. The prevention for this kind of warping is not easy but again consists in trying to get the piece to absorb sufficient moisture to straighten out.

Checking

Much more serious than warping is checking, the woodworker's term for splitting when it happens without the help of any outside agent. Checking, like warping, is caused by the uneven loss of moisture at the ends of a board. When the tendency to contract in one direction is strong and in another weak, the fibers pull away from each other and a break develops on the exposed edge. It will, in time, split the piece from one end to the other.

Techniques for preventing checking are the same as those for warping. In addition, see that all end grains are well protected from the air by finish, wax, and oil. If a piece of wood is fastened down firmly to another with nails or screws, as in a table top, it will split as it shrinks. Another place where splitting takes place regularly is where a wide piece of wood is fitted into a leg with a double mortise and tenon. Since the space between the two tenons cannot decrease, shrinkage of the wide board causes the leg to act like a wedge and ultimately split the side. For this there is no cure.

Shrinking

The final ill from loss of moisture is to be found in just
plain shrinkage. I want to discuss only its effect on glued
joints, which is to tear them apart, usually with some damage
to the joint. Especially serious is the shrinkage of a veneered
core, particularly when it is made of more than one piece. It
often buckles, cracks, and tears the veneer loose. The best
cure is prevention, and this means making every effort to
avoid excessive drying of veneered furniture.

Loss of Veneering and Marquetry

Closely related to core shrinkage and, indeed, partly
brought about by it, is the loss of veneer, marquetry, and
applied ornaments. Glue, like wood, can dry out. It also
picks up moisture from its surroundings, and it is also subject to slow oxidation. The continued swelling and shrinking of
the glue with moisture changes in the air causes glued joints to
let go. Since veneers and cores expand and contract in different directions, the veneer and the carcass often separate.
When not supported by other wood, the very thin veneer checks
and cross-breaks, blisters develop, and pieces of veneer and
applied molding fall off and get lost.

Prevention of this trouble requires controlling the humidity
to keep the glue from drying and the wood from alternately
shrinking and swelling. If you find a piece of lifted veneer,
put a little glue under it and hold it down with a weight.

When glue dries out, all joints that depend on glue to hold
them together will loosen and come apart. To prevent damage
from overdrying (1) protect the surfaces with a finish of
some sort; (2) use moistening or dehumidifying agents within
the piece itself; and (3) maintain a normal level of humidity
in your house during those seasons when it is usually abnormally
low.

Do not place furniture close to a source of heat; keep
pieces out of the sun; avoid overloading shelves or drawers;
avoid setting tables and chairs on an uneven floor; avoid
wrestling with the furniture, particularly the chairs.

Worm Damage

Antique dealers often point to wormholes as proof of age.
Handy as wormholes are as selling points, they are not good
for furniture. Active worms and the larvae of a wide variety
of beetles can reduce a prized possession to sawdust. This
activity may be evinced by little piles of sawdust under the
furniture.

The best way to get rid of worms is to gas the piece; this
is for professionals, and you should stay away from it. Or
you can pour a goodly quantity of carbon tetrachloride into
an airtight box large enough to hold the piece. Since the tetrachloride will kill you as readily as the worms, be careful.

Finish Troubles

Furniture is also likely to suffer damage to its finish. We
care only about the original finish. The old finishes are of
three inherently different kinds. First is the casein or albumin
and water type. These finishes, which are rather soft, need
not cause much worry. They can and should be protected by a
coat of beeswax and oil.

The second type of finish is a spirit varnish somewhat
resembling modern shellac. These finishes are very sensitive
to dampness, sunlight, and oxidation. If the finish is still in
fair condition, there are several things you can do to preserve
it. First, clean it thoroughly with an organic solvent such as
benzine or carbon tetrachloride. The surface can then be
protected with a layer of nondrying oil like lemon oil, or crude
or lard oil. This can be followed with a French polish or with
a heavy coat of beeswax.

The third type of finish made use of a drying oil for its
medium, both for paint and for polished finish. These finishes
tend to check, chalk, craze, and alligator. Clean such finishes and then drench them in raw linseed oil, followed in a
few days with a coat of beeswax, to be renewed from time to
time. Such pieces should receive a coat of linseed oil once a
year.

Stains

Furniture may get stained. Stains that arise from carelessness can be avoided. Occasionally stains seem to develop
out of nowhere and spread within the wood. This kind of ail-
ment overtakes those woods—maple and cherry in particular—
that rot easily. I suppose that it is a kind of dry rot. Treat
such stains with carbon tetrachloride, followed by chloride
of lime and a strong wood bleach, to kill the fungus and to
bleach the stain. If this procedure is used immediately on
discovering the stain, you can stop it from spreading and
bleach it out easily.

You can prevent staining from constant use simply by being
prepared for it. Make sure that the table, for example, is
cleared after every use, that wet or hot objects are not
allowed to come in contact with a table. Be sure that there is
enough polish, and particularly beeswax, protecting the surface. Clean regularly to remove dirt and the old wax and oil
finish before polishing.

Willful Damage—Restoration and Refinishing

There is not a collector or dealer living who has not, on
looking at some once magnificent piece of furniture, now in
almost total ruin, wondered, "What could they have been thinking of to treat a beautiful thing like that?" The top is stained
like a crazy quilt, warped, and dented. The dents in its surface look as if the whole family must have been beating tatoos
on it with ball-peen hammers. The drawers look as if they
must have been regularly opened with pickaxes. As for the
legs and feet, what with chips, dirt stains, wormholes, and
missing parts, they must have dragged it behind the car when
they brought it to the dealer.

Now you buy this decrepit piece of furniture to preserve it.
Well, the first thing it needs is a good repair and refinishing
job. You take the warped top off. The warp you remove by
screwing it down to heavy battens. You have room for them
inside the piece. Sure enough, you get rid of the warp. But
what's this, a crack? A check? A split! Well, that can be

easily fixed. You just run the top right through the power saw and joint and glue it together. Now the battens are no longer needed. The screwholes are inside so they won't show. Of course, the top is now too narrow to fit properly, but you can joint the back edge and glue a new piece on it, taking care to leave enough overhang so that you can rework that battle-scarred front molding.

Now for the loose drawers. The sides of those that are broken are run through the saw to get a straight edge for gluing. You are careful to leave all of the dovetails, because these take time to make, and besides they help indicate age. You glue new pieces on, leaving a slight overhang on both sides to get a nice clean fit. When the glue has set, it is nothing to dress the sides even on the sander.

Now for the drawer fronts. Never mind the dents and cuts. Take care of those later, but just look at the drawer lips—cracked and chipped here and there! Well, the best thing to do is put on new ones, at least at the top. Off with the old, on with the new. These you join with an elegant tongue and groove joint. Better finish them off with the quarter-round router or molding cutter. While they are gluing, take a look inside the chest to see why those drawers stick. Aha! Just as you thought. The drawer slides are worn out. It'll be easy to take them out with a wrecking bar. Before you know it, you have the new set ready. Installing them takes a little time, but think of the satisfaction of being able to open and close the drawers.

Let's look at the feet. Too bad those Dutch feet are so scuffed and dirty. Sure enough there is a bad stain on the knee of the right leg. Better fix them. Look out! Better not go too fast. You can't replace the old feet, you know. Oh, well, you can patch them. Make three little straight cuts to get a good gluing surface. Cut off some more of that old wood, make and glue little blocks onto the flat surface. When the glue has set up, you can reshape the Dutch feet. They'll be much sturdier now—and the old feet have not been replaced!

Well, it looks as if the repairs are finished. Now for the refinishing. Those ax cuts certainly go in deep. Perhaps you'd better plane them off. Now for the stains. The planing

has gotten rid of most of them. The sander will do the rest.
It works fine, too, on the drawer fronts, gets all the dents out.
Be careful! Watch that thumb-nail molding. Better rework
it a bit so as not to lose it. Sides look pretty good too, but
those feet! Well, it did take a lot of work with rasp and file
to clean them up properly, but what a difference!

All ready for the new finish. What's that? It looks a little
light? Well, some of this maple stain will fix that up. Now
for the oil finish. No? Go ahead, shellac and wax it. What?
You wouldn't do that? Oh! That new finish that's just like
wax! Here it goes. It's wonderful, and easy, too. You
wouldn't believe it was the same chest, would you? What's
that you say? It isn't. Well, I suppose with all that work on
it, it is a much better piece, looks like new. What do you
mean, it is new?

Maniacs, Philistines, barbarians, collectors, and restorers—who did the most violence to the antique?

In the imaginary restoration above are committed almost
all the acts of willful violence I can think of. These are done
by conscientious workmen, amateur or professional, going
about the restoration of a chest of drawers. You don't use new
fasteners on old pieces. Power tools should never be used on
old work. Old surfaces should not be scraped or planed to
remove knife cuts or stains. You should never saw a board to
get rid of a warp. No portion of an antique should be discarded
if there is even a remote chance of making it work. When
new pieces must be added, like the drawer sides and lips,
they should be fitted with the breaks and be minimal in size.
No reworking should be done on old surfaces. Finally, the
new finish should be an exact duplicate of the old in materials
and workmanship. The aim in restoring, repairing, and refinishing antiques is not to make them look like new but as
they would look if well taken care of from the time they were
made.

In addition to the damages done in the name of preservation,
there are the following: (1) cutting a piece down from a large
to small size; (2) using parts of a very damaged piece to make
another more elegant; (3) changing the shape of a table top;
(4) turning down a bed post or table leg to make it less clumsy;

(5) replacing usable damaged feet with new perfect ones;
(6) removing veneer or marquetry; (7) removing or adding
parts of a piece on the grounds that this will improve the style,
as, for example, taking the stretchers from a Queen Anne or
Chippendale chair to make it look more elegant; and (8) over-
refinishing. In order to get rid of paint or stain, the refinisher
may remove as much as an eighth of an inch of the outer surface to arrive at today's popular honey color. Think what
such drastic scraping would do to a veneered piece!

The only occasions for removing the finish of an old piece
are when the original finish is completely covered by a new
one, when the old one cannot be revived, or when there are
extensive restorations.

Be extraordinarily careful of how you repair and refinish
and also about whom you allow to repair and refinish for you.
Look out for the delicate surfaces, for the antique is its surface. Remember that your taste is totally unreliable the
moment it varies from that of the original maker of your
antique, whether it is high style or average, elegantly urbane
or provincially simple!

GLASS

In contrast to wood, glass has only two inherent defects.
One is its tendency to dull and exfoliate under certain conditions and the other to chip, crack, or break, often apparently
spontaneously. Glass will occasionally develop cracks from
the deforming effects of its own weight. It also develops chips
from the same cause. Old glass scratches quite readily.
Scratches can go right through the glass at a speed frequently
exceeding that of sound (as in cutting glass with a glass cutter).

Old glass is extraordinarily susceptible to damage from
changes in temperature. The temperature difference does not
need to be very great. A warm sun shining on one part of the
glass while the other is in the shade may do it, especially if
the piece is large. Atmospheric acids will attack the surface
of glass and cause it to flake off. The glass becomes cloudy
and is said to be sick. This chemical degradation is accelerated

where the glass is exposed to ultraviolet light. Glass sickness afflicts glass used for the storage of wines. Two pieces of glass in close contact under pressure will cement together. This causes bottle stopples to stick permanently. The same thing can occur when similar objects are nested in storage. Strong light may modify and sometimes startlingly change the color of glass.

Preventing the damage to which glass is susceptible is easy; not so the curing. To prevent glass from becoming sick, do not use it for storage of liquids. Remember to wash glass occasionally. Ancient (for example, Roman) glass cannot be washed without serious risk. Instead, use a dry or dampened camel's hair brush, or even a shaving brush. Handle it carefully and store in a dust-free place.

Repairs ?

If damage has occurred, what can be done to correct or repair it? Chips and scratches can be removed by polishing, but this is questionable practice and of dubious value. While you can cement broken pieces back together again, you cannot disguise the fact that the glass has been broken. It will never be as good as new from the standpoint of use.

There are in existence a number of cements that fulfill part of these requirements. For example, epoxy resin glues are stable, strong, transparent, and will adhere to nonporous substances. They do not make perfect surface contact and do not have refraction indices equal to glass. This is true, however, only for the present. The future may bring some process for permanent repair. Such processes are almost within our grasp. Perhaps by the time you read this it will be available.

While I would not, except for ancient glass and other types of comparable scarcity and difficulty of finding intact, recommend the purchase of mended glassware, I would equally strongly urge you, should you have the misfortune to break a piece, to glue it together and keep it, both because it is still valuable as a study specimen and because the time may come when it can be repaired in a more permanent fashion.

Sick glass can be cured if enough effort and time are spent on it and if the glass is not too sick. All that has to be done is to polish off the scaling surfaces. Fill the object with lead shot and a series of fine abrasives, using them in order from the coarsest to the finest. By tumbling the shot and abrasives about in the bottle long enough, you can finally eliminate the flaking that causes the glass to look sick.

CERAMICS

Ceramic wares are tougher than glass. Most chip easily, lose their enamel decoration, and discolor from continued use. Break and stain they will. Otherwise, they do not deteriorate. Methods of care are identical with those for glass, with some additions. For one thing, overglaze decoration may wear off, especially where pieces are stacked without protection or where they are exposed to strong soaps or ammonia. Do not hang cups from hooks unless you want the handles broken off. Glazes also crack on sudden changes of temperature, with a resultant train of unpleasant effects. First, the china may stain. Second, the glaze, broken into such tiny pieces, may come loose from its supporting body, and result in typical exfoliation. Third, the cracking allows moisture to enter the clay body and sometimes causes the piece to break or chip. It is therefore imperative to treat ceramic wares with loving care. Fragile, elaborate pieces can be cleaned with soft brushes (a shaving brush will do).

Damaged ceramic wares can be mended with rivets or cemented together with any of a variety of cements. Missing pieces may be made of cement, glazes or chipped areas restored with paint and liquid (nonceramic) glazes. Chips or scuff marks can be filled with plastic wood or tile cement, filed or sanded smooth, painted over and glazed with some substances resembling lacquer.

The best repair is the ceramic repair. However, the difficulties of making ceramic repairs are sufficient to raise their cost to the point that they are warranted only by the extraordinary value of a piece, historic, aesthetic, or

sentimental. For all practical purposes, a ceramic piece
once damaged is damaged for good except in the case of
small chips or a little scuffing. Stains may be removed by
soaking the piece in a strong bleach for some time. However,
the piece cannot be used again, as it will stain on its first
use. Do not buy damaged ceramic ware with the notion of
having it repaired, for the expense is unwarranted. Finally,
I would like to caution you against willfully defacing china and
glass by boring holes in it in order to make lamps. This is
inexcusable vandalism.

METALS

Things made of metal seldom warp, twist, split, crack,
bend, or break under ordinary conditions, though they _may_
do any of these things. They are more likely to tarnish or
corrode.

All metals save gold and platinum tarnish. The first stage
in the tarnishing of silver, copper, brass, tin, pewter, and
lead is caused by sulphur-containing gases in the air.

One way of prevention is to make sure that the air to which
the metals are exposed is free of sulphur, as is done in
museums with sealed cases. This is not practicable in a home,
where the objects displayed may even be used. Actually,
using metals helps to prevent tarnish from accumulating. For
little-used pieces, a coat of lacquer will delay tarnishing.

Regular cleaning will take care of tarnish. Most metal
polishes are good and are a necessity if you want the surfaces
to remain bright. The loss of metal from cleaning is so slight
that it is usually discounted. Where the object is very worn or
the tarnish very heavy, you can resort to electrochemical
means. In a weak acid such as lemon juice or a weak alkaline
solution such as you can get with soda bicarbonate, and a
metal such as aluminum, the aluminum will replace the silver
in the tarnish. Lemon juice and carpet tacks will clean small
objects of silver or copper. Larger pieces can be placed in a
glass pan on crumpled aluminum foil, and covered with water
to which bicarbonate of soda has been added and boiled.

They will come out clean, ready for polishing. This method is not to be used on silver-plated ware of any kind and won't work on pewter or tin. The one method you should never use is buffing by machine.

Corrosion is the end result of tarnishing. The metal becomes not just dull and discolored; its surface is rough, scaly, and deformed, the body of the material erose. Although all metals will corrode and ultimately end in compounds that do not resemble metal in any way, the most susceptible is iron, with tin a good second. Tinned sheet iron is perhaps the most vulnerable, since both its coating of tin and its core rust readily. Except for these, the treatment for corrosion is electrochemical as mentioned above. For iron and tin, there are elaborate methods for reversing the oxidation processes, but these take considerable time and are impractical for private persons. Iron can be kept from rusting by keeping air away from it. In practice, this means polishing and covering it with a film of oil from time to time. Iron so treated will rust very slowly if at all. This treatment is not practical for pewter, tin, and tinned ironware. Pewter can be cleaned and polished as suggested under <u>Metals</u>. Objects of tin can be kept bright by cleaning and when not subjected to heating, can be protected with lacquer.

Tin plate and iron are also often protected with paint. Painted tin has a tendency to deteriorate both in regard to its material and decoration. If the paint is kept from being damaged, the surface beneath is likely to be protected. Once in a while, the tin does go to pieces under the paint. Here there is little hope of saving the decoration. The decoration itself can best be treated as is painted wood. (See p. 000ff.)

Care of pewter requires that it be kept from the fire, because it melts so easily. This applies to soldered tinware as well. Metal objects may come apart at the soldered joints. To prevent this, be careful how you use such pieces, even though they can be soldered together again.

Bronze or tin disease may manifest itself in green or blue patinated bronze. The surface boils up, becomes spongy, and flakes off. Untreated, this disease will destroy the object. Since it most often attacks patinated bronzes, the remedy

would seem to be the removal of the patina. But the patina
is one of the charms of old bronze, and removing it does not
always cure the trouble. Keeping the metal in a very dry place
will help; the cure is electrochemical, done by professionals.

Finally, plated metals, including Sheffield, should be used
sparingly. Store them in a box or bag containing gum camphor
to delay tarnishing. In case the plate wears off here and there,
it is under no circumstances to be replated.

Chapter X

REPAIRING AND REFINISHING FURNITURE

Repairing antique furniture has always been a happy field of activity for the amateur craftsman. This is partly because it is assumed that almost anyone can scrape, paint, sandpaper, and shellac or varnish. If it doesn't come out right, someone else can fix it. Thus, one is not discouraged by the fear that a false move may be fatal. Besides, consider the fine work done by persons without professional training in this field.

Unfortunately, these encouraging assumptions are not true. One false move _can_ be fatal. It is because so many false moves are made, by professionals as well as amateurs, that I feel it important to include very specific directions for the repair and refinishing of furniture. All too many antiques have been ruined by incorrect repairs and refinishing jobs. Of the two, the refinishing is more deadly to the furniture. Before you refinish, consider whether it is really necessary. Often cleaning and waxing plus a little touching up here and there may save the work of refinishing and avoid risks.

REPAIRS

Regluing Joints

The difference between a repair and a restoration is that in a repair you have all the parts, although damaged, while in a restoration some parts are missing. The most common repair required in antique furniture is regluing. If the joint has come completely apart, the problem is simple. If the joint is merely loose, it will have to be taken apart to be reglued. Where the joint is pinned, remove the pins and take out the tenon. Use a dowel of slightly smaller dimensions than the pin and pound out the pins from the inside, since they usually taper. The mortise and tenon is the only joint regularly pinned. Doweled joints and miter and butt joints are usually glued.

If only one joint is loose, try to spring it apart without breaking other portions. Not infrequently, the tenon has pulled apart with the grain, leaving one piece inside the mortise. To repair such a joint, you must extract the other piece. Cautiously, with a wood chisel, break the old glue loose. If the tenon breaks, keep all the pieces.

Remove all old glue from both mortise and tenon with a hook-type scraper, or use a cabinet scraper. Sharpen it as follows: use a file and true up the edge at right angles to the face of the scraper. Finish with an oilstone and polish with a white Arkansas stone. With a polished steel rod, put a small sharp thin burr on both edges by rubbing on the trued edge. Clean the mortise with a chisel or a cabinet scraper small enough to fit inside the mortise. Now, reassemble the joint to see how it fits. If the tenon is loose, a shim made of a small sliver of wood should be placed in the mortise. Be careful that the shim does not make the tenon too thick and split the mortise.

With the shim in place, mark and bore pinholes in it. If the tenon has come apart, this must be fixed first. Put glue on the split portions and clamp together with a small C clamp (Fig. 90) and blocks. The blocks will not stick to the work if paper is put between block and work. When the glue has set, reassemble. Put glue in the mortise and on all contact surfaces. Put the pegs in place before you clamp the work together. Put "C" clamps across the mortise to forestall splitting when the bar clamps are tightened (Figs. 91, 92). When the clamps are tight, place the piece on a level surface and adjust the angles of the clamps until it does not rock.

Do not attempt to drill out pegs that cannot be removed, but work glue into the joint without taking it apart. You can try, with a flexible thin blade such as a palette knife, to work glue back into the joint, until the joint resists efforts to move it. Put clamps across the sides of the mortise. Clamp these and then the clamps across the joint. Epoxy glue may make it hold. Or bore a 1/32 hole or holes into the mortise from inside the piece. Then use a pastry tube to force glue in through the holes

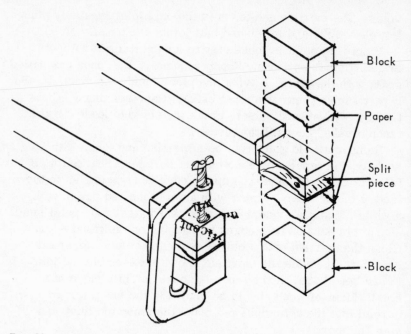

Fig. 90 — Method of using "C" clamp to repair split tenon

until it appears at the joint. Then clamp. Third, use a glued block on the inside of the piece. The block will hold better if it is made of two pieces glued together. Make the block with either a half-lap and miter or with a gain and miter (Figs. 93, 94). Fit the block very carefully into the corner in which it is to go and then clamp it tightly. This type of block permits side-to-side gluing at all contact points.

Corner Blocks

Perhaps the joint you are repairing was made with corner blocks. If they seem to be tight on one side, place a thin shim between the corner block and rail against which it is to fit, and tighten the clamps.

The ornamental corner blocks between leg and skirting are often just glued in place, hence easily lost. Occasionally, they are also nailed. If these are still held by the nails, you

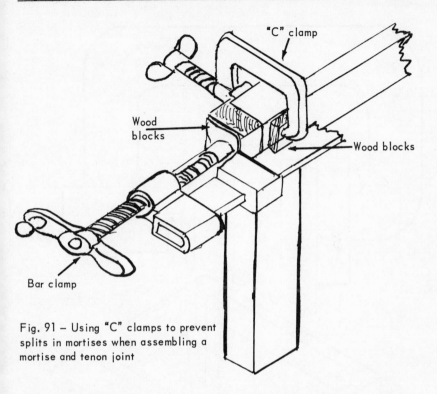

Fig. 91 – Using "C" clamps to prevent splits in mortises when assembling a mortise and tenon joint

can remove them before regluing—or better, leave them alone, clean out the glue, drive the nails home, and clamp. Where these nailed blocks help to hold the piece rigid and are mortised into the leg and nailed to the seat rail, you should remove the blocks before regluing.

Other Glued Blocks

When the glue lets go on both sides, the block will fall off. Cleaning and regluing is simple except where the block is hard to get at, as when it is deep inside a casepiece. Here you must remove the block and replace it. Glued joints, in order to be strong, must be glued under pressure. If the back boards are in place, they should be left that way. Clamp the sides of the piece together in two places, protecting the surface with wood blocks. With bar clamps, clamp the top

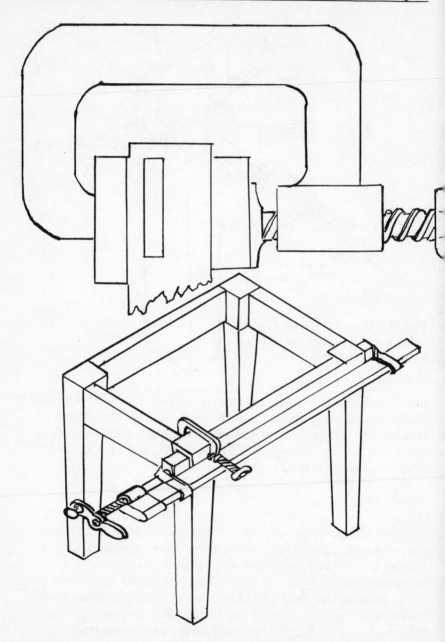

Fig. 92 – Use of "C" clamp across mortise to prevent splitting on assembly

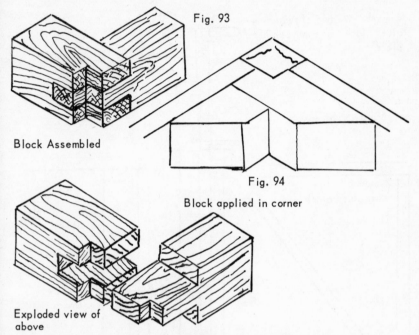

Fig. 93

Block Assembled

Fig. 94

Block applied in corner

Exploded view of
above

Constructing and installing a glued block to reinforce a loose mortise and
tenon joint when the joint cannot be disassembled

onto the sides, placing heavy boards between clamp and top.
Cut a piece of wood not quite long enough to reach diagonally
from the block to the base of the piece. Then cut two wedges.
Put glue on the block, put it in place, put the stick against it,
insert the wedges facing each other, and tap them until you
have sufficient pressure on the block. Variations of this technique will enable you to reach any inaccessible place to glue
blocks or anything else that needs gluing (Fig. 95).

If the top is completely off, the problem is simpler. First,
glue the block to the sides individually with "C" clamps. Then
when set, glue the top onto the blocks, using one bar clamp over
each block, tightening until you see a little glue forced out of the
joint. If you do not have enough clamps, run the clamps
vertically from top to base with a two-by-four between clamps
and work. If, on examination, one block is not surrounded by
a rim of extruded glue, drive a wedge between the two-by-four
and the top directly above the block until the glue appears.

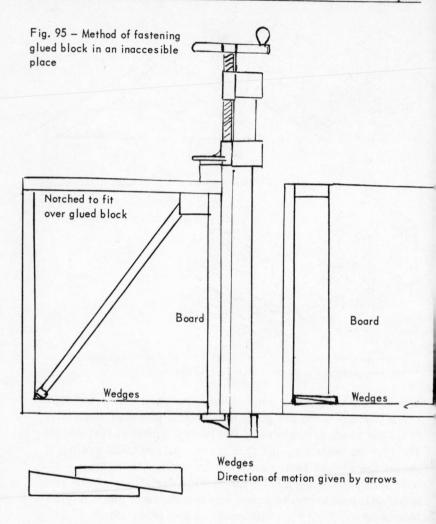

Fig. 95 — Method of fastening glued block in an inaccesible place

Notched to fit over glued block

Board

Board

Wedges

Wedges

Wedges
Direction of motion given by arrows

Miters

Since miters are not strong, they are often doweled, dove-tailed, splined, or most commonly nailed together to add strength. In good furniture, they are glued to a supporting block. Miters are often very difficult to glue with clamps; as you tighten the clamp, the pressure moves the part along the miter and does not hold. Adjust the clamp to one end and very

slightly tighten the clamp until the piece starts to slip. Now
quickly place a clamp at right angles to the first and clamp it.
By taking up a little on each clamp, you can get the miter to
close exactly at the corner (Fig. 97). If the mitered parts are
glued against a rectangular block for support, apply glue to the
miter and the block, which is then clamped at right angles to
meet the other mitered piece. With the miters thus prevented
from moving, clamping them is easy (Fig. 96). Still another
method is to use a spline. Cut a groove, stopping it short of
either edge of the boards to be mitered. Make the groove
perpendicular to the miter joint surface on each board. Cut a
piece of wood to fit in the groove. This spline is slipped into
the slots thus made. It is an elegant repair on antique pieces
(Fig. 98). Neither miters nor corner blocks should be nailed.

Butt Joints and Tongue and Groove

Regluing butt and tongue and groove joints presents no
problem. Clean off the glue and clamp together. Since the
clamps often cause this type of joint to buckle under pressure,
the boards should be clamped across the joint (Fig. 99). Where
butt joints are used for the sides of case pieces and some
table tops, especially those of tripod tables, butt-jointed
together and supported on battens, the only way to close such
joints is to rebuild the piece—and this is not acceptable. .

The best and most acceptable thing is to leave the joint
alone. The next is to fill the joint with appropriately colored
beeswax. The crack is almost invisible. The third is to fill
the crack with a thin piece of wood. This last job does not
effect a permanent repair because the older pieces and/or
the fillers shrink and become loose more often than not.

However, if you decide on this kind of repair, here is the
way it is usually done. Cut the filler from slightly thicker
stock than the boards between which it is to go and so that it
has a slightly wedge-shaped cross section. Now put the glue
on and, using a block, tap it down as far as it will go. There
should be a small portion of it rising above the old surface.
While the glue is setting, sand this down with a sandpaper
block. If anything will close the gap, this should.

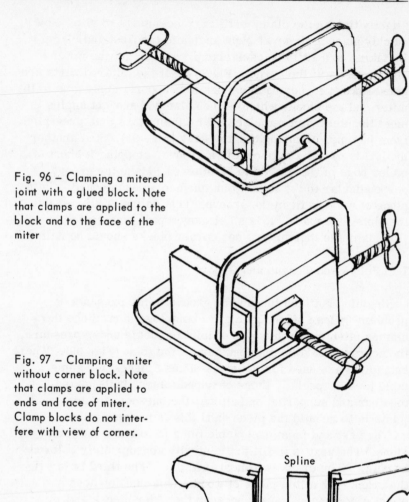

Fig. 96 – Clamping a mitered joint with a glued block. Note that clamps are applied to the block and to the face of the miter

Fig. 97 – Clamping a miter without corner block. Note that clamps are applied to ends and face of miter. Clamp blocks do not interfere with view of corner.

Spline

Fig. 98 – Using a spline in a mitered joint. Note that the direction of the dado for the spline is perpendicular to the face of the miter not parallel to face of the wood, and the grain of the spline runs across the joint. Dado does not run to ends as shown. This is only to show location of dado.

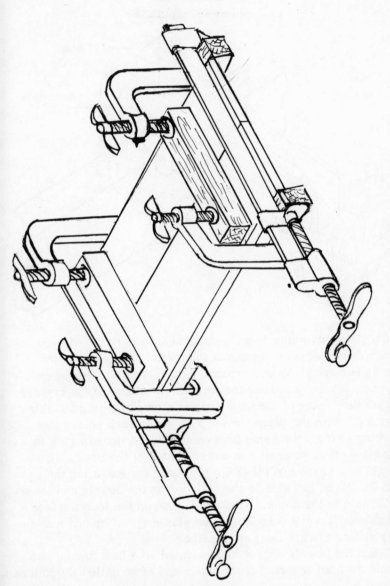

Fig. 99 — Method of preventing butt joint from buckling in the clamps

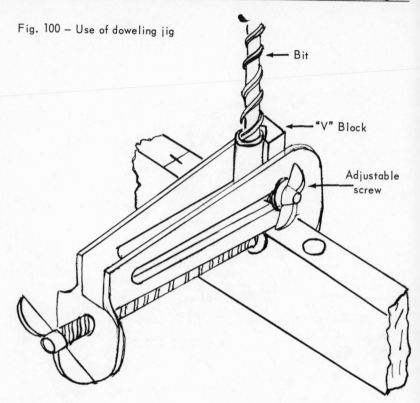

Fig. 100 – Use of doweling jig

Bit

"V" Block

Adjustable
screw

To keep butt joints from opening again where boards are glued edge to edge, you can put in dowels. To get them to line up perfectly and be perpendicular, clamp the two pieces together and mark across the joint the locations of the centers. Locate the center of the edge and set a marking gauge at this distance. With the gauge, make a cross on each center line, marking in from the same face each time. A doweling jig is now set so that its center is on the center of the cross. With the aid of a brace and bit (Fig. 100) bore the holes for the dowels. Next, put glue in the holes or on the dowels and insert the dowels in the holes. Then place glue on the joint surface and assemble very quickly, as the glue may set up and make it very difficult to get the joint together.

When the boards cannot be separated, the best device is a double dovetail inserted from inside and often called a Dutchman.

Fig. 101 – "Dutchman"

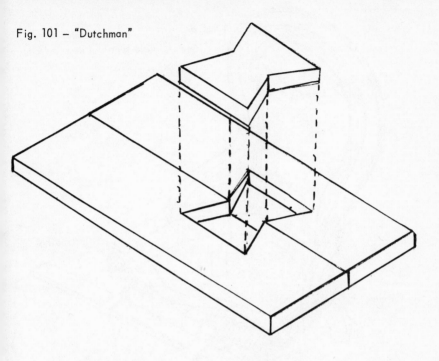

Shims for
Loose Dovetail

Fig. 102 – Dovetail repairs

When dovetail is
broken

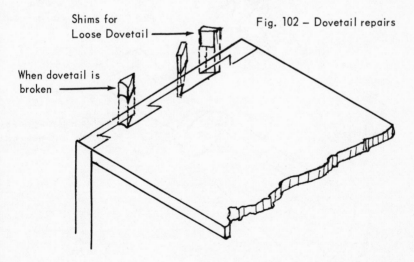

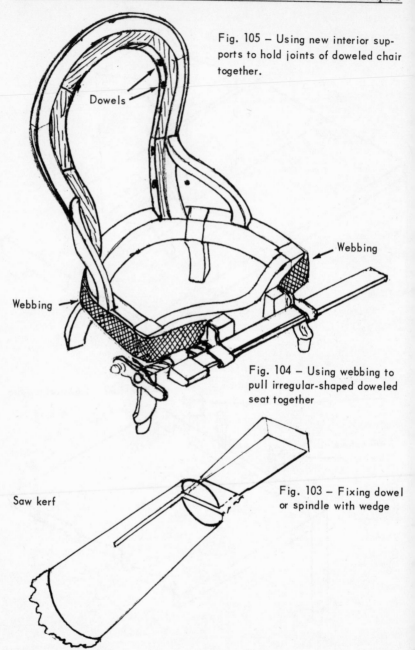

Fig. 105 – Using new interior supports to hold joints of doweled chair together.

Dowels

Webbing

Webbing

Fig. 104 – Using webbing to pull irregular-shaped doweled seat together

Saw kerf

Fig. 103 – Fixing dowel or spindle with wedge

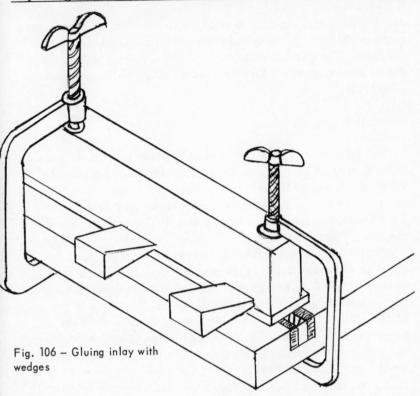

Fig. 106 — Gluing inlay with
wedges

Use a block about 5/8" x 1/2" x 1-1/2". Mark the center line
on this piece, then lay out the dovetails with the small ends
together. Use an angle of about fifteen degrees for the dovetail.
Set the dovetail block so that its center (the narrowest portion)
is in the joint line. Mark the size of the Dutchman, using it as
a pattern. Marking should be done with a knife held against
the edge of the block. Use a 1/2" firmer chisel to make the
socket. Cut it about 9/16" deep. Place glue on the bottom of
the dovetailed piece. Tap the block in and forget about it
(Fig. 101).

Dovetail joints in a piece of furniture were not usually glued
in place. When properly fitted, they hold without glue. Sometimes they work loose. If they have been allowed to remain
loose, constant use thereafter will have worn the edges. In
this case, the dovetails have to be glued. Apply the glue,

reassemble, and clamp. In addition to the glue, the piece may require shimming. Assemble the joint and insert wedges in the gaps. The grain should run the same way as the socket. Shims should be placed on the sloping sides of the dovetail (Fig. 102).

Doweled Joints

The last type of joint that comes unglued is a dowel joint. Dowels may be part of the piece being doweled, as in a chair rung, or they may be separate pieces fitted into holes in each of the pieces to be joined. The chair-rung type of dowel is very common. Rungs, spokes, and spindles are all joined to chairs in this manner.

When loose, one solution is to saw a slot into the dowel, equal to about the depth of the socket. Insert a small wedge in the saw kerf. When glue is applied and the dowel driven home, the wedge forces the dowel against the sides of the socket and helps to hold it there (Fig. 103). This is the best way to correct the trouble, but it is not always effective because the wedge can expand the rung in only two directions and the wedge may split the rung. When the rung cannot be made to hold, you can bore holes through the chair leg and into the dowel, preferably on the inside to almost the outside, and then put in dowel pins.

Pieces of doweled furniture may have been nailed together in exactly the places I have suggested placing wooden pins. Nails must, with whatever difficulty, be gotten out. If finish nails have been used, you can often drive them through with an appropriate-sized nail set, or if you can't drive them through, you can drive them far enough to see where the point is and then drive them out. Where the nails have been driven into the seat, boring or drilling a hole on either side of the nail will enable you to get the jaws of a small, round-nose pliers around the nail and pull it out. There are plier-like nail pullers that can grasp the nail and pull it out also. Both of these methods damage the piece, but this cannot be helped when the piece cannot be used without repair. The use of a separate dowel carries us out of the antique period for the most part, but it is just as well to see how to fix these things.

The swelling curves and odd shapes of the furniture of the 1850's make it difficult to clamp together when it comes loose, as it inevitably does. The dowels have to be removed and replaced with others just a bit larger. If the dowel is scored with a saw, the glue will hold better. You can use a strip of webbing, clamped or nailed onto two substantial blocks. The length of the band should be such, that when wrapped around the thing to be glued, it leaves a 5-8" gap. Across this gap you can run two bar clamps. As you tighten these clamps, all joints will close (Fig. 104).

For regluing Victorian furniture, which was frequently composed of pieces of wood glued together before it was shaped, you need to make an elaborate jig. It often requires ingenuity to see how to clamp the pieces together so that they will not slip out of line. One device is to clamp blocks to the odd-shaped pieces and then run the clamps from one set of blocks to the other. Once you have made this setup, you can get the joints to close. After the joints are glued, I recommend putting a spline across the joint. The slot for the spline should be cut from the inside, both to strengthen the joint and to be inconspicuous. The original joints were never doweled to begin with and are thus not very strong when reglued without a spline. If the chair back or seat is overstuffed and the inner surface out of sight, dowels can be run across these joints to hold them on even better. New pieces of wood can be shaped to fit the inner contours and glued and doweled to the original frame (Fig. 105).

Veneering, Cross Banding, Etc.

Regluing applied pieces like moldings and crossbandings, or pieces of marquetry and inlay, is extremely difficult. Where the missing piece is readily accessible to clamps, there is no problem. When a metal inlay comes loose, it frequently proves very recalcitrant. The wood in which it is placed may have shrunk. If the metal has become too large for its location, it will have to be cut down before it can be clamped in place. Here is another place to use epoxy glue.

Clamping the inlay in place may prove to be a difficult job; it is hard to get an even pressure throughout its length. The best way (outside of a veneering press) is to cover the inlay with a strip of wood not much wider than the inlay—a piece of 1/4" plywood is good here. Then clamp onto it a heavy piece of wood such as a two-by-four. Between this and the plywood, you can insert wedges at frequent intervals to insure an even pressure. If the surface is curved, you must cut a jig to fit accurately against the surface (Fig. 106).

If an edge of a large loose area can be lifted, scrape the surface free of old glue, insert fresh glue, and press the piece down by hand or with a roller, working from the secure to the loose edge to force out excess glue and air bubbles. If the piece will not lie flat because there is no longer room for it due to shrinkage of the core, some of the veneer will have to be removed. Allow the edge to overlap the joint and then carefully cut it along the joint. It frequently happens that the loose veneer forms a blister with no exposed edge because the veneer is too big for the space it is occupying. Separate one veneer from another to get an edge. Now, push down that veneer forming the background, and cut around the pattern at a slight angle to make up for the knife cut.

If the veneer is solid, you will have to cut the blister, perhaps in several places. Make the cut along the natural figure. Once you have the pieces flat, cut out the excess, following the figure.

Clamping veneer if the area is large presents a problem. Weights piled on the veneer will help to hold it down. One of the best weights is sand. The sand can be placed in a sack or in a frame of wood about ten inches deep. With the veneer in place, the glue will usually hold it from springing up. Place the sand over the spot, pile weights on the sand. This will distribute the pressure evenly over the surface. In using sand on curved surfaces, you have to remember to place the sand and weights in such a way that the force applied is perpendicular to the surface.

To correct a warped, buckled, twisted, and shrunken core and its torn and lifted veneering is extremely difficult, unless you force live steam into the veneer to loosen it and then remove it in order to fix the core. The best you can do is to dampen the surface with wet sawdust or sand. If you can't get

the veneer loose easily, don't try. The glue can be got to the
core through the veneer by forcing it through under pressure.
If the core is broken and the veneer with it, reassemble the
core. Let the veneer overlap and correct the trouble by cutting around the figure.

When serious warping has developed because of the relation
between veneer and core, the veneer has to be removed from
the core or else the piece must be left as is. If you cannot get
the veneer loose, cut it away with a fine saw. The core must
be clamped flat, at which point the veneer can be sawn loose.
Straighten out the core and reglue the veneer. This technique
I would recommend as a last resort only.

Breaks

Next to regluing, the most common repairs needed in furniture are repairs of breaks.

The commonest breaks at joints involve the breaking of the
mortise and tenon joint. If the mortise is merely split open,
it can be glued back together. If you clamp it well, the joint
usually holds as well as it did before. If one part of the mortise
has broken off, this may also be replaced and is fairly strong.
Occasionally, the mortise is so badly damaged or a piece has
been lost, so the portions containing it will have to be discarded. Here a new piece will have to be added.

The best joint for this type of addition so that it will show as
little as possible is a scarf joint. To make it, cut off the damaged portion on a long bevel of about three to one. Next, cut a
similar piece, very slightly thicker and a little larger than the
rail. Fit the joint accurately. Lay out and drill two dowel
holes. Assemble, dry-clamp and check. Be careful that the
piece is straight with the rail in both directions, then apply
glue and assemble. When the glue has set, work the new surface down to the old cautiously. Cut to the correct length, cut
the new mortise or mortises and reassemble the piece.

When the tenon is broken, the problem is simpler. If the
tenon has been broken off completely, you should cut a mortise
in the piece of wood where the tenon was. Lay this out carefully—if possible, slightly larger than the old tenon. It is

advisable here to clamp the blocks across the stick in both directions so that the wood will not split. The mortise should be at least two inches deep. Bore a hole or holes down to the proper depth with a brace and bit or a power drill. When the drilling is complete, use a proper-size chisel 1/4" to 1/2" to clear away the remaining wood. Do not pry against the edges of the mortise in making the chisel cuts or you will mash them.

Now, fit in a block of wood long enough to serve as a tenon also. You should have a little extra wood so that when the glue has set the new tenon can be fitted accurately to the old mortise. Remember that it should fit tight at top and bottom but not on the sides. During assembly and gluing, it is well to have clamps across the mortise in both directions (Fig. 107, cf. 91, 92).

When dovetail joints break, the damage is usually to the pins. If pieces are missing, you will have to make shims as above, only this time the direction of the grain has to be the same as that of the pins. Wedge-shaped or square pieces can be glued in the disassembled joint and the dovetails recut.

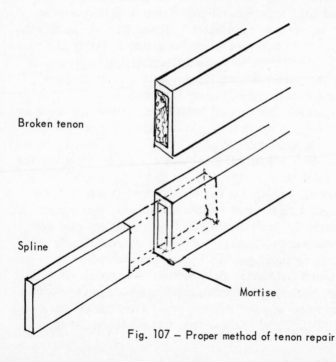

Broken tenon

Spline

Mortise

Fig. 107 – Proper method of tenon repair

If the break extends the whole width of the board and is exactly at the line of the dovetails or very close to it, the board will have to be repaired first with a doweled scarf joint and the dovetails recut.

To lay out dovetails, square the end perfectly, then clamp it to the piece containing the socket. Mark the position of the wide ends of the dovetail, using a knife. With the knife, square the lines across the edge. With the marking gauge set to the depth of the dovetail, score a line on both sides of the board. With an adjustable angle square set to the angle of the socket, lay out the lines with a knife. Do this on both sides. Now take a dovetail saw or a back saw with virtually no set on the teeth and cut along the lines. Cut right outside the lines. The inside pieces across the grain are removed with a chisel, cutting from both sides.

If the directions have been followed carefully, the dovetails will fit the first time. Accurate layout and caution are all you need. If the dovetailed piece was a drawer side, you will need to recut the dado for the drawer bottom in the new portion. This should be done last with the dovetail saw by making two saw kerfs in line with the dado in the old piece and cleaning out the space between the kerfs with a chisel.

Another type of joint frequently in need of repair is a table joint. Sometimes the nose of the quarter-round molding has split off. It is worth while, however, to investigate why it split off. If the splitting was due to loosening of the hinges, the replacement of the hinges in the wrong way, or the wrong kind of hinges, correct this fault. Table hinges are made with one valve longer than the other. The position of the pin is reversed as compared with other hinges.

If the screw holes have worn out due to rusting of the hinges and wear and tear, the screws may have to be replaced. The holes can then be filled with glued pieces or plastic wood. Dowels can be inserted from the edge of the piece to hold the screws. Drill a hole of about 1/4" diameter down from the edge through the screw hole, parallel to the face of the leaf. Insert dowels and glue. When the glue has set, drill lead holes for screws and replace the hinges (Fig. 108).

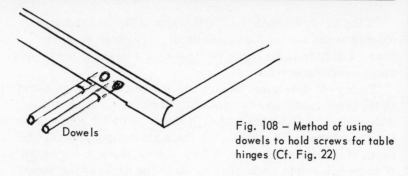

Dowels

Fig. 108 – Method of using dowels to hold screws for table hinges (Cf. Fig. 22)

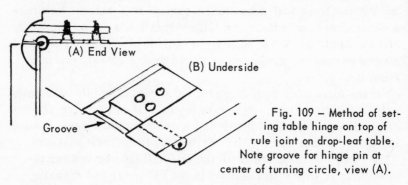

(A) End View

(B) Underside

Groove

Fig. 109 – Method of setting table hinge on top of rule joint on drop-leaf table. Note groove for hinge pin at center of turning circle, view (A).

In setting a table hinge, the short flap goes on the top, the long one on the leaf. The pin has to be set in a groove cut in the top. The groove should be so placed that the center of the hinge pin will be at the center of the circle, one quarter of which forms the quarter-round nose of the rule joint (Fig. 109).

Broken dowels where the dowel is part of a rung or spoke, are usually broken off down into the rung or spoke. The spokes can be repaired in two ways, neither of them very satisfactory, but they are better than replacing the rung.

The first is simply to bore a hole for a dowel of as large a diameter as can be got, into the spoke or rung, without weakening it. If you get a good fit and clamp the dowel or spoke in two directions while it is being glued, the likelihood is that this repair will be satisfactory if the piece of furniture is not abused.

The other way is to glue the broken spindle together however you can, and then cut a slot about three inches long with the break in its center. The direction of this slot should be toward the greatest strain, that is, up and down in a rung, back

to front in a chair spindle. A spline is
made to fit in this slot. The piece is
clamped end to end and across the slot.
This again will usually hold, especially
if pinned (Fig. 110).

When the break is near the end, it is
best fixed with a dowel. The portion that
replaces the old dowel has to be the same
size. The piece that fits into the rung
should be as large as you can get. This
would normally be about 1/4" less than
the spoke.

Where the tacks used in upholstery
have damaged the rails to the degree that
the mortises are badly weakened, the
mortises can be reinforced by using corner blocks to hold the rails together at
the corners. If these are carefully fitted
against and doweled onto the legs from
above, the chair can be saved. Otherwise, the legs must have new mortised
ends fitted to them. Such rails require
new wood to be glued underneath for
fastening the upholstery. This is to be
preferred to replacing the seat rails. The
mortises may also be completely spoiled.
In this case, you must cut away the portion in the leg containing the mortise.
Mortise the leg to take a large tenon close
to the diameter of the leg. Then, in the
upper end of the new block, cut new mortises. This reconstruction is foolproof
and strong. The chief objection is that it
is drastic (Fig. 111).

Damaged (split) rails of cane-seat
chairs cannot really be fixed satisfactorily.
Just give up and, after gluing the split
together, use screws to reinforce it. Drill
holes in the portion toward the center of

Fig. 110 – Use of
Spline to repair a
broken chair spoke

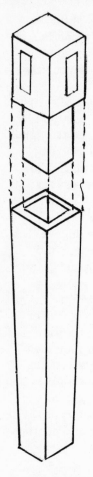

Fig. 111 – Mortise restoration at top of broken leg. New mortise is tenoned into mortise in old leg.

the seat, the size of the screw shank, then drill lead holes in the other portion. This inelegant job will hold the rails together.

The feet of some case pieces and legs of chairs are doweled onto the base or the seat rail. If breaks occur in the dowels, bore holes in the legs and insert new dowels. Where the sockets are too worn to hold the dowels properly, try plastic wood or even putty to hold the legs steady. You can also set a piece of wood into the rail, seat, or base and bore a new hole for the chair or table leg. The best out of poor choices is to wedge the leg as well as possible from below and then pin it by running a dowel in from the side to hold it.

Where the back top rail is made of bent wood as in hoop-back, bow-back, and New England arm Windsors, the bent piece may crack at the point of greatest bending. The best repair is the spline as described in connection with the repair of spokes. The spline will be strongest if made of several pieces assembled to fit the curve.

First, saw your plies of wood, making them a little less than 1/8" thick. The grain in the plies should run at right angles to each other. Make a jig of the same curvature as the spline is to be. Assemble the pieces and glue them up. Steaming will make them sufficiently flexible not to break on bending. In this case, it is better to bend and dry them before gluing (Fig. 112).

Once your spline is made, you can insert it in the slot cut for it. Glued down tightly into the slot with "C" clamps, this kind of repair is elegant and not too conspicuous. Wrapping such breaks with wire is both inelegant and impermanent.

Since in furniture of the 1840's the dowels are harder than the wood in which they are used, and also often placed in one

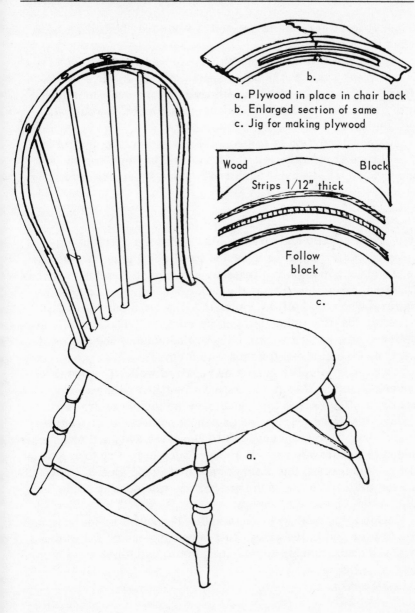

b.

a. Plywood in place in chair back
b. Enlarged section of same
c. Jig for making plywood

Wood   Block

Strips 1/12" thick

Follow
block

c.

a.

Fig. 112 — Repairing bent wood breaks, as in backs of Windsor chairs, with
a plywood piece

piece at least across the grain, the wood may be broken badly when the joint breaks.

Regluing a <u>broken</u> doweled joint is never very satisfactory. It can break again at the same spot. Rather, remove the dowels, glue the broken pieces together, and cut a mortise into each joint. Make a spline and reassemble. I would also peg the spline.

A second solution is to leave the dowel in place and run a 5/8" brace across the joint. This should be sunk into the surface and finished flush. Such repairs are acceptable and strong.

Splits

Checks usually end up as splits. When the check is discovered early, it can be arrested by slipping glue into the end of the check, clamping it together and using a Dutchman across it, either from the edge or the underside, whichever looks better. When the split is complete, it is not a bad idea to dowel or insert a spline across the joint too. The slot for the spline can be cut with a grooving or dado plane, for the most part, and the corners finished with a chisel.

Two kinds of splits cannot be repaired well. The one that occurs on sides of case pieces must be filled with wood or beeswax. The second type occurs in the middle of drawer dados. Since the original piece cannot be reglued, drawer linings will have to be cut back to above the dado and new pieces added to the drawer as well as new dados cut. Try to reglue the broken pieces, cut them down a little, and glue 3/4" by 1/2" pieces to the bottoms of the drawers as was done in some furniture of the eighteenth century.

Molded lips on drawers can split. If a saw kerf is made in the drawer and in the piece, thin veneering can be set in place with the grain running across the joint to reinforce it.

Cross Breaks

Cross breaks must be doweled for a strong repair. This can best be done by cutting mortises in each of the pieces to be put together and making a rectangular dowel to go in the space. It is standard for all broken legs, backs, pedestals, etc.

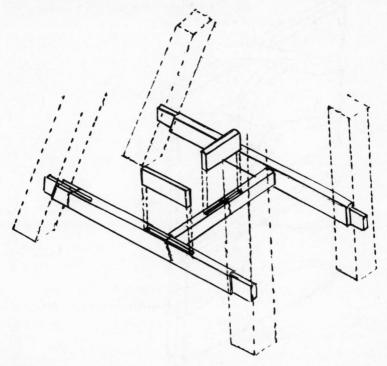

Fig. 113 – Use of splines in repairing
broken stretchers

Repairs of cross breaks in stretchers, rails, and slats will
be fixed with splines as described for spokes (Fig. 113). Cross
breaks occur at the ankles of cabriole legs, especially those
with very many curves, such as snake feet on candlestands and
tripod tables. These should be glued as described above for
broken spokes (Fig. 110). Cf. Fig. 119.

In general, the way to repair splits and cross breaks is to
save all of the outside possible and add the strengthening
pieces inside, where they can do their work without being seen.

Shattering

It often happens that a broken piece is completely shattered.
Repairing this requires another technique. First, assemble

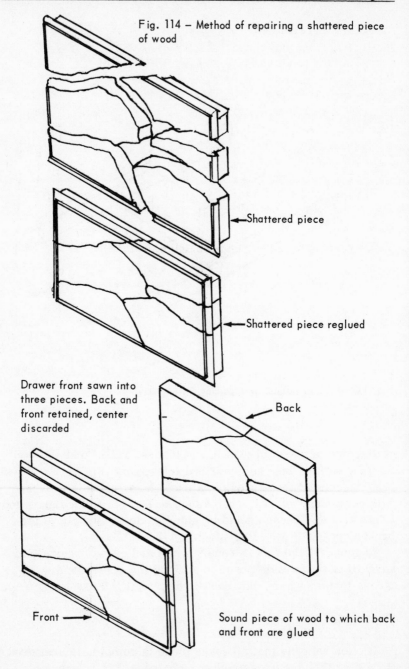

Fig. 114 – Method of repairing a shattered piece of wood

←Shattered piece

←Shattered piece reglued

Drawer front sawn into three pieces. Back and front retained, center discarded

Back

Front →

Sound piece of wood to which back and front are glued

the pieces and find how they go together. Once this is settled, shattered pieces may be glued temporarily to a board for support. Put paper in between to facilitate taking it apart. Apply paper again and another board on top. Each of these boards should be slightly smaller than the assembled piece. The result will now resemble a sandwich with the broken piece corresponding to the filler. Place blocks around the edges and apply clamps in both directions. The shattered piece is now fastened together, but the nature and multitude of the breaks and splits render it unlikely that it will stand any strain.

A backing of sound wood glued to it will perhaps be a little unsightly but it is superior in every way to a new piece. As an alternative, you can saw off the front face to a thickness of about 3/16". The back is treated similarly. Front and back can now be glued to a core thick enough to bring the piece to its original size.

Always try first to put splines across the breaks. In the event that this is impossible, resort to the last method of repair recommended for the drawer front (Fig. 114).

Correcting Warps

Many pieces of antique furniture have been ruined by hare-brained attempts to correct warping. This is disgusting, especially when the cure is so simple.

For a good repair job, take the warped board (if the finish is missing, it will help), and set it out in the sun with the concave side down. Wait until the board warps slightly the other way. Set it on two boards to lift it off the floor, pile weights on it to keep it flat, and let it dry for a week or so. This usually cures the warp. The underside can be protected with oil or finish.

When the board is warped one way on one end and the opposite way on the other, a hot iron or an infrared light will do the trick, provided you do not burn the wood. Place the heat on the convex side. Putting a damp cloth on the underside will hasten the job but is not necessary. Do one end first and then the other. Again, weight the leaf and cure it until it is stable. Oil it on the unfinished side. Do not be disturbed if the job has to be done twice—that will end it.

Restorations

Some of the above repairs require so much new lumber to make a piece serviceable that they lie on the borderline of restorations. Sometimes pieces are missing something to make them complete. When this occurs, the temptation is strong to restore them to their pristine glory.

Acceptable restorations are given in the chapter on furniture. Here are suggestions on how to make some of them. First, old wood should be used for all restorations. The best possible restoration of a part is the part from a similar piece. If you are unable to get old wood, the new wood should be worked with hand tools in the old manner.

Occasionally, a whole new piece has to be made, such as a fall front for a desk, doors for a cupboard, a base for a desk or chest of drawers. Here you don't know what the height, shape, contours, or construction were. All of these are serious restorations and should be undertaken only after study of other similar pieces. Construction should follow that suitable for the piece in question. Since each restoration is peculiar to the piece needing it, the directions that follow are general ones.

Finials and Feet

Before making a restoration, it is worth while considering what it will accomplish. Sometimes pieces are damaged rather than helped by restoration. Restoring a half inch to a worn down foot is a waste of time.

Replacing missing rungs is a different matter. You have the pattern of those missing in the ones that remain, and the chair needs them for strength. When the lost rungs or stretchers are elaborately turned or shaped, restore the most common form.

Many chairs otherwise in fine condition come down missing the finials. Replacing the finial, once a new one is made, is a relatively simple matter. The base of the finial must be cut to fit exactly. If the area to which the finial is to be applied is circular in section, it can be doweled on. If it is rectangular, a doweled scarf joint is the best.

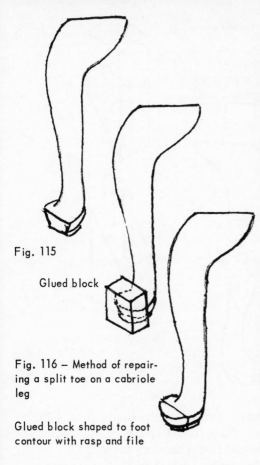

Fig. 115

Glued block

Fig. 116 — Method of repairing a split toe on a cabriole leg

Glued block shaped to foot contour with rasp and file

The doweled scarf joint is the most usual for lengthening legs. Restorations of feet are of two sorts. In the first instance, the leg is complete to the ground but a piece has been split off. The split part is made smooth and a block or blocks glued on. When the glue has set, the block is worked to the contour of the leg (Figs. 115, 116). In this case, you will have an indication of the size and contours. If the feet are missing, you have to use your imagination. An almost finished duplicate of leg and foot can be made and then joined to the original with a doweled scarf joint (Fig. 117).

I prefer another method, although it is more difficult. Cut a mortise in the original piece. Where the face of the joint is normally square to it against the shoulders of the tenons on the new piece, bring them to a feather edge. The new piece will have its shoulders brought to a corresponding slope. This joint is stronger than a scarf joint and discards none of the old surface. Always make the new piece 1/16" to 1/8" larger than the old piece and work the new surface down to the old. Never touch the old (Fig. 118).

Many restorers and dealers prefer to replace a damaged leg entirely. This has the advantage of not showing a joint,

Fig. 117 – Scarf joint used in repair of
broken leg

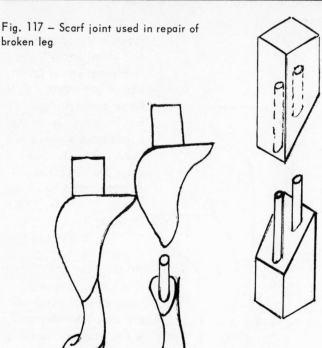

since there is none to show. Better let the joints show a little
than discard the old part. Plain or elaborate, a scarf joint
is almost imperceptible, and that's the way it should be.
Restorations should be detectable, but they don't have to be
obvious.

Drawer Lips, Linings, and Back Splats

A common kind of damage is the chewing up of drawer lips.
Restorations of only the damaged portions are not detrimental
to the piece; replacing the whole lip is. To make this repair,
plane or saw off just enough of the damaged surface to get a
smooth bed. On this bed, glue a block of wood. If you want,
you can cut a saw kerf in the drawer and then in the block, and
join them with a spline.

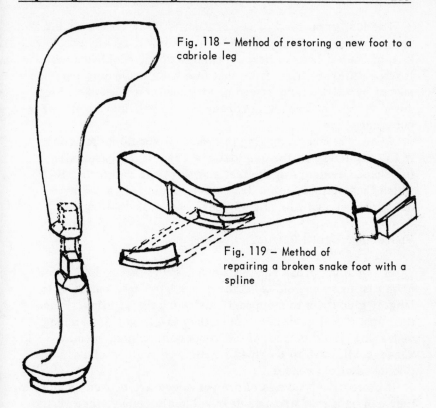

Fig. 118 – Method of restoring a new foot to a cabriole leg

Fig. 119 – Method of repairing a broken snake foot with a spline

In replacing drawer linings, it is well to see whether this is necessary. Where the lining has been damaged, repairs are possible as described above. Sometimes, the drawer lining is only worn. Cutting a piece of wood to fit under the side of the drawer and filling in the worn space is a good plan. Glue it in place after fitting. When drawer slides are worn, they should not be replaced but turned. This can usually be accomplished by taking the slide from the right side, turning it over, and using it on the left.

Occasionally, the back splat of a chair is so hopelessly damaged as to demand replacement. If you have the original, use it for a pattern. If not, you must invent one. Try to follow the form suggested by the rest of the chair and keep the restoration as simple as you can.

The last great need of restoration is that of bases or bracket
feet. Traces on the underside of a piece will be a clue to the
kind of base it had. A bracket base with corner blocks will
leave a different trace from that of a base made with legs connected by skirting, mortised and tenoned into the legs. Legs
doweled into the base with corner blocks will leave still different traces.

When it comes to making the base, it should be fastened
in the same way as the original one was. If the base calls
for shaped contours of the feet and skirting, remember to
finish these either with a draw shave or chisels and knives,
not with rasp and file. Never leave saw cuts showing.

Veneering, Cross Banding, Beading

In replacing cross banding or veneering that has fallen off
or gotten lost, use old wood for cross bandings, cut them to
length, glue them to a support, and work the profiles. Remove
the support and glue them where they are to go. In patching
veneering on old pieces, if old veneer is lacking, modern
veneers will have to be glued together to make up the greater
thickness of old veneer.

If protective beadings of drawer edges are broken or chipped,
they can be turned around. If missing altogether, they should
be replaced. For this purpose, 1 1/8" by 1/8" stock of the
proper wood is required. Round it on the front edge and
miter it at the corners. Glue and nail it in place.

Making the New Look Old

Now, when old furniture has been properly restored, it is
serviceable, but the new work sticks out like a sore thumb.
Restoration involves so much work even on old wood that the
additions are considerably different in color from the wood
they are supposed to match. Stains must be used to make them
match. Use commercial oil stains similar to paints. Color
tones are named for the woods they are intended to match,
such as red or dark mahogany, cherry, maple, light or dark
oak.

You can also use alcohol or water-soluble dyes in a wide assortment of colors. These are described as Bismarck brown (red mahogany), nigrosine (black), walnut (walnut), yellow (maple) and green. They give a good choice of colors, tints, and shades. These color the wood unevenly, emphasizing irregularity in grain or porosity unlike the uniform color of age. In addition, they fade.

Another method of aging uses such chemicals as ammonium dichromate, chromic acid, picric acid, sulphuric acid, hydrochloric acid, potassium permanganate, and a combination of lead acetate and dichromate to color the wood. On most mahoganies, dichromate will develop the natural color very quickly. The dilution and length of time on the wood will control the depth of the stain. Chromates will also tend to deepen the color of cherry, maple, and white walnut (butternut). The chromic acids tend to yellow all woods, as does picric acid. Picric will develop a deep yellow color on any organic substance, including the skin. Hydrochloric acid tends to deepen the color of any wood. Potassium permanganate and lead acetate combined with a chromate both color by the same process. The permanganate decomposes on contact with the wood, depositing microscopic particles of manganese dioxide within the wood. The colors obtained are suitable for maple, mahogany, walnut, oak, pine, chestnut, and beech. Lead acetate and a chromate make a yellow color suitable for French walnut, maple, cherry, pear, apple, satinwood, and holly. The wood is first coated with a solution of lead acetate, then with the chromate to develop a yellow color within the wood. Citric acid added to the wood, which is then heated, will darken most woods.

Chestnut, oak, cherry, walnut, and mahogany, particularly the last three, color up very rapidly when exposed to strong sunlight. It does not require a great deal of time before the color comes close to matching the old. Very often an oxidizing agent, such as peroxide, can develop the color. Peroxide usually bleaches, but it can assist in deepening the color. Heating the woods with infrared lamps and hot irons or dipping them in hot sand will also develop color. Using ultraviolet light on wood will change its color and will even invalidate the use of ultraviolet light as a test for age. For the amateur, the sun, hot iron, and sand are practical.

A fifth method is to introduce transparent colors into the varnish. After the wood has had one coat of finish or varnish, you can tell pretty well how the colors of the old and new wood differ. While the varnish is still wet, you can introduce transparent color over the new areas until you get a match. With an oil polish, you can introduce colors into the oil. You can introduce alcohol-soluble colors into French polish.

The dyes and chemical stains can also be used on bare wood, but will not stand up under close scrutiny. Heat treatment will also color, but leaves a detectable new surface.

Any of the ways described will conceal repairs from casual observation but not from critical examination, which is what is wanted in an honest restoration. Use the chemicals cautiously, use heat and sunlight lavishly, and correct any irregularities with varnish or other finish.

Refinishing

A resplendent finish has often concealed faults of material, construction, and workmanship. Antique dealers often put a brilliant new surface on their antiques to convince you of their importance. Unfortunately, this finish has often been achieved at considerable cost to the antique and more often conceals unacceptable restorations and repairs.

Perhaps these are reasons why you should do your own refinishing, as many collectors do. Yet it is in refinishing that most of the damage to antique furniture is done. Often the dilapidated old finish is worth saving, as in the obvious case where it comprises a painted decoration. The following techniques will help you decide whether or not to refinish.

Renewing Old Finishes

Dusting, followed by gentle washing with a mild soap and water, will do quite a lot toward renewing an old finish. If the surface looks good when wet, it will look good varnished or shellacked. If, after the first washing, the surface still looks dull and grimy, scrub it with soap and a stiff brush. Then try going over the surface with fine steel wool and pumice stone.

Cloudy, rough, and dirty varnishes may often be brought up by treating them with tincture of benzoin. Protect the renewed surface if painted with a good coat of oil, perhaps even an oil polish. Use boiled linseed oil for the purpose and rub it well into the surface with a felt pad (chiropodist's felt is the best). Give the surface all it will absorb. (Cf. Oil Finish.)

For a shellac spirit varnish or a spirit varnish, use a French polish. Coat it with lemon oil or lard oil. Rub it to a smooth surface. Now take some horsehair, cover it with cotton batting, then with muslin, to make a pad. Charge the pad with a solution of dry shellac in 190-proof denatured alcohol of about one part of shellac to five of alcohol by volume. Let the solution stand overnight, shake thoroughly and let settle. Go over the surface with a quick circular motion, never touching the same place twice, until you reach a polish. In removing the pad, slide it off the surface, do not lift it. You can tell whether all is going as it should by watching the pad. As long as the pad is clean, the finish is going on. At the end of this operation, run your strokes the way of the grain.

French polish leaves a very high luster. If you don't like it, you can either shellac or varnish it with flat or rubbed varnish. Be sure to remove all the oil first or the varnish will not dry.

If you wish merely to wax the cleaned finish, use beeswax in preference to the commercial polishing waxes, as it is more suitable for old furniture.

Removing Finish

If the finish can't be cleaned, it must be removed. If the piece is the kind that has a painted decoration, remove the finish cautiously. A mechanical method is to take a sharp knife or similar tool, examine the painted surface for checked or flaked paint, and press the edge of the knife against the edge of the crack or chip. A piece will flake off. At the start, use something less radical than ordinary paint remover. After soap and water, try ammonia on a small area. This is slow but has the advantage of leaving no residue to spoil later finishes, and it may uncover designs. If probing shows no signs of decoration, it is safe to go ahead and use a regular paint remover that will take all the paint off.

Alcohol can be used next. For special cleaning, there are also acetone and ether. All of these substances are volatile and highly poisonous and, except for ammonia, explosive, so they should be used with adequate ventilation or out of doors away from fire. If cotton saturated with ether is brought against the varnish and sealed up for eight to twelve hours, it will soften the top layer, which can be wiped off with a cloth dampened in carbon tetrachloride

Taking off the paint cautiously is justified only if there is a reason for suspecting decoration under the paint. For removing finish right down to the wood, there are two types of paint remover. The safest are oil-soluble, organic solvents. These will hurt nothing but the paint. The objection to them is that cleaning up the paint remover is sometimes more of a job than removing the paint. If the residue of paint remover and softened former paint is not removed, new finishes will not dry. After removing the finish, use alcohol or gasoline and steel wool to remove all residue of paint remover and paint.

Quite different are the so-called wash-off paint and varnish removers, which can be washed off with water. The emulsion thus formed is harmless and can be easily disposed of. They will not harm anything that water won't hurt. But water does cause joints to become unglued and veneers and marquetry to loosen, so keep this in mind. With due caution, these paint removers can be used on all furniture.

Another way of getting rid of paint is to scrape it off. In all scraping operations, you should work exceedingly cautiously at all times, but particularly when you get close to the wood. The best type of finish scraper is a cabinet scraper with the corners ground off and the edge slightly convex. This will take the paint down without risk. When you are close to the original surface, give up scraping and finish cleaning with steel wool and alcohol.

Often a residue of finish remains in the pores. If you cannot get it out by this method, leave it. Overscraping the wood will cause you to ruin the patina and the antique.

The cleaned wood may be cut, scratched, stained, and dented. The temptation is to take your handy scraper and scrape off all scratches, stains, dents, and cuts. Don't do it! Accidental stains can be removed by bleaching. Any good two-solution bleach will do the trick. Remove the color from cuts and scratches with paint remover and bleach. These can then hardly be seen.

If the stains are caused by earth pigments, like Venetian red, they may not bleach out. In this case, the wood will have an all-over tinge, which you can camouflage easily by using a dye stain of its complimentary color. This will make the wood very little darker. If the residual color exists only here and there, such as in blemishes filled with putty, you can paint it out with your first coat of varnish.

To do this, you mix a color to match the ground color of the wood, a little lighter if the spot you wish to eliminate is darker, or a little darker if the spot is lighter. Use colors ground in japan. While the varnish is still wet, introduce the color at the spot, starting at the center and brushing it toward the edges. A No. 3 water-color brush is about right for this work. With a little experimentation, you will be able to paint the spot right out.

Putting on the New Finish

The choice of new finish is up to you, but your piece of furniture will look its best if the finish you put on is a duplicate of the one the piece originally had. Old finishes were made of many varied materials and applied in several ways, but they were all polish finishes having a fairly high luster.

Oil Polish

The most common of the old finishes was an oil finish. The material was linseed oil and the process was simple. Fill the wood if a filler is needed, or use oil as the filler. Sand the oiled surface smooth, using fine grades of sandpaper. Then clean off any sawdust with a tack rag, made by dipping cheese-cloth in linseed oil and then in varnish. When the surface seems

smooth and even to the touch, wipe off the excess oil. Allow
to dry for twenty-four to forty-eight hours and rub down with
pumice stone, oil, and finally rotten stone. Clean off the oil
and abrasive mixture. Next, rub oil into the surface with a
felt pad until you get a polish. Allow the work to stand for some
days until it no longer feels oily. Sand very lightly with the
finest sandpaper. Again, rub oil into the surface until it comes
to a polish. Set aside and let it dry. A final polish may now
be applied.

An oil polish requires a great deal of work. As a reward,
it is both beautiful and durable. It's chief disadvantage, aside
from the work involved, is that the oil tends to darken the
wood. Those pieces, seen in many an antique shop, that are
said to be finished with oil, have in reality only been smeared
with oil.

Simpler than oil is a wax finish. Sand the surface smooth,
fill the wood and sand again. Open-grain woods require fillers.
The best is a paste filler. This should be brushed on with a
short, stiff brush and worked into all pores. As soon as the
surface dulls, the filler should be wiped off across the grain.
After drying for twenty-four hours, it may be sanded. After
the filled surface has been prepared, it can be given a thin
coat of shellac and sanded. The surface is then waxed with
beeswax, thinned with alcohol and turpentine. When the wax
has dried, it is polished with a soft cloth to such luster as
desired. Both oil and wax finishes will benefit from regular
polishing with beeswax or lemon oil.

Varnish

For a good varnish finish, the wood must be well filled,
sealed, sanded—and clean! Varnish should be flowed on with
a clean brush. Hold the brush just close enough so that a film
of varnish will flow from the tip. Flow the varnish with the
grain, then across it, then with it again. Brush off all excess
varnish, bubbles, and dust flecks. Let dry for forty-eight to
seventy-eight hours. Try to rub down with sandpaper. If the
finish does not roll off in little pellets, it is dry; if it does,
it is not dry yet. When the varnish dries, sand it down. Give

the work three coats like the first. Do not use more than three coats as the varnish will check. Rub with sandpaper, then pumice stone and oil (lemon or lard oil), followed by rotten stone and oil. Finally, finish off with oil.

To get the best results, use spar varnishes for the first two coats and polishing or rubbing varnishes for the last coat, unless you want a dull finish.

Shellac

While shellac finishes are not so durable as those of wax or varnish, they are often more beautiful. The wood should be prepared as for varnish. Apply the shellac quickly, stroke in one direction, do not go over the work. Let it dry for eight to ten hours, and sand or finish with steel wool. Shellac again, brushing at right angles to the first coat. Allow to dry, sand, and reshellac.

There is no limit to the number of coats of shellac you may use. If you polish between each coat and make the coat thin, you can achieve a richness with shellac that no other finish can rival. Remember that ready-mixed shellac is good only when fresh. If it is more than a year old, the shellac won't dry.

Shellac will turn white if water gets on it, and it scratches easily. These disadvantages are more than offset by its great beauty. If the surface is exposed constantly to water, heat, or alcohol, you can use a number of alcohol-and-heat-resistant materials, such as lacquers and plastic finishes. Directions for their use will be found on the container. Lacquers cannot be used over other finishes and paints.

Polish on Varnish

Related to French polish but somewhat easier of accomplishment, is the polish-on-varnish finish. Prepare the wood, fill, and sand, and clean as described under Varnish. Give one coat of varnish and sand. On top of this finish put the French polish as above described.

Painted Finishes

To duplicate the old red, black, and green of painted furniture, use milk-and-egg-type tempera finish. Mix it yourself, thus: First take the dry pigment and mix with either
sour milk or egg. Put a little egg or milk on a glass slab,
add the pigment, and grind the powder around with a flat glass
or paint grinder, until it is all incorporated in the medium.
Add more medium until it is the right consistency to paint with.
Some fresh, slaked lime (a gill to a quart of milk) should be
added to the milk. The paint can be applied either with a
brush or with a cloth pad to get a polished surface. When the
paint dries out, sand it lightly and give another coat. These
paints are tricky to use and may give trouble. The same
effects can be achieved with colors ground in japan, thinned
with turpentine, and protected with varnish.

At least as many pieces of furniture were painted with oil
paints as were painted with casein and tempera paints. The
colors were ocher reds, greens, blues, ocher yellows,
browns, and black. The blues were of an order of ultramarine
and slightly purplish blues. Occasionally, they were greenish.
The greens were dark, grayed, often containing a great deal
of black. Browns ranged from chocolate to maroon, and the
black was ebony. Some white seems to have been available,
but whether it was white lead, chalk, or calcium hydroxide,
I do not know. At present, it is quite chalky.

Occasionally, a piece was grained. Very early graining
was done by painting on the ground color, and, while this was
still wet, the second color was applied in loops and swirls
around focal points of blobs and spots, to get an effect like
finger painting. A second fashion was to paint the ground and,
when that was dry, to use a sponge or a crumpled-up piece of
stiff cloth dipped in another color of paint to make splotches
and spatter marks.

One step from this was rose and white graining. The earliest had a white ground color. When the ground color is almost
dry, take a brush from 1/2"-1" wide, charge it with red paint,
and locate and mark spots for centers of the design. Drag the
brush in an irregular ellipse about the spots, thus making a

patterned grain, something like the graining about a pine knot. Where there isn't room for this kind of graining, the design consists of a series of irregular parallel lines, usually crossing the work at an angle. This rose and pine graining is symmetrical; if there is a knot-type pattern on one panel of a door, the design appears reversed on the matching panel.

Somewhat later, red and black graining was employed. The piece was first painted red. When the red was dry, it was overpainted with black. The black was then wiped off with wads of cloth. Use japan colors for graining.

In addition to graining, other backgrounds for decoration were provided. One of these was the tortoise shell. This effect is achieved as follows: On the ground color, usually black, apply japan gold size with a cloth in splotches. When these become tacky, apply bronze, gold, silver, or copper powders with a piece of velvet or suede. Start in the center of the splotch and shade off toward the edges. When it is dry, give the surface two coats or more of alphaltum varnish, allowing it to dry between coats.

A completely different kind of ground, the smoked ground, is used for decoration in paint, but never in parcel gilt or stencil. To do this, paint the ground with white oil paint, enamel, or enamel undercoat. While the surface is wet, hold the painted object over smoke from an oil lamp and shift it around to let the smoke form an all-over design. When dry, use as a ground for painted decoration.

For marbleizing, paint the area with a ground color, and while this is slightly soft, draw in the designs of the veining with a feather quill dipped in paint. The bold veins were painted with a brush or feather on slightly tacky ground, so that they merged slightly with the ground color. After the paint is dry, varnish and japan are applied over the entire surface. With the varnish still wet, the fine cloudy veins are painted; these fade and float over the ground color. With a little practice you can become quite clever at this work.

Japanning

Most of the decorative painted work falls under the classification of japanning, of which there are three kinds. The first and earliest is in imitation of Oriental lacquer work. The ground color is often blue, occasionally cinnabar or some other color. The blue is deep and slightly grayed, like the color of the blue chalk a carpenter uses, but much deeper. On this are drawn pagodas, trees, people, fantastic animals, rocks, birds, etc. The drawings are then filled in with a brush charged with gesso. You build them up to the thickness you wish them to be, then, with a series of well-sharpened tools, you carve in the details on the raised motifs. The next step is to gild the raised areas. Mix a little oil with some varnish and paint with this, or, if you prefer, use an oil gold size.

For painting designs in gold leaf (parcel gilding) in addition to the modeled and carved ornaments, use the following technique: With some japan gold size, paint the designs. Wait until the size snaps at your touch but does not stick to your finger. Then, take the gold leaf—you can pick it up with wax paper or brush—and touch it to the areas to be gilded until all are covered. Let the whole dry and then brush off the loose gold leaf with a soft brush. Next, you may wish to make little spots here and there, which you cover with some japan gold size. When they are tacky, sift onto them gold, silver, and copper colors. When the whole is dry, apply a little varnish to which asphaltum has been added. Three coats of such varnish will leave the ground quite black, decorated with raised and flat patterns in gold leaf.

All parcel gilding is done in this fashion. Shading is accomplished both with paint (mostly burnt umber) and engraving. You can use a crow quill pen (dipped in India ink) for heavy engraved lines and a No. 10 needle for finer lines. Three No. 10 needles soldered together and mounted in a wooden handle are convenient for shading and crosshatching. Transparent gold ocher, burnt umber, Prussian blue, alizarin green, and alizarin crimson will give you a fairly complete palette for shading gold leaf.

For later decorative techniques in japan work, stencils and bronze powders are used. In doing this work, a separate stencil is made for each part of the motif. For example, if a basket of fruit is to be stenciled, the basket, each fruit, and

each leaf is a separate stencil. Paint the ground ivory drop-
black, ground in japan, and allow to dry. Next, give the area
to be decorated a coat of varnish or japan gold size. Allow
the surface to dry to the point where it is tacky. Lay the
stencil on the work. Roll a piece of suede, chamois, or velvet
over your finger or make a tiny pad of it, dip it in the bronze
powder, and tap it gently on a newspaper to remove excess
bronze. Apply the bronze through the stencil, lap it over the
first stencil, and stop applying the bronze as you approach
the first one. In this way, you can shade from light to dark
evenly and elegantly. When the varnish has set completely,
blow off any excess bronze (there shouldn't be any), clean the
surface with a tack rag, and varnish.

Some chairs were not decorated in gold, but were instead
painted in color with brush strokes. For this purpose, your
colors should be mixed with varnish to a consistency that will
flow readily from the brush but will not run. Use round water-
color brushes No. 3 or No. 4, and follow the shape of the
brush to make the strokes. The design may be worked out on
paper and transferred to the chair by pouncing through the
perforated design in the way embroidery patterns are sometimes transferred; or white or yellow impression paper can be
used for a better job. When the work is finished, you should
give it at least one coat of varnish.

Trays are japan work and can be treated exactly as described,
except for one thing. The tray is often rusty. Rust can be
cleaned off with oxalic acid and steel wool. When the rust is
removed, the tray should be cleaned of all reagents and dried.
If it is pitted, the pits should be filled with metal surfacer,
thickened with lithopone to the consistency of putty. After
the pits have been filled and sanded smooth, the whole surface
should be covered with the primer. When this dries, it can
be sanded smooth. On this surface, you can paint with whatever medium you choose.

A great deal of tinware had a thin coat of asphaltum varnish
(japan) over the bright tin. To achieve this effect, varnish the
tray, let dry to the tacky stage, and apply silver or aluminum
leaf to the entire tray. When the tray or other tinware is
covered completely and dry, give one thin coat of asphaltum

varnish to the surface. You should get a rich metallic brown.
Your decoration can be placed on this.

Some of the elaborate painted trays of the eighteenth and
nineteenth centuries combined gold leaf borders, stencil
techniques, and painting. I shall try to describe briefly the
method of painting the floral bouquets and dazzling birds. The
grounds are most often black. Old tinware was cured at between
300° and 500° F. and thus had a surface very like enamel.

Some trays have a tortoise shell ground or a ground shaded
with bronze powders from the center to the edges. For this, the
prepared tray should be painted and varnished or given three
coats of japan. The last coat should be tacky. Start in the
center and spread the dry powder on evenly, shading out
toward the edges. In the center, use bright gold or gold and
silver mixed; about a third of the way out blend medium gold;
and at the edges allow dull gold or dull copper to shade off
into the black of the background.

Next, trace the design onto the ground with carbon paper
or with white or yellow impression paper. Paint on the design
all the opaque colors that are to be used. Chrome green,
chrome yellow, a little Prussian blue, and raw umber make the
greens. Use Philip's white for highlights and underpaint all
flowers in white, except those to be painted in opaque colors.
The birds' feathers are underpainted in white. Where you want
iridescent colors, underpaint with bronzes and silver powders,
applied dry with suede or velvet on a tacky japan gold size.
The medium for all colors should be japan gold size or varnish
thinned with turpentine.

Transparent colors should be applied in a medium of japan
gold size washed carefully over the underpainting. When dried,
coat the whole area of each motif with a little varnish thinned
with japan gold size. While this is wet, use Philip's white
with a little gold ocher to make the highlights. Allow to dry
and then use a fine brush charged with whatever colors are
necessary to paint stamens of flowers, veins of leaves, and
feathers on birds' wings.

If you want curlicues and fine calligraphic brushwork in
gold, you can use bronze powders and a fine striping brush.
You can also use japan gold size and apply gold leaf to these,

again when tacky. Still another method is to use gum arabic and water mixed to the consistency of drawing or India ink. Use a pen to draw the lines. When they have dried, breathe on them to moisten the gum and immediately apply the gold leaf or gold ink applied with a pen.

If you start by copying an old tray in gold leaf, stencil, or paint on a practice sheet, you can later try your hand on a tray or chair. You will find that anyone can learn to do this work well.

Gilding

To repair gold leaf gilding as on a mirror or picture frame is a job that requires both knowledge and skill. If you send things in need of regilding out, you will receive them back in beautiful shape, but the surface is apt to be new. Here are ways to restore without regilding. Reglue any loose pieces of gesso with a china or glass cement. Missing plaster ornaments can be replaced. Take some modeling clay such as is used by children. Press it on top of an ormanent similar to the missing one. Remove it carefully. You now have a clay mold for the plaster ornament. Fill this mold with plaster of Paris. When the plaster is set, remove. Make enough molding or ornament to fill the empty spaces. Allow the plaster a week to cure. Then glue the new plaster in place.

Flat areas should be built up in gesso. You can buy prepared mixes for this that are good, or you can make your own by dissolving about one-quarter of a cake of rabbit-skin glue in three quarts of water. Add enough whiting to make a hot mixture about the consistency of heavy cream. Keep it hot in a container over boiling water. Apply while hot. With this process, you can slowly build up the gesso to the required thickness. When the gesso has set and dried, in about twenty-four hours, you can sand it smooth with the finest grade of sandpaper.

Next, cement on the new plaster moldings with china cement. Varnish all new work, that is, new gesso and plaster ornaments. When the varnish is dry, take some oil gold size or some varnish to which a little oil has been added. Carefully coat all

new surfaces with this medium. When it has reached the tacky
stage, in from twelve to twenty-four hours, apply the gold leaf.

First cut the gold leaf with a silver table knife on a piece of
chamois. Cut the leaf into strips or squares of the right size
to cover the area required. Take a dry camel's hair brush,
brush it in your hair, pick up the gold leaf and drop it on the
surface to be gilded. Repeat until all areas have received a
coat of gold. Set the work away until thoroughly dry. This may
take as much as a week. Now brush off all the excess gold leaf.
The new work will be brighter than the old. You can antique it
with burnt umber or asphaltum varnish.

There is also a way of getting the effect of gold leaf by using
bronze powders. On your smooth prepared gesso surface or
molded plaster surface, put a coat of varnish. When this is
dry, apply a second coat, thinned with a little japan gold size.
While this is still wet, sift or blow on gold powder so that it
floats on the surface. You can select a bronze powder that
matches or very nearly matches the color of the rest of the gilt.
Be stingy with the bronze, use it while the varnish is wet, and
be sure to _float_ it on.

With either of these methods, you can repair the gilt and
retouch as little surface as possible. This is of considerable
consequence where the frame, as in some mirrors, is mostly
old.

Furniture Polish

A good furniture polish should do two things: keep the furniture looking nice and clean and protect the finish from deterioration. Some of the new silicoid polishes may be excellent
for saving the finish. I cannot be sure, since I have not used
them enough.

The rest of the polishes contain wax and pick up dust from
the air. Repolishing builds up a coating that covers the furniture with alternate layers of wax and dust to the dullness and
detriment of the furniture. Polishing oils such as lemon oil do
not do this.

You can prepare a good polish that will last a long time.
Combine equal proportions of turnpentine, linseed oil, vinegar,

190-proof denatured alcohol, and lemon oil. Mix this as
needed, since it deteriorates on standing.

Below is a list of essential tools and materials required to
carry out the repairs discussed in this chapter.

Tools

Brace and Bit:	Bits range in size from 1/8" to 1" by sixteenths, expansion bits from 1 1/8" to 3".
Brushes:	For painting and varnishing—2" to 3" flat brush. Water-color brushes with round tips, from the very finest up to about No. 5. Quill stripers with bristles as long as possible. Broad 1" sable, squirrel, or camel's hair brush for brushing off gold leaf and for picking it up.
Chisels:	Firmer chisels from 1/16" to 1" as follows: 1/16", 1/8", 1/4", 1/2", 1". Carving tools in a variety of forms, contours, curvatures, and handles. You will need a gouge and a parting tool.
Clamps:	Six 3" "C" clamps; twelve 6" "C" clamps; twelve bar clamps 12" to 18"; eight bar clamps 4' or over. Pipe clamps can substitute for the long bar clamps.
Dowels:	Two sorts, long ones 36" by 1/8" and 1/4", and short ones of assorted odd sizes and approximately 2" long.
Drills:	These are occasionally useful to work in end grain where the bits will not cut easily. In sets ranging from 1/4" to 1/2" in sixteenths. Best sizes are 1/16", 1/8", 3/16", 1/4", 5/16", 3/8", 7/16", 1/2", 9/16".
Doweling Jig.	
Files:	Several mill files, two saw files and one half-round and a rat tail file.
Gauge:	A marking gauge is useful.
Hammers:	An ordinary claw hammer and a tack hammer.
Knives:	A pen, stencil, and veneering knife.

Mallet:	Useful for carving and cutting mortises.
Planes:	Several planes—jack, smoothing, block, rabbet, adjustable dado, fillister.
Rasps:	Shoemaker's rasp and fine half-round rasp.
Sandpaper:	A supply of flint and garnet papers, from fine to the very finest.
Saws:	Rip, cross cut, back, dovetail, keyhole, and coping saw.
Scrapers:	Several cabinet scrapers and a hook scraper.
Squares:	An adjustable angle square, a try square, and a steel square.

Materials

Bronze Powders:	Silver, copper, and gold in many varieties. It is important to get the finest lining bronzes.
Gold and Aluminum Leaf:	Indoor type sold in books.
Glues:	Epoxy, casein, and synthetic resin glues.
Paint:	Venetian red, chrome green, white lead, chrome yellow, raw and burnt umber. The same colors plus ivory drop black, ground in japan.
	Artists' oil colors: Alizarin crimson, alizarin green, burnt sienna, burnt umber, cadmium red, cadmium yellow, chrome green, chrome yellow, cobalt blue, gold ocher (transparent), Harrison red, Indian red, Philip's white, Prussian blue, raw sienna, raw umber, scarlet vermilion, ultramarine blue, Venetian red, viridian, and yellow ocher.
Varnishes:	Cabinet rubbing and polishing varnishes.

Don'ts

The following is a list of things not to be done under any circumstances:

1. Make no attempt to improve on the original design by removing or adding ornament.

2. Do not substitute one kind of leg or foot for another.

3. Do not add carving, veneer, or any embellishment not original.

4. Do not cut down pieces to make them more desirable.

5. Do not cut up table or chest tops or table leaves to get rid of warps.

6. Do not disassemble a piece to close a crack on its side.

7. Do not replace or repair anything unnecessarily.

8. Never discard anything original unless it cannot be repaired.

9. Do not scrape or clean a piece below its original surface.

10. Do not try to remove dents, cuts, scratches, and stains by scraping or planing.

11. Never use power tools on old furniture.

12. Never restore in place of repairing.

13. Never leave a piece to be repaired without a clear understanding of what is to be done and how.

Chapter XI

GETTING A COLLECTION TOGETHER

FROM AMBERINA TO ZITHERS

So far, what I have said has been aimed mostly at telling the difference between the true and the false antique. Beyond these lies a larger if less immediate aim—the aim of making a collection of antiques.

To be profitable, a collection need not be extensive. A few carefully chosen things selected for their meaningfulness and interrelation may make an elegant collection, for example, half a dozen pieces of blown glass. Selected to illustrate the forms, techniques, and metals of glassmaking, they can be as important and useful as a hundred odd bottles, goblets, or sugar bowls of pressed glass. Therefore, a <u>collection</u> is typified by its exclusiveness rather than its extensiveness.

At its worst, a collection can feed our pride and give us status by making us members of an exclusive set—that of the collector, the patron of the arts (albeit the arts of yesterday). It can serve as a magic carpet to carry us away from a painful present to a romantic past, for the collector is an incurable romantic. There are many more compelling reasons for preserving the relics of antiquity. Out of the foregoing personal interests, it comes about that as the collector learns to know his collection and the times it represents, he slowly comes to regard himself as its custodian rather than its owner. There is still a further reason. In putting together a group of objects to reveal new meanings or uncover richer aesthetic significance, the collector satisfies the urge to create that seems innate in most human beings.

What should be a collection's scope? There is no limit to its size, richness, or variety. The number of objects in museums and private and semiprivate displays will testify to this. The limits are set for you by the amount of time, money, and display space you have available. Each individual will do well to confine himself within his own known limits. For example, an individual with a three-room apartment would find collecting pianos a problem. Persons with limited incomes would find collecting eighteenth-century French furniture difficult. However, no matter what limitations may exist for you, there are none that preclude having, enjoying, and displaying artifacts from times past.

Perhaps the best kind of collection is one with a dual or even triple purpose. If we collect useful antiques, we can, with some exceptions, use them as we would new pieces. A homeowner will find that many pieces of antique furniture may be had for little more than modern pieces cost (not infrequently for less). In addition, as time goes on, the pieces he is using every day, instead of becoming less valuable, become more so, until that moment is reached when he can sell the furniture in his house for more than he paid for it.

If you furnish a house with antiques, what should be the basis of selection? It should be the same as if you were buying the things as antiques only, that is, you should try to maintain quality within the limits of your budget. What do I mean by maintaining quality? I mean making no compromises with the antiquity of an object. This includes avoiding the heavily restored and the not-quite-antique piece. If you consider the function of what you buy, you can use many antiques that may by modern standards seem uncomfortable or impractical.

Naturally, you will want the over-all appearance of your home to be attractive as well as to exude an aura of the past. This brings me to the consideration of what part good taste plays in the selection. Remember that the only constant thing about good taste is that it changes, a fact that makes it possible to distinguish the past from the present styles.

If you find several especially good antiques, you can exercise your taste to select the best one or two. How will you tastefully select the best? Try always to choose the piece that best embodies the taste of the period in which it was made <u>as you understand that taste.</u> In struggling to make such a decision, and it will be a struggle on more than one occasion, you will be almost certain to come home with better pieces.

I should like to put in a word here for variety. At all times, men have liked things put to similar use to be similar in appearance. We have sets of dishes, sets of parlor chairs, dining room furniture en suite. This can lead us slowly to the deadly dull monotony of tone, color, and form that was so often the result of good taste in the early twentieth century. The past was, whatever else it lacked in taste, never monotonous. Take advantage of its variety in selecting the pieces you will use for furnishing.

In picking furniture, do not be seduced into selecting mediocre things because the real antique seems unobtainable or too expensive. It is better to buy a good early blanket chest than a poor Victorian or Empire sofa. You can sit on the blanket chest in case of necessity, and the whole room will look better. Slat-back, banister-back, and simple urn-back chairs of the eighteenth century may not be comfortable to lounge in, but they make the dining room look handsome.

Things in poor condition are not good buys for any reason, but are to be especially avoided when you intend to use them, for this condition is certain to get worse in use. By poor condition I mean something heavily in need of restoration.

The Specialized Collection

A collection is a creative unity when it is limited to some one item that expresses a central theme. For example, you might try to collect a number of case pieces to illustrate the variations in form of blanket chests. Or you might show the evolution from the blanket chest to the tall chest of drawers or highboy. You can select chairs to show the different types made in the seventeenth century or choose them for some motif, such as the fan, to show variations on a theme. Again, it would be interesting to illustrate the evolution of the chair through many forms and transitions.

In contrast to furniture, glass is wonderful to collect if you have limited space, because you can use it in so many decorative and informative ways to show the history of taste or even of events. A few shelves of a china cabinet can house a magnificent collection.

The first and most obvious type of glass collection is based on function. Drinking vessels show variety in form, technique, historical development, or embellishment—or even bizarre forms and comic qualities. Another collection might be made of forms like cup plates, salts, or lamps to show a wide variety in form, color, or techniques of manufacture. Bottles are a favorite with collectors, who collect for type, color, or historical association.

People have made collections of pitchers, tumblers, plates, perfume bottles, bowls, and the myriad other forms that glass is used for. Often a series—for instance, tumblers—does not close down quickly enough, so you soon have a very large number of tumblers with the end not in sight. Consequently, further limitation is necessary, such as collecting only one type of glass or one kind of metal. Still, you will find a need to limit further the types of tumblers. Or, if you want your collection to run the gamut of types, it is possible to select a piece that is an example of several things at once. Six or eight goblets or tumblers, carefully selected, could give you an illustrated history of glass blowing over the last three centuries in Western Europe.

Many collectors have endeavored to collect enough of one pattern to use as table settings. Pattern glass was made in forms for table settings. Here, the aim is completion and the result is certainly impressive. Such collections are possible only in later glass, such as blown three-mold and pressed, where matching patterns exist.

Similar special collections may be made of ceramic wares as to types of bodies, decoration, glazes, factories, table settings, and the like. Special collections of metal objects from silver tea services to wrought-iron door locks and keys to go with them are equally worth while.

We could have glass collections that are related to currency, fruit, or birds. From this it is but a step to the heterogeneous collection of a wide variety of different classes of objects related by a theme. Such themes as commerce, astronomy, whaling, highwaymen, or the American eagle can serve as the center of such a collection.

You can gather things that honor a public historical figure such as Washington or Lincoln, or that belonged to one, such as Lady Hamilton's snuffbox or fan. Those objects that use the famous person as subject matter are naturally more easily found than those that actually belonged to him.

Lest you feel discouraged at this sort of collecting, remember that any collection has one powerful unifying factor, and that is the personality who has assembled it. Your taste and judgment will themselves give a sufficient theme, provided you exercise them.

Quite different is collecting with a view to creating another world. We can be most successful if we conjure up a completely new reality, a magic made in the moonlight resuscitation of things past. Here you use some particular past time as your central theme. To try to recreate a room or a house as of June 30, 1754, is palpably insane, but to furnish a room as it could have been in the middle of the eighteenth century is quite possible. A generation or two ago, the period room was the natural goal of antique collecting. Today, the aim is rather to use many periods together. Still, one-time collecting is worth while, and museums and historic restorations certainly encourage emulation.

For best results, our enchanted room or house should be contemporary with its furniture, as should be all the accessories. Many practical difficulties, such as the fact that old fabrics cannot be used for upholstery or that old lighting devices are inadequate, add difficulties. This sort of thing can be carried out to its logical conclusion only in museums. You can also cram too many treasures into one room. Museums frequently fall into error in this respect, but private collectors are less likely to since they are less likely to have so many things on which to draw.

If you can't fill a room, try a portion of a room; for example, have a seventeenth-century corner or grouping. Various seventeenth-century furniture, glass, china, and prints can be grouped together. Here, on a smaller scale, is the period room, the magic effect dramatically heightened by its contrast to the rest of the room. Or collections of Oriental and Western antiques can be juxtaposed. Relations between the

East and West can be brought out in a collection of Orientalizing styles in the West and Occidentalizing styles in the East.

Wolves and Sheep, Black and White

For whatever purpose you collect, you are most certainly going to have to buy the antique somewhere. What are the sources? In the long run, you will find that most of your purchases will be made from antique dealers. This would seem to be obvious, yet an enormous number of persons avoid buying from dealers. The reasons given are that dealers will overcharge and outsmart collectors in every way possible; that dealers have secret knowledge that they will not share; that dealers are utterly unscrupulous and rapacious.

Dealers do charge more than they pay. The retail price of antiques ranges from about fifty to thirty or twenty percent profit. This seems inordinately high, but is actually no higher than ordinary retail profits. When you consider the difficulties of locating antiques and the slow turnover, the profits do not seem so exorbitant. But prices may be. The reason is that there is no standardization of prices. Average modern commodities seldom show a great difference from the bargain basement to the highest-class store for the same item. An antique may cost a hundred times more in one shop than in another. Of course, not all antiques that are similar are the same. Also, many dealers have prices adjusted to suit the customer's purse. It is often customary to mark the price in a code that tells the dealer his cost price at a glance. He can raise or lower his price without seeming to do so.

There is reason for expecting the dealer to overcharge us, for dealers have made a practice of buying something for ten dollars and selling it for a thousand. It is also generally true that dealers who have high-class (expensive) shops, offer no more than a small dealer, although they get more. On the other hand, such dealers can and will pay the enormous sums for outstanding pieces that the small dealer cannot touch because of lack of capital. Such shops are about the only places to find really rare and valuable antiques.

Dealers have a number of tricks for ramming a high-priced article down one's throat. One of the commonest is to say, "Yup, that there commode is a museum piece," or, in another locale, "Believe me, madam, there is a piece quite comparable to this in the Trevelyan Collection in the Biscayne Museum, though in my opinion ours is of a somewhat higher style."

Another method is to appeal to the avarice of the collector by saying, "Yes, that's a mighty fine piece you're looking at there. Manville and Sayers have offered me within a few dollars of what I'm asking for it, and you know very well they won't sell it for no such price." Still another device is to say, "Well, I don't know as I ought to give you a price for it. I'm expecting a visit from Hiram Jones of the Bayside Museum and I suppose he'll want it!" The soft sell is often successful: "Considering the difficulty encountered today in finding things of this quality in such condition, I believe that you will find the price quite reasonable." Finally, there is: "Well, I was quite lucky when I got it, so I can let you have it real cheap."

In all such cases, the dealer is exaggerating to the best of his ability. But there are other similar occasions when he tells the truth. It is up to you to recognize the difference. One thing is true: in order to buy successfully and reasonably from dealers, you must know both your antiques and your dealer. The responsibility for high prices lies in the inexperience of collectors. When customers overpay, the dealer is also likely to overpay, with the result that dealer prices are often higher than the scarcity of the commodity warrants. There are too many ways of finding out the prevailing prices for you to overpay.

While some dealers are quite willing to outsmart the buyer, it is worth remembering that the majority of dealers are as honest as anyone else with something to sell, perhaps even more so. Here are a few ways in which the unscrupulous dealer outsmarts the unsuspecting amateur. The most obvious way is to get an antique price for a fake. The dealer with any experience at all can tell very quickly by what you pick up, by the way you examine it, and by the way in which you ask questions, exactly how much you know about antiques. His approach

will vary with the individual, but will be something like this:
"Well, sir, I am glad once in a while to see someone come
into my shop who knows what he's about. Tell me, what do you
think of this? I bought it last week. It's a little out of my line,
but I liked it so I thought I'd take a chance on it."

Another good way to help the buyer deceive himself is to
pretend complete ignorance: "No, sir, I ain't got no idea what
it be. Got it off an awful old lady over in Sayville. She said it
come down in her family. Bought an awful lot of stuff there,
too. Sold it all but that." Another way of feigning ignorance is
to misstate the piece belligerently. As you examine a piece
of dirty translucent china somewhat the worse for wear, the
dealer says, "That's a lovely piece of white earthenware.
With such lovely underglaze decoration." It has overglaze
enameling. Finally, "I am sure it is Copeland." Obviously,
the dealer does not know what he's talking about. Thus you
take home what needs only to be washed properly for you to see
—even before you remove the strategically placed price label
—that it was made in Japan.

Another trick in misdirecting your scrutiny is to call your
attention to some small defect. "You know, that's a interesting
piece over there. Did you notice how the top is made? I
never saw one made just like it before. That's why I bought it.
Unusual, ain't it?" or "Too bad that top is so dented. Wonder
if I ought to turn it!" The poor condition of the top, the dark
shop, the dust, all of which hinder a careful examination, may
convince you to buy the piece (especially as it will be reasonable).

In complete contrast to this chatty approach of inviting you
into his world is the taciturn, reluctant dealer, who, as soon
as you go to examine a thing, orders you summarily to put it
down. "If you want to see anything, I'll show it to you," he
growls. "That's not anything you would want, it's very expensive." Or, in a tone that brooks no contradiction: "That
chair is a New Hampshire piece clearly made by someone
close to the Dunlops." You wonder how a dealer like this
ever gets anyone to buy anything. But before you know it, he
has you so annoyed that you buy something just to show him
you are not to be bullied.

Then there is the whimpering old lady who comes tottering
to the door in an old kimono and cap. She is likely to greet
you with "Oh, dear, I haven't been feeling myself all day and
I was hoping no one would bother me. Oh, yes, you can come
in, but I don't think I've got anything you would want." Her
pieces are unmarked, the store is a shambles and, on inquir-
ing the price of anything, you are likely to get this sort of
answer: "Oh, dear, I don't know. So many people look at it
but don't want it. Would five dollars be too much?" (It usually
is.) The antiquer thus buys out of embarrassment. He'll be
lucky to get out with his fingers.

A variant approach is that of the sweet, absent-minded old
lady who has a story for every piece. Kind and trusting, she
has much of her stock marked, but will usually quote a price
much less than the marked price. Look out for her, too.

One is not to suppose that such dealers handle nothing but
fakes; the risk is too great. But they do heavily stock their
collections with spurious, overrestored, and doubtful pieces.

Then there is the name-dropper. His technique is to follow
you around the shop. If you evince any interest in a particular
item, he will say, "I think that's pretty good, don't you?
Mr. Pickalemon, who wrote the standard work on Early
American vinegar bottles, was here only last week and he said
to me, "Well, Cheatham, that's one of the best examples of
the old acidosis bottle and it's got the S wrong side to. You
sure earned a day's pay when you got that one!" Or: "Well,
how do you like that? I had quite a fight to get that one. I
found it down in the cellar of the old Cock and Bull Tavern
here in Clinton the day of the sale. I waited for a lull and
asked the auctioneer (he's a personal friend of mine) to put it
up. It almost got out of my reach, but Harry Pokes (you know,
the big bag manufacturer over in Leverett) had stepped out to
make a telephone call, so I got it."

There are other tricks of the trade that are used more often
abroad or in wayside shops where the traveler is in a hurry,
which in itself gives the smart dealer his chance. That is, to
make a switch. It works so often that he can take the risk. The
shop is elegantly immaculate—a first-class showroom. It
contains outstanding pieces with appropriately outstanding

prices. However, here and there in this august assemblage may
be a sleeper. The item is usually small and breakable and
will be taken in back to be wrapped. While your attention is
engaged elsewhere, the proprietor or assistant wraps up a
duplicate item. The chances are excellent that you will not
discover the substitution for some time. This stunt works
even better if the item is to be shipped. It is a timeworn
trick, and the old writers' advice always was "If you want it,
pay for it and take it with you."

So far as knowing all the tricks of the trade is concerned,
the dealer must, because if he doesn't, he will himself be
victimized. He is very chary of letting his customers in on
any of his secrets, not only because he may wish to use them
on customers, but also, and more importantly, because he
wants to have his customer in his own vest pocket.

The dealer wishes to be the sole authority on genuineness.
He will do all in his power to make certain that all exchanges
of antiques take place through him. This is probably the most
serious charge of all against dealers, because it is a fault
that is more generally true and is as likely to include reputable
as it is disreputable dealers. What are some of his tricks?
The smartest have to do with buying antiques.

Buying well is very important because the less paid, the
greater the profits and the more latitude in turnover. The
dealer will often offer an exorbitant price for an object he
has no intention of buying. His approach to the items he really
wants will be stealthy. He can offer various excuses for not
taking the overpriced item so that he gets what he wants and
leaves behind nothing but vanished hopes.

You may think that this will work only on the ignorant and
uninformed, but it can be worked on you also. For the dealer,
in touch with a fluctuating market, knows to the fraction of a
cent about what he can get out of a piece, whereas you, who
buy only occasionally, have no such knowledge.

A more subtle variation of the above stunt is for the dealer
to offer a good price for the first piece you show in the hope
that the impression thus made will give him an entree to the
rest of your collection. He will, in this case, pay you immediately and try another shot. This often works and is legitimate.

Illegitimate stunts are also worked, especially on the lowly, the aged, and the infirm. The dealer walks in, gathers up what he wants, throws some money on the table, and walks out, completely disregarding the protests of his victim. This is, of course, theft, but very difficult to prove, especially if the victim is loath to complain. Pestering an owner into selling is not far removed from this, except that the seller consents. Another method is cajoling or flattering people, especially elderly persons, with a view to buying their antiques. The dealer thus gets into a favored position. He will make many social calls before even suggesting that he may be more interested in the antiques than in the people in the house.

Dealers use various devices to bid against themselves at auctions. I remember one dealer in particular. He was a Goliath of a body upon which sat an undersized head that somehow seemed to go to a peak. He had the loose jaw and vacant stare that suggest a low-grade moron. Yet he had the most discriminating taste. He also seemed well supplied with money. It was not until much later that I discovered that he was in the employ of a very well-known dealer. He kept raising the bid until signaled to stop by his boss.

Dealers also induce persons to buy antiques at higher prices than they would ordinarily pay by carefully setting the stage. The simplest trick is the plant. Here, a dubious old antique is farmed out to a place that has the proper atmosphere for selling. An old couple can act as salesmen. Grandpa can take the old rocking chair that belonged to his great-granddad and rock in it comfortably, if not in the middle of the road, close enough so that no one can miss the fact that it's an old hoop-skirt rocker and being simply ruined. Grandpa can sell quite a few of these in a season at prices that dealers would never have the face to ask.

This method eliminates examination, since Grandpa is not asking anyone to buy anything. He is the very picture of reluctance. Two, the purchaser has no comeback if something is wrong. Third, the dealer can get good pieces by buying poor ones along with them, since he can do so well with the junk. Depending on the stakes, enormously complicated stage settings have been erected to market spurious pieces. These have

included old houses furnished with genuine antiques, complete
with motheaten carpets, moldy wallpaper, dust, and cobwebs,
for the sole purpose of selling one or two important—and
expensive—spurious pieces.

One can create a demand for something not previously much
sought after. The steps are, first, to acquire large quantities
of a class of antiques not currently popular and thus low-
valued. The next step is to send excellent examples to prominent
galleries to be sold. The firm then sends two or more agents
(who are not known to one another) to the sale with instructions
to buy the object. This results in establishing a high price
for the particular type of antique. Such methods are obviously
only for very large concerns. But they have been used more
than once.

Another way of artificially creating a demand for a certain
kind of antique is to have it written up in a magazine with a
wide circulation—not necessarily one dealing with antiques.
A dealer can submit the article or induce a well-known expert
to write one. In either case, a sudden demand for the featured
object will follow within six to eight months. This gives him
ample time to assemble junk that will sell as antiques. Once
the desired result is achieved, the action pyramids. Collectors
want egg cups, and dealers struggle to get enough, causing the
price to rise.

Sometimes a single sale will raise the price of all classes
of objects. Such a sale can be rigged; but the sale of a famous
collection often does the trick. Witness how art glass rose in
price after a sale of it in Ohio.

If you have been shocked at some of the things antique sellers
will do to make money, it is as nothing to what customers will
do to get a bargain. These range from outright theft to altering
or removing price tags, haggling for lower prices, and above
all, belittling the dealer's merchandise.

Many of you may have concluded that antique dealers are
never to be trusted. Nothing could be farther from the truth.
As I said at the beginning, dealers are your one biggest aid.
You will learn most from them, you will find your best pieces
through them, and you will have the greatest help from them.

The following are some suggestions for getting along with dealers: First, be frank about what you are looking for and what you expect to pay. If the dealer does not have it but thinks he can get it, give him a chance. He will frequently find for you what you would not find for yourself. If he finds your widget and it is genuine, thank him for his efforts and buy it. Finally, don't try to take advantage of a dealer; don't disparage his wares—rather, admire them; don't continually ask him prices if you don't intend to buy.

Once the dealer gets the idea that you are a good customer (this does not necessarily mean that you spend a lot of money or are easily fooled or make a good place to get rid of junk), he will do quite a bit to keep you one.

Grand Slam at Auction

The second largest source of antiques is auctions. These range from simple country sales to sales in famous galleries where only the finest of antiques change hands.

An auction is a place to get antiques at your own price if you can keep your head. For, if a few fakes are sold to an unsuspecting public by dealers, the number of fakes sold at auction is a hundred times greater. If dealers overcharge, the auctioneer can get the patron to overpay in dozens of ways. Some auction houses hire people to liven the bidding if prices start lagging, although I doubt if such devices are used by reputable firms.

One fault of the sale is that the sales talk of the auctioneer is traditionally irresponsible. You cannot hold him to account for any kind of misrepresentation as to age, genuineness, or condition. All sales are final. You can't reclaim your money for a fake bought.

Presale exhibitions give you a fair chance of not getting caught with a lemon. Printed catalogues with identification dates and condition indicated give you a comeback. Such catalogues exist mostly for important sales, and while you are reasonably safe as to quality, you may pay the very highest possible prices, for you must compete with large-scale operators, agents for museums, and wealthy private collectors, to all of whom price is of little consequence. However, you may still find bargains, particularly in odd things in the collection. For example in a sale of a collection of eighteenth-century European porcelain, odd pieces of American silver or simple pieces of furniture may sell at less than market price because the specialist did not attend the sale.

The typical auction at which most people buy is the one-day, one-place, country sale with no opportunity provided for seeing the goods beforehand. Auction houses in cities differ from this in providing you with a chance to examine things before the sale. Where you have no chance to examine a piece before it is placed on the block, and then only a minimal opportunity, since the auctioneer tries to get bids from the audience and sell the piece in the shortest possible time, you have to buy on faith, for unless you have clairvoyance or phenomenal vision, you often are doing well if you can tell what an object is, let alone whether it is an antique or not.

Sales are frequently held by dealers for the sole purpose of getting rid of second-class pieces. These are honest sales, with no forcing of bids other than the forcing that a skillful auctioneer can do. In contrast to these are the sales that purport to be part of the settling of estates. These, unless run by the state, may not be exactly what they appear to be. Often those things that are good enough are disposed of privately before the sale begins, and near fakes or poor items replace the pieces taken out.

The quality of a few good pieces well-advertised and judiciously placed in a sale will keep the prices of most of the other things high. Also, when two similar items are sold in succession, the first in good condition and the other a wreck, the second piece will bring very nearly the same price as the first. Similarly, if identical pieces are put up for sale, the second will usually bring more than the first.

The risks of buying at auctions are these: you are likely to buy fakes or damaged pieces, you are likely to overpay for what you do buy, and you may often find that you have bought something you don't want.

Like connoisseurship in general, buying at auction requires attention to business. If you have an opportunity to examine

the objects before the sale, do so. Set down a sum that you
think you should pay for each item. Now, once you have picked
your top figure, <u>do not raise it</u> once the bidding has begun. If
you do this, you will not regret it. At the beginning of your
career at auctions, bid cautiously and do not get alarmed if
you lose.

In bidding, there are as many tricks as there are experienced bidders. The best trick of all is to know accurately the
current price of the antique you are bidding on. If you can find
the piece in any reputable shop for fifty dollars, it would be
foolish to pay that much for it. Try to get it for little more than
a dealer would give and for quite a bit less than what he would
have to get.

The art of bidding is to discourage the opposition bidder or
bidders as soon as you can! In these days of cheap money and
rising prices, this usually takes some doing. I notice that
experienced salesgoers who are buying for resale and so are
out for money tend to use three tricks. One is this: when
there have been a few small raises or a reasonable starting
figure, the experienced bidder steps in and doubles or triples
this increment. This usually slows down the bidding. He may
return with sharp increases until he reaches his present limit
or the others give up. The purpose of the sharp increase is to
surprise the other bidders and to give the impression that the
new bidder is able and willing to pay and determined to get the
object.

A second way of entering the bidding is to wait until the
competition is limited to two bidders who are just managing to
keep ahead of each other. Then, as one seems to be entering
the home stretch, the new bidder knocks them both dead with
a triple raise.

The third trick is to open the bidding with a bid that is about
half of your limit. Your next step, whatever is bid by others—
unless they overreach your mark—is to increase the bid to
three-quarters of what you expect to pay. At the next bid, you
raise it to seven-eights. This approach may, if you try it
early in the sale and on a number of items in succession, discourage competition by suggesting that the sale is rigged.

Here are some points to remember: Be careful—you can get hurt. Know your antiques (that is, the types at the sale). Know the current prices. Stay within your limit.

For beginning collectors, an auction is a wonderful place as long as they do not bid. Take a notebook and list what the things bring. Note the pattern of bidding and who wins. Write down what you think the piece will bring and then compare it with what the final bid is. Later, you can compare prices with those in shops.

Auctions sometimes serve the useful end of exhibiting similar things together, as when famous collections are sold. This will enable you to see a collection as you could in almost no other way. It will give you ideas of what to collect and suggest how to go about it. If you learn nothing else from them, auctions will give you an idea of what you are likely to have to pay.

Finding the Golden Fleece

While the last source from which you may get antiques is from individuals, it is almost the only source through which the market is supplied. The bulk of the antiques bought by the public from dealers, auctions, or individuals (including estates), is new to the market. In spite of this, you will not find too many opportunities to buy from individuals.

Why do people sell their antiques? The least likely reason is to get rid of them. Someone wants to clean his attic or cellar of all the junk stored therein and will call in a dealer. The only way you will get these opportunities is by accident or by knowing a lot of people. When people moving from larger to smaller quarters are forced to dispose of some things, the last person they will think of selling them to is a collector. In general they are right, for collectors are almost certain to make the lowest offers and to want to take only a few things.

The most common reason for selling antiques is to turn them into something else, which is quite different from getting money for them. Although sentimentally attached to grandfather's card table or grandma's old tea set, it may seem better to turn it into a new car or a television set. The old armchair in the second-best bedroom may help put Johnny through college. It is usually when a person is faced with such problems that he decides to part with family antiques. A final reason is just plain need. The individual or the family is in desperate need of money for this, that, or the other emergency.

These reasons will give you some insight into what you will run into when buying from an individual. Take the last reason. The person in dire need of money is usually in need of a fixed sum. He has two fixed sums of money in his mind: the sum he wants to get and what he thinks the antiques are worth. If they are worth as much as he thinks, it will be remarkable. If he thinks the antique is priceless and you offer him a reasonable price, you will be shown the door. If you offer him more than he needs or he thinks the antique is worth, he may decide not to sell it at all. Often, what people have—with many misgivings—decided to turn into cash is not antique. Finally, the price is almost sure not to meet their double expectations. Frustrated in attempts to transform their heirlooms into a solution to their problem, they end up by keeping them.

There are other difficulties. Caveat emptor applies here as nowhere else. Some of these desperate families regularly take in experienced antique dealers. Buyers may have to examine objects that are covered with dust and dirt, with the aid of a flashlight in a dark attic without a floor.

At best, you will give the individual a free appraisal with your offers. However, if you do get an opportunity to buy from an individual who has something worth while, and in your offer you hit on the magic number, you will find that you will not have had all your other disappointments in vain.

Regardless of how or what you collect or where you find it, your success as a collector will depend on the degree of exclusiveness in choosing your collection. The limits can be enlarged as your collection, knowledge, and experience increase. In fact, they can be made as large as you choose. Great oaks from little acorns grow; just be sure that it is an acorn and not a thorn apple that you plant.

CHRONOLOGICAL TABLES

Styles derived from the names of the ruling monarch are, with few exceptions, shown by the monarch's names and dates.

ITALY

Due to its political development from the Medieval period on, Italy was divided into provincial regions under the nominal control of hereditary rulers. In each of these regions, there arose a number of city-states and/or communes, each one having different organization, political control, historical experiences, and trade connections. Thus Italy, in the period of its greatest achievements in the arts, comprised no single unity of outlook, thought, or style. For this reason, Italian styles are as varied as the centers that produced them. Artifacts from Italy are usually identified by date and the city or region in which they originated. The style development in cities tends to be in advance of the regional development by about ten to thirty years.

Writers on Italian art frequently use the terms trecento, quatrocento and cinquecento (literally three-hundredth, four-hundredth, five-hundredth for the thirteenth, fourteenth, and fifteenth centuries. This differs from English usage. For example, 1365 is in the fourteenth century in English but in the trecento in Italian.

Principal Geographic Divisions and
Styles of Their Chief Regions

North Italy: Provincial Styles: Emilia, Liguria, Lombardy, Piedmont, Trentino, Veneto

	City-State Styles:	Bologna, Parma (Emilia)
		Brescia, Milan, Monza,
		Pavia (including Certosan)
		(Lombardy)
		Genoa (Liguria)
		Turin (Piedmont)
		Venice (Veneto)
Central Italy:	Provincial Styles:	Abruzzi, Marche, Tuscany, Umbria
	City-State Styles:	Ancona, Urbino (Marche)
		Assisi, Gubbio, Orvieto, Perugia (Umbria)
		Florence, Livorno (Leghorn), Lucca, Pisa, Siena (Tuscany)
		Rome
South Italy:	City-State Styles:	Kingdom of Naples
		Kingdom of Sicily

In the following table, five regions of Italy have been selected, together with their leading cities. Styles A represent conservative, more provincial types. Styles B, high fashion, florid and leading styles.

ITALY

North Italy Styles A	North Italy Styles B	Central Italy Styles A	Central Italy Styles B	South Italy Naples
Lombardy (Brescia, Milan, Monza, Pavia)	Veneto (Venice, Padua) Genoa	Tuscany (Forence, Livorno, Lucca, Pisa, Siena)	Rome	Naples
Late Gothic				
Lombardy To c. 1470	Venice (Late Byzantine, Flamboyant Gothic) to 1460	Florence To c. 1340	Rome To 1447	Naples To 1440

North Italy Styles A	North Italy Styles B	Central Italy Styles A	Central Italy Styles B	South Italy Naples
		Transition to Early Renaissance		
To c. 1500	———	To c. 1404	To c. 1460	To c. 1460
		Early Renaissance		
To c. 1525	To c. 1500	To c. 1470	To c. 1500	To c. 1500
		High Renaissaince		
To c. 1550	To c. 1550	To c. 1530	To c. 1530	To c. 1530
		Baroque		
		To c. 1730 in all styles—last Italian style		
		Rococo		
To c.1760-1770	To c.1750-1760	To c.1760-1770	To c. 1750	To c. 1845-1850
		Neo-Classic		
		To c. 1790-1810		
		Classic Revival		
		To c. 1840		

SPAIN

Late Gothic

(Hispano-Moresque, Mudejar, Flamboyant Gothic Styles)

House of Castile-Leon	House of Aragon
Henry III (1390-1406)	Martin I (1395-1410)
John II (1406-54)	Ferdinand I (1412-16)
Henry IV (1454-74)	Alphonso V, King of Naples (1416-58)
	John II (1452-79)

(Uniting of Castile and Aragon)

Isabella (1479-1504)	Ferdinand II (1452-1516)

Early Renaissance

(Italian Lombardian   Hispano - Moresque = Plateresque Style)

Philip I, Austria—House of Hapsburg—(1493-1506) and Joanna of Castile (1504-55)

Charles I of Castile and V of Hapsburg, Holy Roman Emperor and King of Naples (1516-56)

High Renaissance

(Herreran, Hispano-Moresque Styles)

Philip II (1557-98)
Phillip III (1598-1621)

Baroque

(Churrigueresque Style)

Philip IV (1621-65)
Charles II (1665-1700)

Rococo

(Churrigueresque Style + French influence brought in by Bourbons)

Philip V (Bourbon) (1700-46)
Ferdinand VI (1746-59) (Beginnings of Neo-Classicism)

Neo-Classicism

Charles III (1759-88)
Charles IV (1788-1808) and Napoleon's brother, Joseph Bonaparte (1808-14)

Classic Revival

Ferdinand VII (1814-33)

FRANCE

Late Gothic

John the Good (1350-64)⎫
Charles V (1364-80)   ⎬   End of Rayonnant Gothic Style

Charles VI (1380-1422 ⎫
Charles VII (1422-62) ⎬   Flamboyant Gothic
Louis XI (1461-83)   ⎭

Early Renaissance

Charles VIII (1483-98)⎫   Transitional Renaissance
Louis XII (1498-1515) ⎭

Francis I (1515-47) ⎫
Henry II (1547-59)   ⎬   Renaissance Proper
Francis II (1559-60) ⎪
Charles IX (1560-74) ⎭

High Renaissance

Henry III (1574-89)
Henry IV (1589-1610)
Louis XIII (1610-43) Transitional to Baroque

Baroque

Louis XIV (1643-1715)

Rococo

Regency for Louis XV (1715-23), Regency Style
Louis XV, from 1723 to 1754

Neo-Classic

Louis XV, from 1754 to 1774
Louis XVI (1774-93)

FRANCE

Classic Revival

Directory (1795-99)
Consulate (1799-1804)   Directory Style

First Empire—Napoleon I (1804-14), Empire Style

Louis XVIII (1815-24)
Charles X (1824-30)   Eclectic Classic Revival Style

Eclecticism

Louis Philippe I (1830-48)

ENGLAND

Late Gothic

Henry VI (1422-61 and 1470-71)

Edward IV (1461-70 and 1471-83)   Flamboyant,
Richard III (1483-85)   Perpendicular
Henry VII (1455-1509)   Gothic

Henry VIII (1509-47)   Italianate
Edward VI (1547-53)   Tudor Style
Mary 1 (1553-58)   Strapwork
                                                                            Oak
Early Renaissance   Period

Elizabeth I (1558-1603)   Elizabethan Style

James I (1603-25)
Charles I (1625-49)

Commonwealth—Cromwell   Puritan, Cromwellian,
    (1642-60)   Protectorate Styles
                                                                  Jacob-
Transition to Baroque   ean
                                                                  or
Charles II (1660)   Stuart
James II (1685-88)   Style
William III and Mary II (1689-1702)
                                                                            Wal-
Baroque   nut
                                                                            Pe-
Queen Anne (1702-14), Queen Anne Style,   riod
    extending to c. 1760

ENGLAND

Baroque (continued)

George I (1714-27), Transition to Rococo,
   Georgian Style, extending to c. 1760

Rococo   Mahogany
                                                 Period
(Chippendale Style)

George II (1727-60)
George III (1760-1820), beginning of
   New-classicism, 1763

Neo-Classicism (1763-1820)

(Satinwood Period)

(Adam, Hepplewhite, Sheraton Styles 1963-1812)

Regency (1811-20)

Classic Revival

(Rosewood Period)

George IV (1820-30)
William IV (1830-37)
                              ### Eclecticism

Victoria (1837-1901)
                              ## GERMANY

Late Gothic

(Curvilinear, Flamboyant)

      Sigismund (1410-37)
      Albert II (1438-39)
      Frederick III (1440-85)
      Maximilian I (King of Austria, 1486 to 1493,
         when he became Emperor, to 1519)
      End of Middle Ages

GERMANY

Transition to Baroque

(Early German Renaissance)

(Strapwork Style)
Charles I of Spain <u>or</u>
   Charles V of Hapsburg (1519-56)
Ferdinand I (1558-64)
Maximilian II (1564-76)
Rudolph II (1576-1612)

(High German Renaissance)

Mathias (1612-19)
Ferdinand II (1619-37)
Ferdinand III (1637-57)

Baroque

Leopold I (1658-1711)
Charles VI (1711-40)

Rococo

Austria	Germany Proper
	Independent Princes:
Maria Theresa (1740-80)	Frederick William of Prussia— 1740 on
and	Frederick Augustus II of Saxony— 1733 on
Francis I (1740-65)	Charles Albert VII of Bavaria— 1745 on
Joseph II (1765-90	League of German Princes—1785

Neo-Classic

Leopold II (1790-92)	Chief States in the League of German Princes:
Francis II (1792-1835)	Prussia, Hanover, Saxony, Saxe-Weimar, Saxe-Gotha, Palatinate

GERMANY

Classic Revival (c. 1825–45)

(Biedermeier)

LOW COUNTRIES—THE NETHERLANDS

Late Gothic
(Flamboyant)

Belgium		Holland
Burgundian Dynasty	Philip the Bold of Burgundy (1428–67) Philip the Good (1467–77) Mary of Burgundy (1477–82)	
	Philip I of Castile (1482–1506)	
	Charles I of Castile or V of Hapsburg (1506–56)	

Transition from Gothic to Baroque

(Mixture of Gothic, Renaissance and Baroque) beginning c. 1530

Philip III (or II, of Spain) (1556–98)

Governors General	State's Generals

(Strapwork Style c. 1530 on)

Governors General	State's Generals
Margaret, Duchess of Savoy (1530–1564) Duke of Alba (1568–73) Don Luis Requesens (1573–76)	William of Orange (1559–73) William of Orange—independent ruler (1573–84)

(Netherlands split into Belgium and Holland in 1579)

Don Juan (1577–88) Farnese (1588–92) Philip III of Spain (1598–1621)	Philip William (1584–1618) Maurice of Orange I (1618–25)

LOW COUNTRIES—THE NETHERLANDS

Governors General

Archduke Ernest (1592-95)
Albert and Isabella, daughter of Philip III (1595-1633)

Baroque (beginning c. 1625)

Philip IV of Spain (1621-65)   Frederick Henry (1625-47)
Charles II of Spain (1700-01)
Philip V of Spain (1701-06)   William II (1647-50)
Louis XIV of France (1706-13)   William III (1650-1702)

Transition to Rococo
(Baroco)

English-Dutch Conference   Interregnum (Peace of Utrecht—
  (1706-13)   1713)
Charles VI of Austria
  (1713-40)
Maria Theresa of Austria
  (1740-80)

Neo-Classic

Joseph II of Austria (1780-90)
Leopold II of Austria (1790-92)
Francis II (1792-99)

Classic Revival (beginning c. 1800)

William I, King of Holland   William VI or William I, King of
  (1815-31)   Holland (1815-44)
Leopold I, King of Belgium
  (1831-65)

AMERICAN (Colonial and U.S.A.)

Late Gothic

1621—c. 1650 (Pilgrim)

AMERICAN (Colonial and U.S.A.)

Styles of Renaissance Character

(William and Mary) Colonial

1650-1700

Transitional to Baroque

(William and Mary) Colonial

1700-25

Baroque

(Queen Anne) Colonial

1725-55

Rococo

(Queen Anne, Transitional, Chippendale) Colonial

1756-87

Neo-Classic

(Hepplewhite, Sheraton)

Also Federal, Roman Revival or Early Republican

1787-1825

Classic Revival

(Greek Revival)

1825-1840-50   American Directory
                  American Empire

AMERICAN (Colonial and U.S.A.)

Eclectic

Rococo Revival—to 1865

Victorian (1840-1900)	Italianate Gothic Revival Medievalism Naturalism Antiquarianism

Dates of the Emperors of the Manchu (Ching) Dynasty

K'ang Hsi	(1662-1723)
Yung Ch'eng	(1723-36)
Ch'ien Lung	(1736-96)
Chia Ching	(1796-1820)
Tao Kueng	(1820-50)

GLOSSARY

Acanthus. (a) Thistle-like plant of the Old World. (b) Ornament
derived therefrom. Found primarily in architecture and
furniture.

Adz. Cutting implement used as an ax, but with a blade set like
a hoe.

Aeolic. Classic style of architecture, characterized by its
palm capitals.

Agate ware. Ceramic ware made by working different-colored
clays into a marble-like pattern, glazing with transparent,
slightly bluish glaze in imitation of agate. Made by Thomas
Whieldon. Early eighteenth century.

Ajouré. Pierced. Used of architecture or furniture.

Alabastron. Small ointment jar of Ancient Greece.

Alligatoring. Developing scaly cracks suggestive of those on
an alligator hide and caused by shrinking of paint or varnish
on furniture.

Amberina. Glass shading from ruby to amber, made by the New
England Class Company, c. 1878-88.

Annealing. In glass, the slow cooling to prevent crystallization
and breakage. In metals, the use of heat to draw the temper
of work-hardened metals so that they can be hammered
without breaking.

Anthemion. Classical ornament of alternating conventionalized
honeysuckle and palmettes.

Antiquarianism. Style of the late nineteenth century, characterized by copying of antique styles.

Antiquing. Process of making surfaces appear aged by use of
stains, paint, and abrasives, particularly on furniture, with
or without an attempt to deceive.

Apron. Portion of table or chair that holds the legs in place.

Aquatint. Kind of etching that deals in areas rather then in
   lines.

Architrave. In architecutre, the portion of the superstructure
   that rests directly upon the columns in a colonnade.

Armoire. French clothes press or wardrobe.

Armorial forms. Making use of (a) coats-of-arms; (b) crests
   from coats-of-arms; (c) forms characteristic of heraldry.

Art glass. Glass designed primarily to be looked at. Used particularly of certain types of glass popular in the late nineteenth century in Europe and America.

Art Nouveau. Style of art in fashion c. 1900, based primarily
   on free-flowing forms but not naturalism.

Astbury. (a) Staffordshire potter, sometimes credited with being the inventor of the use of white clay washes and of the
   addition of calcined flint to the Staffordshire clays. (b) Figurines and teapots in brown and tan, decorated with a brilliant lead glaze in cream-colored ware of the early eighteenth century. Attributed to John Astbury's son, Thomas.

Atlantes. In architecture and furniture, male figures, sometimes grotesque, used in place of columns or pedestals.

Aubusson. (a) Town in France known for its rugs and tapestries.
   (b) The type of tapestry and tapestry-woven rugs made there.

Aurene. Iridescent art glass made at Corning Glass Factory,
   Corning, New York.

Baccarat. Glass factory in France, known particularly for its
   paperweights. Nineteenth century.

Bail brass. Drawer pull of brass, making use of bail or loop
   handle.

Baluster. (a) Profiled short column, usually circular in section
   but frequently polygonal, used in stair railings, balustrades.
   (b) Having the form of a baluster, as a stem of a goblet, pedestal of a table, shaft of a candlestick.

Banjo clock. Wall clock of Neo-Classic period, with round upper
   section for the works and dial, a trapezoidal section for the
   pendulum rod and a rectangular section at the bottom for the
   pendulum bob. Late eighteenth, early nineteenth century.

Banister-back. American chair, the back of which is made up
   of split turning running between a top and bottom rail and

with turned sides facing back of chair. Descendant of cane-
and leather-back chairs of Charles II, c. 1700-25.

Baroque. In architecture, the use of Classical forms for coloristic effects in fanciful and theatrical fashion. In furniture,
the use of swelling, curving lines. In decoration, dramatic
contrasts of light and dark. Irregular and lopsided.

Baryta. Naturally occurring barium sulphate used as a natural
ingredient in ceramic bodies, particularly jasperware.

Battens. Pieces of wood, applied, nailed, or screwed across
the grain of planks, (a) to hold several together, (b) to prevent or cure warping.

Bay. (a) Projecting or organized space in a wall, separated
from the next section by columns, pilasters, or piers. (b)
Bay wood. Honduras mahogany named for Bay of Campeche.

Beading. Small molding of semicircular section. Thin projecting strip, the outer edge having a half-round profile, used as
ornament on drawer edges or blades to prevent veneering
from being torn off. An astragal.

Beaker. Cylindrical or baluster-shaped drinking vessel without
a handle.

Beehive. (a) Symbol of industrial activity, occurring as decoration on ceramic ware and glass. Early nineteenth century.
(b) Mark of several factories in Germany and Bohemia for
china and glass.

Beer tray. Round or oval tray with a stand-up rim, for carrying beer glasses, and more particularly used as a field for
decoration. Eighteenth and early nineteenth centuries.

Bennington. Pottery made in Bennington, Vermont, by U.S.
Pottery Company, both flint ware (Rockingham glazed ware)
and Parian (soft paste), usually unglazed. 1852-88.

Bergère. Round-backed French armchair, caned or upholstered.
Reign of Louis XV through the Empire period.

Bermuda chest. Type of chest made in Bermuda during the late
seventeenth and early eighteenth centuries, and famed for
the ornamental use of dovetails.

Bevel. Slanted surface on the edge of a board or panel, used
ornamentally and structurally.

Biedermeier. Style popular in Germany during the period of
Classic Revival, c. 1825-45.

Biscuit. The ceramic body after the first firing.

Bisque. Unglazed procelain.

Block front. Style of Baroque case pieces originated by the Townsend Goddard family of Newport, Rhode Island. The front is ornamented with alternating projecting blocks, often carved with shells, between which are re-entrant forms of the same pattern as the blocks. Eighteenth-century American.

Block print. Wood or linoleum print, making use of areas rather than lines.

Bloom. White, clouded appearance, caused by the deterioration of painted, varnished, or shellacked surface.

Blue-banded. Oriental export porcelain decorated with a blue band at the rim.

Bohemian. Used of enameled cut and engraved glass made in Bohemia. Particularly flashed overlay or luster-enameled ruby cut through to clear glass, wherever made. Eighteenth and nineteenth centuries.

Bolt brass. Brass with round bolts rather than cotter pins for holding the bail.

Bombé. Term applied to case piece that swells at the base and curves inward at the top like a pot or kettle. Typical of Baroque and Rococo furniture, particularly of Holland and France.

Bone china. Soft paste containing large amounts of bone.

Bonnet top. Broken arch, whose contour is carried back through the depth of the piece. Seen on clocks, highboys, chests on chests, secretaries, cupboards.

Boston rocker. Factory-made rocking chair with straight side posts and spindles, usually with arms, and decorated with stencils. 1830's and '40's.

Boule work. Elaborate marquetry in tortoise shell and brass, originated by Boule family in France. Seventeenth and eighteenth centuries.

Bow-front. Furniture of which the front is convex.

Bracket. (a) Ornamental, angular support for holding up shelf, cornice, pediment. (b) Bracket foot constructed of a plank, found at the corners of case pieces.

Brass. (a) Alloy, composed chiefly of copper and zinc. (b) Piece of furniture hardware made of brass.

Bristol. (a) Soft-paste China, English, eighteenth century. (b)

English glass manufactory of the eighteenth and nineteenth centuries. (c) Type name, used loosely, for different varieties of semiopaque glass.

Britannia. Alloy of tin, copper and antimony, mass-produced from the end of the eighteenth and through the nineteenth century.

Bronze disease. Deterioration in bronze caused by chlorides imbedded in the metal.

Buckle. To bend or warp, particularly under pressure.

Bucranium. Ornament in the shape of an ox head or skull.

Buffing. Machine polishing with rouge or crocus to obtain a high luster on metal. To be avoided on antiques.

Bull's-eye mirror. Convex circular mirror. By extension, any mirror with convex glass. Popular in Classic Revival period in 1830's in England and America. Frequently ornamented with carved and gilt eagle, gilt chains, and gold drops. When mirror contains candle holders, it is called a girandole.

Burmese. Nineteenth-century art glass, shading from lemon yellow to orange, made at Mount Washington Glass Works, New Bedford, Massachusetts.

Butt joint. Joint made at right angles to the faces.

Cabriole. In furniture, a leg having an S-shaped curve in two directions.

Cameo glass. Cased glass of contrasting colors, carved like a cameo. Used in ancient times by Greeks and Romans and recreated popularly by John Northwood in the 1870's.

Canopy. Wood support and cloth accouterments making a cover for a high-post bed.

Canton. Type of Oriental porcelain exported by China during the late eighteenth and early nineteenth centuries. Usually decorated in blue and white.

Carnival glass. Cheap iridescent glass made in the late nineteenth and mostly in the early twentieth century, in imitation of Favrille (Tiffany) glass. Also called taffeta glass.

Cartouche. Ornamental medallion, in form of unrolled scroll, found in architecture, furniture, painting, etc. Often contains inscription.

Carver. Name describing arm or side chair, the back of which
is made up of spindles set between rungs in one or two
ranges. Seventeenth century. The name derives from a
chair in Pilgrim Hall, Plymouth, Massachusetts, said to belong to Governor Carver.

Caryatid. Female supporting figure serving in place of column
or pilaster.

Case piece. Furniture consisting of an outside, fixed portion
and movable parts, either doors or drawers.

Casing. Used of architecture or furniture. Outside framing of
door or window.

Cast. Something made by pouring liquid into a mold.

Caughley. Factory of second half of eighteenth century producing soft-paste porcelain at Caughley in Shropshire, England.

Cauliflower ware. (a) White earthenware made in Staffordshire
during the eighteenth century by Whieldon, so called because
of its cauliflower form. (b) Late nineteenth-century majolica
of same type.

Cavetto. Concave molding.

Ceramic. Made of fired clay.

Chalk. Used of paint. To become powdery and rub off.

Chamberlain, Robert. (a) Founder of rival factory to Worcester,
called Chamberlain-Worcester, c. 1783. Factory operated
till 1840 when Chamberlain returned to original factory.
(b) China made in Chamberlain-Worcester factory.

Chamfering. Planing, carving, adzing, or hewing off the corner
of a plank, timber, post, or other member of a building or
piece of furniture for ornament.

Chantilly. Soft-paste porcelain of eighteenth-century France.

Charger. Large platter or plate, generally of metal, and larger
than 15 inches.

Chasing. Hammering, with properly shaped tools, designs on
metal.

Checking. (a) Partial splitting of wood from the end. (b) Fine
network of cracks all over in paint.

Chelsea. (a) English soft-paste porcelain factory, c. 1742-70,
famous for its figurines and polychrome-decorated china.
Periods: Triangle mark to c. 1750. Raised anchor—1753-54.
Red anchor—1753-58. Gold anchor—1758-70. (b) Chelsea-

Derby ware produced after Duesbury took over the Chelsea
factory, 1770-1848.

Chiaroscuro. Theatrical contrast of lighting in painting or carving. Artificial as opposed to natural lighting or plein-air.

Ch'ien Lung. Emperor of China 1736-96, of the Ching dynasty.
Applied to wares of China during his reign, specifically to
small sprays in polychrome scattered over a white ground,
showing strong European influence.

Chinese export. Porcelain made in China during the seventeenth,
eighteenth, and early nineteenth centuries for export to Europe and America.

Chippendale. Furniture designs based on the published designs
of Thomas Chippendale, Sr.

Classical. Pertaining to the culture of Ancient Greece and
Rome and styles derived therefrom.

Claw-and-ball. Foot appearing in European furniture early in
the eighteenth century, along with other Orientalizing influences from China, where it represented a dragon holding the
world.

Colorism. The making of strong contrast of light and dark or
highlight and shadow for decorative, dramatic effects.

Commode. Long chest of drawers on high legs, containing usually two ranges of drawers. French in origin, associated
chiefly with, but not limited to, the Rococo style. Made in
France, England, and wherever French styles were fashionable. Eighteenth and nineteenth centuries.

Composite. Roman order of architecture, richly ornamented,
combining Ionic and Corinthian elements.

Coping. Fitting two pieces of abutting molding together by sawing one out to fit the contours of the other, instead of miter-
ing.

Copperplate. Describes printed textiles, the designs of which
were printed from engraved copper plates.

Copper wheel engraving. Used of type of etching, engraving, and
cutting of glass done with abrasives and copper wheel.

Corinthian. The richest of the three Greek orders of architecture.

Cornice. Crowning molding of a room, building, or piece of
furniture.

Counterpane. Ornamental woven bedspread.

Country Chippendale. Type of simple, transitional Chippendale chairs, frequently displaying elements of much earlier styles. Found in country districts of America. Eighteenth century.

Cotter pin. Piece of metal bent together with a loop at one end.

Courting mirror. A mirror the frame of which was made up of pieces of glass painted from the back. Often accompanied by carrying box. Allegedly brought back by seafaring men as presentation pieces for sweethearts and wives. Eighteenth and early nineteenth centuries.

Crackle glass. Pressed or blown glass covered with ornament imitating a fine network of crackles.

Cranberry. Clear, somewhat purplish, gold ruby glass. Appears extensively in English and American glassware of the second half of the nineteenth century.

Crazing. Fine network of cracks, as in paint, varnish, and ceramic glazes.

Crewel. Embroidery on linen, worked in a variety of stitches in Orientalizing patterns with a two-stranded twisted wool, which gives its name to the work. England and America. Seventeenth and eighteenth centuries.

Crocket. Leaf-formed ornament resembling an opening bud, used on pinnacles, cornices, etc., in Gothic-type architecture and furniture.

Crosshatching. Lines crisscrossed at a constant angle for shading in pen and ink drawing, etching, engraving, and woodcutting.

Crystal. (a) Extra fine quality of soda-lime glass containing potassium, colorless and virtually flawless, of sixteenth into eighteenth century. (b) Flint or lead glass.

Crystallized. To have atoms arranged in a specific three-dimensional pattern or lattice.

Cullet. Broken galss used in the glass industry for starting batches of glass.

Cup plate. Four-inch diameter plate to hold a teacup after the tea was emptied into the saucer.

Currier and Ives. Most famous American lithographers and the lithographs produced by them.

Cyma. S-shaped curve forming profile of moldings. Contours
of legs in furniture, modillions in cornices. Characteristic
of Classical, Renaissance and Neo-Classic design. When
lower section is concave and upper convex, it is a cyma recta;
when lower is convex and upper concave, it is a cyma reversa.

Dado. Groove.

Delft. Tin-slip or tin-enameled redware. Faience made in Holland and wares like it. Seventeenth and eighteenth century.

Dentils. Row of evenly spaced, projecting cubes forming the
base molding of the cornice in Ionic, Corinthian, and Composite orders. Also used as ornament in furniture.

Deruta type. Majolica named from town in Italy where it was
made.

Diamond point. Engraving used on glass, done with a diamond-
pointed graver.

Die. Metal form used in stamping or drop-forging, into which
the work is pushed or pressed rather than poured, as in
casting.

Doric. The simplest of the three orders of Greek architecture.

Dovetail. Wedge-shaped piece to hold two pieces together in
construction work.

Dowel. Small piece of wood, usually cylindrical, for fastening
two pieces of wood together.

Drawshave. Knife with two handles, that cuts when pulled toward the operator. Used for smoothing curved surfaces.

Drawer lining. Sides, back, and bottom of drawer.

Dress. To bring to an even surface. To plane.

Drop-stamping. Process of giving form to metal part by placing sheet metal between two dies and pushing metal into dies
by force of falling weight.

Dry point. Engraving in which the graver's tool scratches rather than engraves the plate.

Duck foot. Flat, circular foot, usually terminating a cabriole
leg, on eighteenth-century-style furniture.

Durand glass. Iridescent art glass made in Vineland, New Jersey, by Durand. Early twentieth century.

Dutch cupboard. Wardrobe with elaborately painted or paneled double doors. A kas, found in America in regions of Dutch influence, for example, Hudson and Connecticut valleys and Delaware watershed.

Dutch foot. A foot in the form of a thickened disc attached to a cabriole leg at the edge of the disc in such a way that the foot appears to turn out toward the corner of the piece it supports. Frequently, the foot rests on another disc, often called a shoe, pad, or cushion. Not to be confused with duck foot, which is much flatter and does not have a pad.

Dutchman. Double dovetail used to hold two pieces of wood together.

Earthenware. Porous, opaque ceramic ware of low fire.

Eclecticism. Creating a design by combining elements of different existing styles.

Egg and dart. Ornament, characteristically carved on an ovolo molding.

Empire. Classicizing style originating in France, in reign of Napoleon I.

Engraving. Print made from an incised drawing on a copper or steel plate.

Ermine cloak. Applied to Oriental export ware decorated with a motif in blue of an ermine cloak in which is a shield containing a monogram, a floral motif or, occasionally, a crest.

Etching. Print made from a design etched into a copper plate with acid.

Ewer. Pitcher, frequently used for ornament.

Exfoliate. Peel or flake off in thin layers.

Faience. Tin-enameled or tin-glazed redware, typically with polychrome decorations.

Fairy lamp. Night lamp of glass, patented by Clarke and Company, England. Lighted with a candle. Late nineteenth century.

Fauteuil. French type of armchair with upholstered seat and back and open upholstered arms. Reign of Louis XIII through the Empire period.

Favrille. Iridescent cased glass, such as Tiffany, Aurene, Durand.

Ferrotype. Glossy photographic print.

Filler. Material, for example, whiting, silica, for filling pores of open-grained wood.

Filigree. Metal ornamental—pierced or wire—work.

Fin. Thin ridge on a cast object of glass, metal, or other material.

Finial. Ornamental carved or turned termination at top of an object.

Fireback. Ornamental cast-iron plate made to go in fireplace, to reflect heat of fire.

Firedog. Andiron.

Fitzhugh. Border of stylized bees and pomegranates on eighteenth-century Oriental export ware.

Flemish scroll. Hollowed out, reversing spiral or volute, used as ornament in Dutch, English, and American furniture of the seventeenth century.

Flight and Barr. Manufacturers of Worcester porcelain in the late eighteenth and early nineteenth centuries.

Flint glass. Lead-containing glass.

Flip glass. Large tumbler-shaped, flaring glasses (in sizes up to a quart), ornamented with paneling and copper wheel engraving. Made for drinking a spiced drink called flip. Eighteenth and early nineteenth centuries.

Flowing blue. Kind of transfer-decorated white earthenware of English manufacture, in which the pattern flows into the glaze. C. 1840.

Flute. Broad, shallow, concave groove, usually on column or pilaster, but also found elsewhere.

Flux. Material used to assist in melting of another material.

Fly-leg. Drop-leaf table whose leaves are supported by legs that swing or fly out from the base. Such tables may have four, six, or eight legs. Found in Queen Anne, Chippendale, Hepplewhite, Sheraton, and early American Empire styles. Often confused with gate-leg tables.

Foliated. Foot type appearing on Rococo furniture in shape of a curled-up leaf tip of the acanthus plant. Somewhat resembles a crocket, except for its use.

Folio. Size of paper on which books or engravings are printed. About the size of a single sheet of newspaper. So-named because standard sized paper is folded once to make a folio.

French polish. Shellac and oil polish applied to furniture during the nineteenth century.

Fret. Geometric, lattice-like design.

Frieze. Architectural term meaning an ornamental border, and usually part of an entablature.

Frosted glass. Glass that has been rendered nontransparent by etching the surface with hydrochloric acid or roughening it by grinding.

Gain. Slot on one piece of wood for receiving another piece.

Gallé. French glass manufactory. One of several firms producing cameo glass. Late nineteenth century.

Gargoyle. Grotesque, peculiar to Gothic style.

Gate-leg. Type of table popular in England and America during the seventeenth and early eighteenth centuries. So called because the support for the drop leaf is braced at top and bottom, like a gate.

Gaudy ware. Highly polychromed ware deriving from the Imari type of decoration and applied to white earthenware (gaudy Dutch), soft paste (with additions of gold), white earthenware (gaudy Welsh) and ironstone (gaudy ironstone).

Genre. Art forms based on everyday subjects.

Georgian. Style fashionable in England under reigns of George I to III and sometimes applied to styles of reign of George IV.

Gesso. Gilding base made of whiting and glue, used for painting, gilding, japanning.

Gilt. Decorated with gold leaf or with bronze powder.

Girandole. (a) Mirror decorated with arms to hold candles. (b) In plural, matching candelabra for mantel garniture.

Glass frit. Decomposed and partly calcined glass, roasted in oven for use in (a) making of glass, (b) making soft-paste porcelain.

Glaze. Glasslike covering on pottery and porcelain.

Glorification. Additions to or subtractions from an antique to enhance its money value.

Glory hole. Oven for reheating glass.

Godrooning. Rounded or oval ornament used in decorating

ovolo and quarter-round moldings in silverware and furniture.

Goffering iron. Cast-brass or cast-iron shoe, into which other irons heated in the fire were placed. Used for ironing ruffles.

Gothic. Style of the later Middle Ages. Its chief characteristic is the pointed arch.

Graining. Painting in imitation of natural grain of wood.

Grooved joint. Table joint usually characterized by a tongue on the leaf and groove on the top of a drop-leaf table.

Grotesque. Fanciful figure, human or animal, used in Classical, Neo-Classic, Rococo, and Gothic decoration.

Guilloche. Classical, Renaissance, Neo-Classic braid pattern.

Half-lap. Lap joint. Notch cut in two pieces of wood to fit them together.

Halftone. (a) Photographic method reproducing light, shade, and color by photographing objects through screen. (b) Hues in prints and textile midway between dark and light.

Hallmark. Mark stamped primarily on silverware in a guild hall, guaranteeing the quality of metal and workmanship.

Hardwood. Trade term for all woods not members of the conifer family.

Harness. Frame together with its pulleys and cords. Holds heddles. Used for raising or lowering a group of threads to make a shed in weaving.

Heddle. Wire or cloth loop for holding a single warp thread on the loom.

Hepplewhite. Furniture resembling the designs published by George Hepplewhite, in 1788.

High style. Piece exhibiting at their best the qualities characteristic of a style.

Highboy. Two-piece case of drawers standing on legs, fashionable from 1680-1780.

Hitchcock chair. American Empire chair made in the chair factory in Hitchcockville, now Lamberton, Connecticut. 1830's. Similar-appearing chairs made elsewhere.

Hogarth chair. Chair in Baroque style of the Georgian period, with rectangular back, trapezoid-set cabriole legs and

Dutch feet. c. 1725-50. Favored by Hogarth in his engravings.

Homespun. Simple fabric made of yarn spun and woven by housewives.

Hoop-skirt rocker. Slat-back rocking chair with short horizontal arms and broad seat. Arm supports pierce seat rails. c. 1725-70.

Hutch. (a) Term misapplied to a cupboard with open shelves above. (b) Kind of table chair, usually called a hutch table.

Imari. Japanesque decoration on china in dark blue, brick red, pea green, yellow, and gold, named after the Imari ware of Japan.

Incised decoration. Chiefly on pottery, made by cutting into soft clay or through slip, before firing.

Inlay. Ornamentation by setting piece of one material into another, for example, inlaying wood, brass into wood, silver into brass, iron.

Ionic. Classical order characterized by use of volutes in column capitals, richly carved ovolo and cyma moldings.

Iridescent glass. Late nineteenth- and early twentieth-century cased glass with iridescent surface, produced by Tiffany and Corning, as well as others imitating these two.

Ironstone. White semiporcelain, originally containing slag from iron mines.

Jacobean. Used of Renaissance and Baroque furniture, particularly of England, during reign of the Stewarts. Name is from Latin form of James I.

Jacquard. A type of woven fabric with elaborate pictorial and other patterns, possible since any thread, as well as groups of them, could be lifted or depressed at will. So called from the fact that it is woven on a loom invented by M. J. Jacquard in 1801.

Japanning. Art of gilding, painting with bronze powders and colors ground in varnishes, containing asphaltum on asphaltum varnished grounds, for example, japans.

Jasperware. Stainable, translucent semiporcelain that could be delicately molded. Novel ingredient used was barium sulphate (baryta) invented by Josiah Wedgwood, about 1775. Stained, colored grounds ornamented in white reliefs by process of sprigging. See Sprigged.

Jig. Pattern of wood or metal to guide in actual working.

Jolier. Machine for pressing clay into plaster mold.

Kaolin. China clay.

Kas. See Dutch cupboard.

Klismos. Chair for reclining, seen on Ancient Greek vase paintings and copied during the Greek Revival as a form for chairs and sofas

Krautstrunk. Cabbage stalk. Refers to German drinking vessel, the stem of which was ornamented with irregular blobs of glass.

Lacquer. (a) Gum obtained from lacquer trees (rhus vernicefera) of the Orient and used in the Orient for varied purposes. (b) Modern synthetic enamel for finishing furniture and painting.

Lambeth delft. Name applied to early English faïence (delft) with cream-colored tin-slip glaze. Frequently decorated with portraits. Known for its plates with portraits of the Stewarts and religious subjects. Late seventeenth century.

Lambrequin. (a) Stiff and shaped valance. (b) Design of pendant, irregular outline, as in lambrequin decoration.

Lantern clock. Small clock of metal, made in England. Run by weights, having a verge and crown wheel escapement instead of a pendulum. Late sixteenth and first half of seventeenth century.

Lathe. Device for rotating between centers a piece of metal or wood for shaping it.

Laticino. (a) Decorated with milk white glass hence name (b) Ornamental latticework used in glass as background.

Leeds. (a) English factory making creamware, polychrome white earthenware and luster-decorated ware of the late eighteenth and early nineteenth centuries. (b) Name describing a blue-bordered, very light cream-colored and lightweight earthenware, made in Stafforshire, much of it by Ralph and James Clewes. Early nineteenth century.

Lesbian leaf. Pattern painted or carved on cyma molding in Classical, Renaissance or Neo-Classic styles.

Ley metal. Pewter containing lead, used for spoons and other ordinary items.

Linen fold. Decoration of Late Gothic and Early Renaissance in form of cloth, hanging in stylized folds.

Lip. Molding around drawer to prevent it from closing beyond a certain point.

Lithograph. Print made from stone plate.

Liverpool ware. (a) Creamware decorated in underglaze, black transfer, sometimes with addition of other colors, made in Liverpool, England, in late eighteenth and early nineteenth centuries. (b) First hard-paste porcelain factory in England and wares made there.

Lowboy. Small table containing drawers. Companion piece to highboy.

Low key. Generally dark in hue. Used of prints.

Lusterware. Ceramic ware decorated with iridescent, metallic glaze of several types. (a) Hispano-Moresque wares of the twelfth and thirteenth centuries—pinkish gold luster in geometric patterns, usually on cream. (b) Gold lusterwares of England, which come in three colors, pink, purple over white ground, copper over terra-cotta and brown ground. (c) Cottage lusterware decorated with scenes in pink luster on white. (d) Silver luster, a platinum luster, either solid or patterned (resist). (e) Sunderland, a deep rose or purple mottled luster. (f) Canary or light gold luster. (g) Wedgwood moonglow luster—pinkish or purplish mottled, very iridescent luster. All lusterwares except for Hispano-Moresque date from the eighteenth and early nineteenth centuries.

Majolica. (a) Italian tin-glazed redware decorated in polychrome. (b) Enamel-decorated white earthenware of late nineteenth century.

Marbleized. Decorated with a blend of different colors of paint or glaze, imitating marble.

Marquetry. Patterned, veneered work in variety of woods. ivory, tortoise shell, brass. Used for furniture decoration.

Mary Gregory. Enameled glass made in Sandwich, Massachusetts, decorated with figures, usually of children. Second half of nineteenth century.

Matting. Woven material made of leaves, bark and other similar fibers, not woven on the loom.

Meissen. Ceraminc manufactory near Dresden, Germany, where true hard paste porcelain was first made in Europe.

Mezzotint. Engraving composed of light and dark areas instead of lines.

Melt. In glass, molten mixture of materials making up the glass.

Milk glass. (a) Translucent, white glass. Second half of nineteenth century. (b) Bristol milk glass. Second half of eighteenth century.

Millefiori. Glass, especially paperweights, decorated with slices of glass canes.

Mordant. Material used in dyeing, to allow cloth to be dyed to take up dyestuff that it would ordinarily reject.

Mold. (a) Form of casting. (b) Negative cast.

Molded glass. Shaped by molding, either by fusing threads of glass together in a mold, spinning them on a molded core, dipping the parison into an iron mold before blowing, or blowing into a full-sized mold.

Molding. (a) Contoured strip of wood applied to furniture, woodwork, door and window casings, wall crowns on exteriors and interiors. (b) Contoured projection of stone or metal, resembling (a).

Mount. Ornamental brass, porcelain, glass, etc., added to furniture.

Nancy. French glass manufactory producing art glass of the late nineteenth century, including cameo glass.

Nankeen. Blue and white decorated Oriental export ware popular during the last quarter of the eighteenth century.

Nappy. Small, oval, or rectangular, uncovered serving dish.

Neo-Classic. Style based on domestic architecture and decoration of ancient Rome, popular in Europe and America during the latter half of the eighteenth century.

Neo Feudalism. Movement in art, popular in middle and end of nineteenth century.

Nonflint glass. Glass earlier than 1862 and not containing lead.

Offhand blown glass. Glass produced entirely by blown methods and free of decoration added subsequent to its blowing.

Ogee. Molding, the profile of which is in the form of two "S" curves, meeting at a point or cusp.

Ohio-type Stiegel. Glass made in Ohio in early nineteenth century, displaying techniques similar to those used in the Stiegel factory and presumably carried there by workmen from the Stiegel factory in Pennsylvania.

Oriental export. Hard paste porcelain made in China under the Ching dynasty for export. Forms and decorations show mingling of Occidental and Oriental.

Orientalizing. Style with elements of design derived from the Orient.

Ormolu. Beaten gold, gold leaf, gold gilt on bronze, brass and ceramic ware.

Overglaze. Ceramic enamel decoration applied over the glaze.

Overlay. Cased glass, the outer portions of which are cut through in a pattern.

Ovolo. Molding with egg-shaped profile usually carved or painted with egg and dart motif.

Pairpoint. American glass manufactory established at New Bedford, Massachusetts, in 1865. Known for paperweights and cut glass.

Palmette. Classical ornament suggesting the leaf of a palm.

Parcel gilt. Gold leaf applied in designs.

Parian ware. Kind of soft paste ware developed by Copeland toward the middle of the nineteenth century and used primarily for figurines and busts. See Bennington.

Parison. Tear-drop-shaped bubble of glass, which is the start of all subsequent operations in glass blowing.

Parquetry. Marquetry composed of rectangular or rhomboidal pieces of wood, applied in a geometric pattern to furniture.

Pattern glass. American pressed glass in which the same

pattern is used on a variety of forms to make sets.

Peachblow. (a) Name given in the West during the nineteenth century to a kind of pink glaze porcelain made during the Ming dynasty. (b) Name given to late nineteenth-century art glass nominally imitating the Chinese wares. Wheeling peachblow—lined glass, yellow to red. New England peachblow—unlined cream to pink. Mount Washington peachblow—unlined pale blue to purple.

Pediment. A gable. Triangular area surrounded by moldings, crowning buildings or furniture parts.

Pembroke table. Fancy small table with short leaves, often in fancy shape, four legs ornamented occasionally with saltire or X-shaped stretchers. First designed by Chippendale and called breakfast tables. Named by Hepplewhite after Earl of Pembroke, c. 1754-1830.

Pennsylvania Dutch. Styles of decoration in furniture developed in the German sections of Pennsylvania during the seventeenth and eighteenth centuries.

Philadelphia style. Rococo furniture based on Queen Anne and Chippendale, but also showing, especially in the carving, influence from France and Ireland. Eighteenth century.

Pick. One passage of shuttle across the web or one thread of weft.

Pickling. Process of using acid to remove oxides from metals after annealing.

Pilaster. Square, engaged column, projecting slightly from wall or case of piece of furniture.

Plaque. Ornamental embellishment of wood, ceramics, or metal. Applied as decoration on furniture and walls.

Planishing. Hammering metals to a smooth, shining surface with a polished steel hammer.

Plate. (a) Metal sheet upon which engravings or etchings are made. (b) Thin coating of one metal upon another. (c) Solid silver.

Plate mark. Mark made by edges of the plate of an etching or engraving on the print paper.

Plein-air. In art, natural, even lighting as opposed to artificial lighting.

Pokal. Large, covered, stemmed drinking vessel of German origin.

Polychrome. Decorated with many colors.

Porcelain. Hard, heavy, nonporous, vitreous, translucent, and high-fired ceramic body.

Portuguese scrolls. Volutes with convex cross sections frequently forming feet of Dutch, English, and American furniture of the seventeenth century.

Post and bail. Brass employing bolts (posts) rather than cotter pins to hold the bail.

Pressed glass. Glass shaped by being forced into a metal mold by pressure from a plunger.

Proof. (a) First trial impressions of a print. (b) Perfect condition.

Quarter round. Molding with a profile having curvature of a quarter of a circle.

Quatrefoil. In Gothic art and furniture, ornament composed of four circular arcs meeting in cusps, suggestive of a four-leaf clover.

Queen Anne. Term used of Baroque Dutch styles, brought into England during the reign of Queen Anne, 1702-14, and its continuation through the first half of the eighteenth century in England and America.

Queensware. Superior type of creamware, notable for its perfection of form and execution. Usually undecorated. First perfected by Josiah Wedgwood but also made by other English firms. Last half of eighteenth and early nineteenth centuries.

Quezel. Iridescent art glass made by the Quezel Glass Company, in Corona, New York. Early twentieth century.

Rabbet. Step down on piece of wood to receive a panel.

Rail. In paneling furniture and chairs, a horizontal framing member.

Raising. Shaping metal by hammering it over metal form or stake.

Redware. Ceramic body, low-firing, porous, coarse-grained and soft. Usual color is red shading from black through red to yellow.

Refectory table. (a) Long table supported on horses or trestles,

used in monasteries in Medieval period and later. (b) Early
table having the same form.

Regency. (a) Period at beginning of eighteenth century when the
Duke of Orleans was Regent for Louis XV. Beginning of Rococo style. (b) Period when George IV, then Prince of Wales,
was Regent for his father, George III, due to the latter's
mental collapse, 1811-20.

Renaissance. Period of revival of Classical learning. In art,
c. 1300-1600.

Repoussé. Ornamented with raised designs, hammered from
the back.

Rinceau. Border design of interlacing acanthus leaves and
flowers.

Rockingham glaze. (a) Lead and sometimes feldspathic glaze
containing driftings, shading, sprinkling, of brown. Used on
creamware, in the potteries on the estate of the Marquis of
Rockingham. (b) Under the name of flintware, a spattered
brown glaze frequently embellished with yellows and greens,
found on creamware made in Bennington, Vermont, Jersey
City Pottery Company, Baltimore, Maryland, Trenton, New
Jersey, and in some Ohio potteries. Second half of nineteenth
century.

Rococo. Style originating in France during reign of Louis XV,
making use of fanciful forms.

Romanesque. Style of art of the early Medieval period, c. 700-
1100.

Rubina. Art glass shading from clear to pale ruby at the edges.
Late nineteenth century.

Rubina verde. Reheated gold glass, shading from pale greenish
yellow to a cranberry color.

Rung. Round stretcher.

Sad iron. Flatiron.

Sagger. Refractory box for holding porcelains during firing.

St. Louis. French glass manufactory in town of that name in
France, credited with being the first to make paperweights,
c. 1820. First dated examples, 1845.

Salopian. Things made in Shropshire or Salop. Specifically:

(a) Caughley soft-paste porcelain. (b) Black-transfer-decorated white earthenware or creamware, overdecorated with transparent colors in orange, yellow, blue, and green, made by Leeds et al.

Salt glaze. Glaze, usually found on stoneware. Applied by throwing rock salt into the kiln.

Salver. Small circular shallow dish or tray, often with feet and an ornamental edge. Chiefly eighteenth century.

Sampler. Small piece of needlework, usually made by young girl, to show off skills learned.

Sandwich. Glass factory operating at Sandwich, Massachusetts between 1825 and 1888.

Sash. Movable part of window.

Satin glass. Late nineteenth-century art glass made of cased glass with inner layer of opaque white glass, outer layer of transparent glass and with an acid-etched surface.

Saw kerf. Cut left by saw.

Scarf. Joint made for purpose of gluing two pieces of wood together, end grain to end grain.

Sconce Ornamental candle holder to hang on wall.

Screen. (a) Network of fine lines, such as occurs on engravings, mezzotints. (b) Pattern of dots making up modern halftone or photoengraving.

Scroll-top. Mirrors, clocks, case pieces, cupboards, with broken arch cresting ending in volutes.

Scrub plane. Plane used by cabinetmakers in past, to cut down quickly the thickness of a board.

Serpentine front. Curve, convex in center and concave at ends, used for fronts of chairs, case pieces and tables. Reversed serpentine or ox-bow is concave in center, bulges outward on sides, and is again concave at ends.

Settle. Wooden bench with arms, sometimes with high back without wings, more often with a low spindle-back. May have rockers.

Sèvres. Royal porcelain manufactory of France during the eighteenth and nineteenth centuries.

Sgraffito. Redware decorated with lines incised through the slip.

Shed. Separation of two or more sets of warp threads in the

loom during weaving for purpose of passing shuttle over one set and under the other at the same time.

Sheffield plate. Silver plate in which silver and copper were fused together into blocks and sheets, before shaping into final forms.

Sheraton. Style of Neo-Classic furniture resembling plates of furniture designs published by Thomas Sheraton, c. 1791-1825.

Shim. Thin piece of wood inserted in joint to tighten it.

Sinkage. Depression struck into back of metal objects for marking purposes.

Size. (a) Gluelike or gelatinous coating used on paper. (b) Type of varnish used in gilding.

Skirting. Apron. Ornamental top stretcher just below top of table and just below seat of chair and pieces having similar appearance in other types of furniture.

Slag. Misnomer applied to marbleized semiopaque glass in two colors, originally called mosaic glass. Blue or brown and white. Made chiefly in Pennsylvania and England in the 1870's.

Slipware. Redware either decorated with poured or molded slip or with slip coating.

Soda-lime glass. Ordinary glass of antiquity and modern times till about 1862. Still made, primarily in Mexico.

Soft paste. Synthetic porcelain made of china clay and various materials, for example, glass, to make body translucent.

Softwood. Wood from any kind of conifer. Has nothing to do with softness or hardness.

Solder. Material used in fused state to fasten two metals together. There are two types, soft solder (lead or pewter) and hard or silver solder. Soft solder has a low, hard solder a high, melting point.

Spanish foot. Three-grooved angular foot on furniture of England and America in late seventeenth and early nineteenth centuries.

Spatterware. China decorated with splotches in blue, green, or deep rose. Frequently containing reserves on which are painted fantastic birds. English white earthenware exported chiefly to America, chiefly during the first half of the nineteenth century.

Spindle. (a) Spinning device consisting of tapered, round-pointed rod. (b) Piece of wood on back of chair having same or similar form to spindle of spinning wheel.

Spiral. Plane curve winding around a point. To be distinquished from helix, which is a three-dimensional curve, like threads on a screw.

Spirit varnish. Varnish composed of gums, such as shellac, dissolved in alcohol (spirits) rather than in turpentine and oil.

Splat-back. Chair the back of which is formed by an ornamental, shaped, sometimes pierced or openwork slab or splat of wood, mortised into the cresting at the top and the seat rail at the bottom. In early versions, the splat does not reach the seat rail but is mortised into a cross rail about 3 inches above the seat rail.

Spline. Thin, flat piece of wood or metal fastening two pieces of wood or metal together. Differs from dowel in shape.

Split turning. Turning made by gluing two pieces of wood together at the ends in such a way that they may be split apart when turning is complete.

Spode. (a) Potters of Staffordshire. Josiah Spode I made creamware, 1797. Spode II made first bone china, 1827. (b) Ware made by Spode, primarily the bone china of the nineteenth century.

Spoke. Spindle. Portion of piece of furniture resembling spoke of wheel, as in Windsor chair.

Spokeshave. Tool for shaping spokes, spindles, or other curved member of piece of furniture. Drawshave.

Sprigged. Ceramic ware ornamented with small thin cast pieces of clay cemented onto the body with slip, for example, jasper and grandmother ware.

Staffordshire. (a) Section in England known for its potteries and the pottery, chiefly white earthenware, made there. (b) Historic Staffordshire, also called Anglo-American Staffordshire. Transfer-decorated wares with scenes of (1) American historical personages, (2) scenes from American history, (3) American landscapes. (c) By extension, wares with similar subjects from other parts of the world.

Stained glass. Glass that has been colored by flashing, enameling, or staining with silver nitrate.

Stake. Polished piece of metal for shaping objects of sheet metal.

State. Version of a print.

Stencil. Paper in which a pattern has been cut, through which paint or powder can be applied to a surface to be decorated.

Stick chair. Chair composed of entirely or almost entirely of spindles and turned members, for example, Windsor chairs of the eighteenth century and turner chairs of the seventeenth.

Stiegel glass. Name of the eighteenth-century type of blown glass displaying characteristics known to belong to glass made in Stiegel's factory.

Stile. In woodwork and furniture, vertical portion of structure or frame, for example, back stiles of chairs, stiles of chests.

Stippling. Painting, drawing, or punching dots with brush, pen, graver's tool, or diamond point.

Stoneware. Ceramic body, coarse to fine, high-firing, nonporous, and opaque.

Stretcher. (a) Member used to brace legs of furniture by holding them apart and tying them together. (b) Stretcher table— a small table, usually with square top, whose base is characterized by stretchers, frequently ornamental and turned, running from leg to leg. Seventeenth and early eighteenth centuries.

Striped Sandwich. Venetian-type glass made in Sandwich, Massachusetts, between 1869 and 1888.

Sunderland. Town in Wales known for its mottled purple and pink lusterware. Also the ware.

Sunflower blanket. Hand-woven woolen blanket embroidered with large sunflowers.

Swirled pattern. Helical ribbing used on blown, molded, and pressed glass.

Tabby weave. Straight, regular basket weave, one over, one under.

Table joint. Joint of a drop-leaf table, formed by fitting a quarter-round nose on center board against a quarter-round cavetto on leaf.

Taffeta glass. Also carnival. Iridescent glass of very late

nineteenth and early twentieth century, imitating more expensive sorts. Name suggested by Mrs. Lee.

Tankard. Hinged, covered, handled drinking vessel, with a
thumb piece for lifting the cover. In silver or pewter.

Tazza. Stemmed, two-handle shallow bowl, characteristic of
Venetian glass and the Renaissance style.

Tear-drop. Early brass pendant pull of seventeenth century.

Tempera. Medium in which paint is ground, consisting of egg
yolk, used especially by Italian painters of Early Renaissance. Applied as water color but becomes waterproof with
time.

Tenon. Piece of wood parallelopiped in shape, forming termination of structural member of furniture, which fits into a
mortise in another member.

Terra cotta. Low-firing, finely levigated, red earthenware,
midway in hardness between redware and stoneware.

Tesserae. Small stone, glass, or ceramic cubes used in mosa-
ics.

Tester. Covering for a high-post bed.

Theorem painting. Painting with aid of pieces of paper in which
holes have been cut, following shape to be painted. Frequently used on textiles.

Three-mold. Glass made by blowing a parison into a three-part
mold of cast iron.

Tiffany glass. Late nineteenth-century iridescent art glass, invented by the man whose name it bears.

Tin disease. See Bronze disease.

Tinware. Utensils ornamental and practical, made of tinned
sheet iron.

Tôle ware. Decorated sheet iron, usually tinned.

Tortoise shell. (a) Mottled, sometimes patterned lead glaze applied to creamware. (b) Similar glazes on white earthenware
of late nineteenth-century majolica. (c) Japan work on a
ground variegated with silver, gold, and copper powders.
(d) Kind of cased glass decorated with splatterings of brown,
amber, gold, in imitation of natural tortoise shell.

Tracery. Openwork in architecture, characteristic of the Gothic
style. Stone lace.

Transfer. Method of printing designs, particularly on china,

by printing on special paper and then transferring design to
china.

Tree of Life. Floral, stylized pattern, originating in the Orient
and popular in the West, as decoration from seventeenth
century on, especially in textiles.

Trefoil. In architecutre and furniture, an ornament composed
of three circular arcs meeting in three cusps. Looks somewhat like a clover leaf. Characteristic of Gothic style.

Tripod table. Pedestal table with three legs or feet.

Trivet. Three-legged, usually ornamental metal stand for
holding kettle.

Trompe l'oeil. Eye-deceiving. Said of painting and decoration
so executed that it appears three-dimensional.

Tucker. American manufacturer making porcelain in Philadelphia, c. 1828-37.

Turning. Contoured shape, circular in cross section, such as
can be turned on a lathe.

Tuscan Doric. Kind of simple Doric order, originating in Ancient Rome, with unfluted columns on molded bases. Popular during Renaissance.

Urn-back. Splat-back chair having splat in shape of urn or
vase. Used of Queen Anne and transitional chairs, particularly American. First half of eighteenth century.

Valance. Ruffled, shaped, or draped hanging for window or bed.

Veneer. Thin pieces of wood glued on furniture to gain advantage of fancy grains.

Venetian glass. Glass characterized by fragile forms and elaborate, applied blown ornament in endless variety.

Vincennes. French soft-paste porcelain manufactory, c. 1738-
56.

Vitrine. French glazed cupboard. Sometimes table with glass
top and compartment below for objects to be displayed.

Volute. Spiral-shaped, three-dimensional curve found in art.
Used on column capitals, handles, furniture decoration.
Spiral helix.

Wainscot. (a) Oak and anything made of oak. (b) Chair of oak with paneled back, carved cresting and wooden seat, made in England and America during the seventeenth and early eighteenth centuries.

Waiter. Tray with two applied handles, usually of silver.

Wall Worcester. Period of earliest Worcester, beginning in 1750. Wall Worcester continued to be made after Dr. Wall's death in 1776, till 1783.

Warp. (a) To bend under stress, as wood. (b) In textiles, the stretched threads running length of fabric.

Waterford. Glass factory in Ireland known for its production of cut glass. Late eighteenth, early nineteenth centuries.

Welding. Fusing two metals together by pressure and heat or by heat alone.

Wheeling. Glass factory in Wheeling, West Virginia, famous for several kinds of art glass, especially peachblow, and for the invention of improved soda-lime in 1864 by William Leighton. Factory was known as Hobbs Brokunier and Company, founded 1844-45.

Windsor chair. Type of chair of which the wood pieces, with the exception of the seat, which is plank, are sticks, either turned on a lathe or shaped with a spokeshave. The seat is of pine, chestnut, beech, or elm. The chairs were popular in England and America since first made in the early eighteenth century. Legend associates the name with George I or II and the town of Windsor. In America, these chairs were also known as "stick" and "Philadelphia" chairs. English Windsors are likely to have a splat in the center of the back in place of a spindle. American chairs never do. Windsors come in a variety of forms, a few of which are as follows: (1) Arrow-back. Late Sheraton Windsor with spokes in shape of arrows. (2) Bird-cage (chicken coop). Late Windsor, where back posts rise above top rail. Spokes usually look like bamboo. Occasionally, top rail made like back posts and matched at the joint. Many have arms. (3) Bow back. Bowed, profiled, bent wood, rising from seat. Forms at once the top, rail, and side posts of the back. When chair has arms, they are doweled into the bow and supported on additional spindles. (4) Comb-back. Chair with high back and intermediate rail, which forms the arms. Through this, the spokes pass to a shaped cresting resembling an old-fashioned ornamental comb. (5) Fan-back. The spokes of the back are arranged so that between two turned back posts, they spread out like a fan to make the chair back wider at the top than at the seat. (6) Hoop-back. The back has intermediate rail from which rises a bent hoop-shaped spindle into which ends of back spindles are doweled. (7) Low-back. Has H-shaped stretchers, an oval seat, and many spindles. The heavy, low, profiled top rail forms the arms. (8) New England arm. The spokes of the back reach up to a top rail, so bent that it forms a rising curved back and horizontal arms. (9) Sheraton. Late Windsors with wide top rail to be decorated in japan in the manner of a Sheraton fancy chair. (10) Slipper-back. Stepped-down Windsor, the ends of which are rounded to a point like the toe of a slipper. May have arms. (11) Stepped down. A fan-back with the top rail stepped down or cut out at the ends. May have arms doweled into the side posts. (12) Writing-arm. Windsor chair of almost any form, in which one arm is broadened out to provide a space for writing and often contains a drawer for writing materials.

William and Mary. Term used of Renaissance and Baroque styles of decoration, showing Dutch influence, popular in England at the end of the seventeenth and early eighteenth centuries. By extension, similar-appearing styles of America, mostly of the early eighteenth century.

Wistar. American glass manufacturer and the glass attributed to his factory, c. 1730-75.

Wood-type figurines. Staffordshire figurines of the kind modeled by Aaron and Ralph Wood. Late eighteenth, early nineteenth centuries.

Wooduct. Print made through carving a wooden block. A wood engraving.

Worcester. Soft-paste porcelain of English manufacture, made during the eighteenth and early nineteenth centuries.

BIBLIOGRAPHY

GENERAL:

Cole, Ann K., Antiques, N.Y., 1959.

Dow, George F., Arts and Crafts in New England, 1704-1775, Topsfield, Mass., 1927.

Downs, Joseph, Pennsylvania German Arts and Crafts, N.Y., 1942

Eberlein, Harold, D., and McClure, Abbot, The Practical Book of American Antiques, Exclusive of Furniture, Philadelphia and London, 1927.

Litchfield, Frederick, Antiques, Genuine and Spurious, London, 1921.

Lockwood, Sarah M., Antiques, Garden City, N.Y., 1925.

Ormsbee, Thomas H., Collecting Antiques in America, N.Y., 1940

Ormsbee, Thomas H., Know Your Heirlooms, N.Y., 1957.

Winchester, Alice, American Antiques, Words and Pictures, N.Y., 1943

Winchester, Alice, How To Know American Antiques, N.Y., 1951.

Winchester, Alice, ed., The Antiques Book, N.Y., 1950.

Yates, R. F., A Guide to Victorian Antiques, N.Y., 1949.

FURNITURE

Bjerkoe, Ethell H., The Cabinetmakers of America, Garden City, N.Y., 1957.

Brackett, Olive, English Furniture Illustrated, London, 1950.

Burr, Grace H., Hispanic Furniture, N.Y., 1941.

Cescinsky, Herbert, English Furniture from Gothic to Sheraton, Grand Rapids, 1929.

Cescinsky, Herbert, English Furniture of the 18th Century, London, 1911.

Cescinsky, Herbert, The Gentle Art of Faking Furniture, London, 1931.

Cornelius, Charles O., Furniture Masterpieces of Duncan Phyfe, Garden City, N Y., 1922.

Cousins, Frank and Riley, Phil M., The Wood Carver of Salem, Samuel McIntire, His Life and Work, Boston, 1916.

Downs, Joseph, American Furniture, N.Y , 1952.

Downs, Joseph, American Chippendale Furniture, A Picture Book (Metropolitan Museum of Art, N.Y., 1949.)

Downs, Joseph, American Furniture, Queen Anne and Chippendale Periods in the Henry Francis Dupont Winterthur Museum, N.Y., 1952.

Eberlein, Harold D., Interiors, Fireplaces and Furniture of the Italian Renaissance, N.Y., 1916.

Eberlein, Harold D., Spanish Interiors and Furniture from the 14th to the 17th Century, N.Y., 1925.

Eberlein, Harold D., and McClure, Abbot, The Practical Book of Period Furniture, Philadelphia, 1914.

Felice, Roger de, French Furniture in the Middle Ages Under Louis XIII (Tr. by F. M. Atkinson), London, 1923.

Felice, Roger de., French Furniture Under Louis XIV (Tr. by F. M. Atkinson), N.Y., 1923.

Felice, Roger de, French Furniture Under Louis XV (Tr. by Florence Simmond), N.Y., 1920.

Felice, Roger de, French Furniture Under Louis XVI and the Empire (Tr. by F. M. Atkinson), N.Y., 1921.

Hayden, Arthur, Furniture Designs of Chippendale, Hepplewhite and Sheraton, N.Y., 1938.

Hornor, William MacPherson, Blue Book of Philadelphia Furniture, Philadelphia, 1935.

Jourdain, M., and Rose, F., English Furniture: The Georgian Period, 1750-1830, London, 1953.

Kettell, Russell H., Pine Furniture of Early New England, Garden City, N.Y., 1929.

Litchfield, F., How To Collect Old Furniture, London, 1906.

Lockwood, Luke V., Colonial Furniture of America, N.Y., 1926.

Lockwood, Luke V., The Furniture Collector's Glossary, N.Y., 1913.

Miller, Edgar G., Jr., American Antique Furniture, N.Y., 1948.

Miller, Edgar G., Jr., The Standard Book of American Antique Furniture, N.Y., 1950.

Morse, Frances C., Furniture of the Olden Times, N.Y., 1943.

Nutting, Wallace, Furniture Treasury, N.Y., 1948.

Odum, William M., History of Italian Furniture, from the 14th to early 19th Centuries, N.Y., 1918-19.

Ormsbee, Thomas H., Early American Furniture Makers, N.Y., 1930.

Ormsbee, Thomas H., Field Guide to Early American Furniture, Boston, 1951.

Ormsbee, Thomas H., The Story of American Furniture, N.Y., 1934.

Riccardi, Saro J., Bibliography of English Regency Furniture, N.Y., 1940.

Rogers, John C., English Furniture (Revised and enlarged by Margaret Jourdain), London and N.Y., 1950.

Schottmueller, Freida, Furniture and Interior Decoration of the Italian Renaissance, N.Y., 1921.

Sironen, Marta K., A History of American Furniture, East Stroudsburg and N.Y , 1936.

Symonds, Robert W., Furniture Making of 17th and 18th Century England, London, 1955.

Winchester, Alice, ed., The Antiques Treasury of Furniture and Other Decorative Arts, N.Y., 1959.

CHINA:

Barber, Edwin A., Marks of American Potters, Philadelphia, 1904.

Barber, Edwin A., Pottery and Porcelain of the U.S., N.Y., 1901.

Barber, Edwin A., Salt Glazed Stoneware, London, 1907.

Barret, Richard C., Bennington Pottery and Porcelain, N.Y., 1958.

Burton, William, Josiah Wedgwood and His Pottery, London, 1922.

Chaffers, William, The Collector's Handbook of Marks and
   Monograms on European and Oriental Pottery and Porce-
   lain, London, 1932.
Clement, Arthur W., Our Pioneer Potters, N.Y., 1947.
Cox, Warren E., The Book of Pottery and Porcelain, N.Y., 1944.
Cushion, J., and Honey, W. B., Handbook of Pottery and Porce-
   lain Marks, London, 1956.
Dormman, Edward A., Blue Dash Chargers and Other Early
   English Tin Enamel Circular Dishes, London, 1919.
Dormman, Edward A., English Pottery and Porcelain, London,
   1918.
Eberlein, Harold D., and Ramsdell, Rober W., The Practical
   Book of Chinaware, Philadelphia, 1948.
Elliot, Wallace, Reproductions and Fakes of Eighteenth Century
   Ceramics, English Ceramic Circle Transactions, Vol. 2,
   1938-47.
Garner, Frederick H., English Delftware, London, 1948.
Haggar, Reginald G., The Concise Encyclopaedia of Continental
   Pottery, London, 1960.
Hannover Emil, Pottery and Porcelain, London, 1925.
Hayden, Arthur, Chats on English Earthenware, London, 1919.
Hayden, Arthur, Spode and His Successors, London, 1925.
Hobson, R. L., and Burton, W., Handbook of Marks on Pottery
   and Porcelain, London, 1928.
Hobson, R. L., Porcelain, Oriental, Continental and British,
   N.Y., 1906.
Hobson, R. L., Worcester Porcelain, London, 1910.
Honey, William B., Dresden China, London, 1934.
Honey, William B., English Pottery and Porcelain, 1949.
Honey, William B., French Porcelain of the 18th Century,
   N.Y., c. 1950.
Honey, William B., German Porcelain, London, 1947.
Honey, William B., European Ceramic Art from the Middle Ages
   to About 1815, London, 1949-52.
Honey, William B., Old English Porcelain, A Handbook for Col-
   lectors, N.Y., 1946.
Honey, William B., The Art of the Potter, London, 1946.
Honey, William B., The Ceramic Art of China and Other Coun-
   tries of the Far East, London, 1945.

Honey, William B., Wedgwood Ware, N.Y., 1949.

Hurlbutt, Frank, Bristol Porcelain, London, 1928.

Hurlbutt, Frank, Old Derby Porcelain and Its Artist Workmen, London, 1925.

Hurlbutt, Frank, Bow Porcelain, London, 1926.

Hyde, J. A. Lloyd, Oriental Lowestoft, N.Y., 1936.

King, William, Chelsea Porcelain, London, 1922.

King, William, English Porcelain Figures of the 18th Century, London, 1925.

Kovel, Ralph M. and Terry H., Dictionary of Marks: Pottery and Porcelain, N.Y., 1953.

Laidacker, Sam, The Standard Catalogue of Anglo-American China, Scranton, 1938.

Larsen, Ellouise B., American Historical Views on Staffordshire China, Garden City, N.Y., 1950.

Litchfield, Frederick, Pottery and Porcelain, Guide to Collectors, N.Y., 1951.

Moore, N. Hudson, The Old China Book, N.Y., 1936.

Nelson, Glenn, Ceramic Reference Manual, Minneapolis, 1957.

Ormsbee, Thomas H., English China and Its Marks, N.Y., 1959.

Phillips, John G., China-Trade Porcelain, Cambridge, 1956.

Pitkin, Albert H., Early American Folk Pottery (Including the History of the Bennington Pottery), Hartford, 1918.

Pountney, W. J., Old Bristol Potteries, Bristol, 1920.

Price, R. K., Astbury, Whieldon and Ralph Wood Figures and Toby Jugs, London, 1922.

Ruscoe, William, A Manual for the Potter, Newton, Massachusetts, 1959.

Savage, George, 18th Century German Porcelains, N.Y., 1958.

Schleiger, Arlene, Two Hundred Patterns of Haviland China, Omaha, 1950-55.

Spargo, John, Early American Pottery and China, N.Y. and London, 1926.

Spargo, John, Potters and Pottery of Bennington, Boston, 1926.

Spelman, W. W. R., Lowestoft China, London, 1905.

Watkins, Lura W., Early New England Potters and Their Wares, Cambridge, 1950.

Wedgwood, Josiah C., and Ormsbee, Thomas H., Stafforshire Pottery, N.Y., 1947.

Wedgwood, Josiah C., Staffordshire Pottery and Its History, London, 1913.

Wedgwood, Josiah and Sons, Ltd., Wedgwood Catalogue of Bodies, Glazes and Shapes. Current for 1940-50, Etruria, Staffordshire, 1940.

GLASS:

Beard, Geoffrey, Ninetenth Century Glass, Newport, England, 1956.

Belknap, Eugene, McCamly, Milk Glass, N.Y., 1949.

Chambon, Raymond, L'Histoire de la Verrerie en Belgique du IIme Siècle à Nos Jours, Brussels, 1955.

Daniel, Dorothy, Cut and Engraved Glass, N.Y., 1950.

Downey, Alan, The Story of Waterford Glass, 1952.

Eisen, Gustav, Glass, Its Origin, History, Chronology, N.Y., 1927.

Fish, Grace, A., Catalogue of Early American Glass, N.Y., 1940.

Gaston, Frederick, Early American Glass, N.Y., 1940.

Hartung, Marion, F., Carnival Glass

Honey, William B., Chinese Glass, London, 1946.

Honey, William B., English Glass, London, 1946.

Jefferson, Josephine, Wheeling Glass, Mt. Vernon, Ohio, 1947.

Kamm, Minnie E., Two Hundred Pattern Glass Pitchers, Detroit, 1941.

Kamm, Minnie E., A Second Two Hundred Pattern Glass Pitchers, Detroit, 1940

Kamm, Minnie E., A Third Two Hundered Pattern Glass Pitchers, Detroit, 1943.

Knittle, Rhea M., Early American Glass, N.Y. and London, 1927.

Lee, Ruth Webb and Rose, James H., American Glass Cup Plates, Northborough, Massachusetts, 1948.

Lee, Ruth Webb, Antique Fakes and Reproductions, Northborough, Massachusetts, 1950.

Lee, Ruth Webb, Early American Pressed Glass, Pittsford, N.Y., 1931.

Lee, Ruth Webb, Nineteenth Century Art Glass, N.Y., 1952.

Lee, Ruth Webb, Sandwich Glass, Northborough, Massachusetts, 1947.

Lee, Ruth Webb, Victorian Glass, Northborough, Massachusetts, 1944.

McKearin, George S. and Helen, American Glass, N.Y., 1941.

McKearin, George S., Early American Glass from the McKearin Collection, N.Y., 1931.

McKearin George S. and Helen, Two Hundred Years of American Blown Glass, Garden City, N.Y., 1950.

Pazaurek, Gustave E., Gläser der Empire und Biedermeierzeit, Leipzig, 1923.

Revi, Albert C., Nineteenth Century Glass, Its Genesis and Development, N.Y., 1959.

Thorpe, William A., A History of English and Irish Glass, London, 1929.

Van Rensselaer, Stephen, Check List of Early American Bottles and Flasks, Petersborough, New Hampshire, 1926.

Watkins, Lura W., American Glass and Glassmaking, N.Y., 1950.

Watkins, Lura W., Cambridge Glass, 1818-1888, Boston, 1930.

Watkins, Lura W., The Development of American Glassmaking (Account of the 4th Exhibition of National Early American Glass Club), Boston, 1935.

METALS:

Silver:

Boivin, Jean, Les Anciens Orfèvres Francais et Leurs Poinçons, Paris, 1925.

Chaffers, William, Handbook to Hallmarks on Gold and Silverplate, London, 1897.

Churchill, Sidney, J. A., The Goldsmiths of Italy, London, 1926.

Ensko, Stephen, G. C., American Silversmiths and Their Marks, 1948.

Halsey, R. T. H., American Silver, The Work of Seventeenth and Eighteenth Century Silversmiths, Boston, 1906.

Havard, Henry, Histoire de l'Orfèvrerie Française, Paris, 1896.

Hughs, G. Bernard, Three Centuries of English Silver, 1500-
1820, London, 1952.
Jackson, Sir Charles, J., English Goldsmiths and Their Marks,
London, 1921.
Knittle, Rhea, M., Early Ohio Silversmiths and Pewterers,
Cleveland, 1943.
Marquet de Vasselot, J. J., Bibliographie de l'Orfèvrerie et de
l'Emaillerie Française, Paris, 1925.
Okie, Howard, P., Old Silver and Old Sheffield Plate, N.Y.,
1928.
Phillips, John M., American Silver, N.Y., 1949.
Rosenberg, Marc, Der Goldschmiede Markzeichen, Berlin,
1928.
Voet, Elias, Jr., Nederlandse Goud en Zilver Merken, 1445-
1951, Nijholf, 1951.

Pewter:

Cotterell, Howard H., Old Pewter, Its Makers and Marks in
England, Scotland and Ireland, London, 1929.
Demman, Carolyn, A Bibliography of Pewter, Boston, Pewter
Collectors' Club of America Bulletin no. 15, 1945.
Downs, Joseph, American Pewterers and Their Marks, N.Y.,
1942.
Hintze, Erwin, Die Deutschen Zinngiessen und Ihre Marken,
Leipzig, 1921.
Kerfoot, J. B., American Pewter, N.Y., 1942.
Laughlin, Ledlie I., Pewter in America, Its Makers and Their
Marks, Boston, 1940.
Moore, H., Old Pewter, Brass, Copper and Sheffield Plate,
Garden City, N.Y., 1935.

Brass and Copper:

Burgess, Frederich, W., Chats on Old Copper and Brass, Lon-
don, 1954.
Clouzot, Henri, Les Arts du Métal Méteaux Precieux, le Bronze
et le Cuivre, Paris, 1934.
Tavenor, Perry J., Dinanderie, A History and Description of
Medieval Art Work in Copper and Bronze, London, 1910.

Iron:

Blanc, Louis, Le Fer Forgé en France, La Régence: Aurore, Apogée, Déclin, Paris, 1930.
Blanc, Louis, Le Fer Forgé en France aux XVI et XVII Siècles, Paris, 1928.
Byne, Arthur and Mildred, Spanish Ironwork, New York Hispanic Society, 1915.
Clouzot, Henri, Le Fer Forgé, Documents Artistiques de Ferronnerie Ancienne du Moyen Age à la Fin du XVIIIme Siècle. Paris, 1927.
Ferrari, Giulio, Il Fero Nell'Arte Italiano, Milan, 1927.
Block, Frank E., Old French Ironwork, Harvard University Press, 1950.
Gardner, John S., English Ironwork of the XVII and XVIII Centuries, London, 1911.
Hoever, Otto, An Encyclopaedia of Ironwork, N.Y., 1927.
Sonn, Albert H., Early American Wrought Iron, N.Y., 1928.

Tôle ware:

Gould, Mary E., Antique Tin and Tôle Ware, Its History and Romance, Rutland, Vermont, 1958.

CLOCKS:

Dreppard, Carl W., American Clocks and Clockmakers, Boston, 1958.
Nutting, Wallace, The Clock Book, Garden City, N.Y., 1935.
Palmer, The Book of American Clocks, N.Y., 1950.

WOODEN WARE:

Gould, Mary E., Early American Wooden Ware and Other Kitchen Utensils, Springfield, Massachusetts, 1942.

PRINTS:

Binyon, Sir Laurence and O'Brien, Sexton, J.J., Japanese Colour Prints, London, 1923.

Briquet, Charles M., Les Filigrams, Dictionaire Historique du Papier dès leur Apparition vers 1282 Jusque 1600, Leipzig, 1923.

Bryan, Michael, Dictionary of Painters and Engravers, London, 1903-05.

Churchill, William A., Watermarks in Paper in Holland, England, France, in the XVII and XVIII centuries, Amsterdam, 1935.

Conningham, Frederic A., An Alphabetical List of 5734 Titles of N. Currier and Currier and Ives Prints, N.Y , 1930.

Fielding, Mantle, Dictionary of American Painters, Sculptors, and Engravers, N.Y., 1945.

Hayden, Arthur K., Old Prints, London, 1956.

Hind, Arthur M., Engraving in England in the 16th and 17th Centuries, Cambridge, England, 1952-55.

Levis, Howard C., A Descriptive Bibliography of the Most Important Books in the English Language Relating to the Art and History of Engraving and the Collecting of Prints, London, 1912.

Peters, Harry T., America on Stone, The Other Printmakers, Garden City, N.Y., 1931.

Slater, John H., Engravings and Their Value, N.Y., 1929.

The Briquet Album of Miscellany on Watermarks, Supplementing Dr. Briquet's Les Filigrams, by various paper scholars, Hilversum, Holland, 1952.

Weaver, Warren A., Lithographs, N. Currier and Currier and Ives, N.Y., 1925.

Whitman, Alfred, Print Collector's Handbook, 1921.

TEXTILES:

Baker, George P., Calico Painting and Printing in the East Indies, London, 1921.

Clouzot, Henri, Metrolpolitan Museum of Art, Painted and Printed Fabrics, N.Y., 1927.

Dunton, William R. Jr., Old Quilts, Catonsville, Maryland, 1946.
Finley, Ruth E., Old Patchwork Quilts and the Woman Who Made Them, Philadelphia and London, 1929.
Flemming, Ernst, An Encyclopaedia of Textiles, London, 1928.
Howley, Walter A., Oriental Rugs, Antique and Modern, N.Y., 1937.
Lewis, George G., The Practical Book of Oriental Rugs, Philadelphia and N.Y., 1945.
Little, Frances, Early American Textiles, London, 1931.
Weibel, Adele C., Two Thousand Years of Textiles, N.Y., 1952.

MUSEUM CATALOGUES

Halsey, Richard T. H., The Metropolitan Museum of Art, N.Y., A Handbook of the American Wing, N.Y., 1932.
Hipkiss, Edwin J., Museum of Fine Arts, Boston, 18th Century American Arts, The M. and M. Karolik Collection, Cambridge, Massachusetts, 1941.
Honey, W. B., Victoria and Albert Museum, S. Kensington, Eng., Glass, a Handbook for Study of Glass Vessels of All Periods and Countries and Guide to the Museum Collection, London, 1946.

DICTIONARIES AND ENCYCLOPEDIAS

Baker, Sheila, S., A Dictionary of Antiques, Edinburgh, 1953.
Boger, Louise A., The Dictionary of Antiques and the Decorative Arts, N.Y., 1957.
Comstock, Helen, ed., The Concise Encyclopaedia of American Antiques, N.Y. 1958.
Ramsey, L. G. G., The Connoisseur, the Concise Encyclopaedia of Antiques, London and N.Y., 1954.

DESIGN, DECORATION, ARTS AND CRAFTS

Brazer, Esther S., Early American Decoration, Springfield, Massachusetts, 1950.

Christensen, Erwin O., Index of American Design, N.Y., 1950.

Lipman, Jean, American Folk Decoration, N.Y., 1951.

Waring, Janet, Early American Stencils and Stencilled Furniture, Springfield, Massachusetts, 1939.

Waring, Janet, Early American Stencils on Walls and Furniture, N.Y., 1937.

Yates, Raymond F., Early American Crafts and Hobbies, N.Y., 1954.

Yates, Raymond F., Hobby Book of Stenciling and Brush Stroke Painting, N.Y., 1951.

DECORATING WITH ANTIQUES

Bjerkoe, Ethel J., Decorating For and With Antiques, Garden City, N.Y., 1950.

Comstock, Helen, 100 Most Beautiful Rooms in America, N.Y., 1959.

Eberlein, Harold D., Colonial Interiors, Federal and Greek Revival, N.Y., 1938.

Gould, Mary E., The Early American House, N.Y., 1949.

Halsey, R. T. H. and Tower, E., The Homes of Our Ancestors, Garden City, N.Y., 1937.

Kelly, F. Frederick, Early Domestic Architecture of Connecticut, New Haven, 1935.

Kettell, Russell H., Early American Rooms, Portland, Maine, 1936.

Winchester, Alice, Living With Antiques, N.Y., 1941.

REPAIR AND RESTORATION:

Ormsbee, Thomas H., Care and Repair of Antiques, N.Y., 1949.

Yates, R. F., How to Restore China, Bric-a-brac and Small Antiques, N.Y., 1953.

PRICE LISTS:

Jacobs, Carl, Guide to American Pewter, N.Y., 1957.

Lee, Ruth Webb, Current Values of Antique Glass, Massachu-
    setts, 1955.
Lee, Ruth Webb, Price Guide to Pattern Glass, N.Y., 1955.
Warman, Edwin B., 6th Antiques Current Prices, Uniontown, Pa.,
    1963.
Yates, Raymond F., Antique Collector's Manual, Price Guide and
    Data Book, N.Y.. 1952.

ART INDEXES:

Chamberlain, Mary W., Guide to Art Reference Works, Chicago,
    1959.
Lucas, E. Louise, The Harvard List of Books on Art, Cambridge,
    Massachusetts, 1952.
The Art Index, A Cumulative Index (Annual).

PERIODICALS:

American Collector (1938-48)
American Heritage (Current)
Antiques (Current)
Antiques Journal (no longer printed)
Country Life (English, current)
Hobbies, The Magazine for Collectors (Current)
The Antiquarian (1923-33)
The Antique Collector (Irregular)
The Connoisseur (English, current)